Language Variety and the
Art of the Everyday

LANGUAGE VARIETY AND THE ART OF THE EVERYDAY

Valerie Shepherd

Pinter Publishers
London and New York

First published in Great Britain in 1990 by
Pinter Publishers Limited
25 Floral Street, London WC2E 9DS

British Library Cataloguing in Publication Data

A CIP catalogue record for this book is available from the
British Library

ISBN 0 86187 984 8

Library of Congress Cataloging-in-Publication Data

Shepherd, Valerie.
    Language Variety and the Art of the Everyday / Valerie Shepherd.
        p. cm.
    ISBN 0–86187–984–8 : £27.50
    1. English language—Variation.   2. Dialect literature, English—
History and criticism.   3. English language—Dialects.   4. English
language—Style.   I. Title.
    PE1074.7.S47 1990
    427'.09—dc20   90–7025
                                                                          CIP

Typeset by Florencetype Ltd, Kewstoke, Avon
Printed and bound in Great Britain by
Biddles Ltd of Guildford and Kings Lynn

For Simon, Nick and Lucy;
and also for David.

Contents

Acknowledgements

I am grateful for the support and advice of many colleagues and students at Loughborough University of Technology. Special thanks are due to David Fussell, and also to Sheila Hermolle, Ronald Chan, Robin Hamilton, Bernard Ratigan and Alan Lilley.

We are grateful to the following for permission to reproduce copyright material: Tom Leonard for extracts from 'Poetry', 'Good Style', 'The Dropout', 'Unrelated Incidents (1)', 'Cold, isn't it', 'The Good Thief', 'A Summer's Day', 'It's awright for you hen', 'Ah knew a linguist once' published in *Intimate Voices* 1984 by Galloping Dog Press, © Tom Leonard 1984; Faber and Faber Ltd for 'Afternoons' from *The Whitsun Weddings* 1964 by Philip Larkin; Macmillan Ltd, for permission to reproduce extracts from *The Complete Poems of Thomas Hardy* 1976, edited by James Gibbs; Lomgman Group UK Ltd for 'Northern Farmer, Old Style' from the *Poems of Tennyson* 1969 edited by Christopher Ricks; Centaur Press Ltd, for extracts from 'The Farewell' and 'Dawn' by William Barnes, published in *The Poems of William Barnes* 2 vols, 1962, edited by Bernard Jones; Virago Press for 'Divorce' copyright © James and George Hepburn, *Songs of John Oland* 1911, published by Virago Press 1984; Robin Hamilton for 'Semantic Fairytale' from *Lost Jockey* 1985 published by Bran's Head, © Robin Hamilton 1985; Harvard University Press and the Trustees of Amherst College for 'A man may make a remark' by Emily Dickinson, reprinted from *The Poems of Emily Dickinson*, Thomas H. Johnson, ed., Cambridge, Mass.: The Belknap Press of Harvard University Press, Copyright 1951, © 1955, 1979, 1983 by the President and Fellows of Harvard College; 'What the Sleeping Beauty would have given her right arm for', by Zoe Ellis, and 'The Spaceman and the Dinosaur' by Alexander Osmond-Brims, © Alan Sutton Publishers Ltd, Gloucester and © The Daily Telegraph plc.

Preface

Circles of Language

A language is not one homogeneous entity. It is more helpful to think of it as a variety of circles, one within another, their perimeters converging and overlapping, fluid and changing. For instance, English includes a number of *dialects*, and these dialects vary, in sound, word or syntax, according to *idiolect*, and also to choice of *register* or *style*. Such variations alter over time: no one now speaks Shakespeare's English.

Dialects are consistently systematic, regional or social variations of a language. So-called prestige *standard* English is itself a dialect: it was never the one and only language of England. Originally, in the Middle Ages, it was both regional and social, used by the educated and the upper-class in London and the Home Counties. But at present it is a prestige social variation without geographical boundary. Its syntax and vocabulary may or may not be accompanied by prestigious 'RP' accent – 'received pronunciation': it is frequently spoken with regional accents. Switching between the prestige and a regional dialect is possible for many people. But there are still more 'circles' of language, related to culture, gender, and the individual.

Nowadays English adds to the prestige standard, and to regional dialects, the varieties of the language spoken by immigrants and their descendants. As for gender, some feminists argue that there is only a male version of English (presumably touching every dialect variety) – and insist there should be an alternative female circle of language. Then, each of us can be said to have an idiolect, our own personal variation on a dialect theme. Moreover, we choose to use our idiolect in particular ways, varying its register in terms not only of subject matter but also in style of presentation. We do so because we have a sense of *appropriateness*, of what we believe will be acceptable language for the situation in which we find ourselves. For example, most of us would not address anyone as 'm'lud' or, as our boss enters the room, remark 'All rise!' – unless we happen to work with a judge in an English Court of Law. We have here 'standard' language in a broad sense: that which we consider to be the norm in a particular context. The users of prestige standard English, like everyone else, may decide to adapt their chosen variety to match this kind of norm.

Non-conformist language – considered inappropriate, abnormal for one reason or another, by someone or other – tends to provoke bewilderment and condemnation. Regional dialect poetry has been dismissed as 'weariful . . . misspelled English' (Lang quoted in the *Times Literary Supplement* 1944: 321). Editors, from Tottel in the sixteenth-century onwards, have felt obliged to sanitize their writer's syntax, neaten their rhymes, and perfect their punctuation. Non-literary non-conformist language has also suffered under the attack of self-appointed custodians of language. The feminist invention 'Ms' was greeted with incomprehension and derision. Jobs may be won or lost according to a rounded vowel or a dropped *h*, and not so long ago a newspaper journalist – spurred on by readers sending him shoals of what he termed their 'pet' linguistic 'abominations' – reacted with pained indignation to language he considered in some way deviant. 'We must', he wrote, 'fight on' to save the standard. He was referring to his particular norm, the prestige standard in, to judge from the examples he quotes, an especially constrained form with all innovation, all adaptation to changing circumstances inhibited. He wrote:

> . . . a language teacher at the University of Bath . . . wrote that standard (i.e.) correct English has "no inherent superiority". But it has. Correct grammar and syntax and the accurate use of words derive not only from history and custom but from logic. They are the mortar which holds our thoughts together. When they crumble, so does our *capacity for thought*. (Italics mine) (Anthony Lejeune, *The Daily Telegraph*, 1 January 1985.)

It is hardly surprising that a circle of language should inspire such passion. There is an Arabic proverb: 'A man by learning a second language becomes two'. According to this understanding of words and syntax, languages and their varieties are not merely descriptive of experience, not merely vehicles to transmit information. Language is personality. It is expressive of the individual. It is expressive of his/her culture. So, protecting one's own norm of language is a preservation of one's self and one's own particular society. Equally, ruling somebody else's usual variations of language out of court is a rejection of that person and that person's way of life.

The nineteenth-century German scholar, Wilhelm von Humboldt, had a related view. He believed that 'each language draws a magic circle round the people to which it belongs, a circle from which there is no escape save by stepping out of into another' (quotation translated in Cassirer 1946: 9, from von Humboldt's *Einleitung zum Kawi-Werk*, VII, 60). Put this way, conformity – to a single, accepted, standard use of language – sounds to be a kind of prison, social and psychological. The newspaper journalist confirms the point. For this writer his circle of language seems admirable because he believes it to be correct for certain reasons. In his opinion it is authorized by history, custom and apparently conforms to a particular logic. Yet here 'logic' appears largely as another word for 'longevity'. If an aspect of language has a long pedigree it has here an authoritative logic as of right. For this reporter, history, custom and logic, seem to refer to much the same thing – that is, to a powerful status quo. He objects, for example, that 'front-runner . . . cannot indiscriminately mean "leader of the field", "favourite" and "pacemaker"; its real meaning is an athlete who likes to race in the front position'. But he is mistaken. For the compound is actually used and understood in these various ways. 'Capacity for thought', in this writer's case, can hardly refer to innovative free thinking, but instead implies standard language formulas. It is not a crumbling of the creative thinking process that he mourns. It is rather the disintegration of established thoughts, through a challenge to their conventional – and therefore assumed to be 'correct' – expression, that is truly feared.

Certainly the restraining effect of language standardization is a very real possibility. But it is particularly so to the unaware, the unimaginative, the uncreative. Choice of language is available – if we acknowledge its availability and when necessary and appropriate take its opportunity. The artist, by definition, takes the opportunity. But it is not closed to the rest of us.

True, John Honey (1989) details the way in which the prestige standard of English, in particular RP, acquired its status and argues that prejudice and misunderstanding would be drastically reduced in England if everyone conformed to the same accent. Honey is quite right in saying that we should all be aware of the advantages of a particular form of language and be able to use it – as and when we wish. Communication would be impossible if there were no shared norms, and if a speaker is aware that in certain contexts a particular kind of English is likely to be advantageous, then it would be foolish not to use it. The Kingman *Report of the Committee of Inquiry into the Teaching of English Language* insisted in 1988 that one of a school's duties 'is to enable children to acquire Standard English, which is their right' (14). And the National Curriculum proposals of the Secretary of State for Education and Science and the Secretary of State for Wales, together with the Report of the National Curriculum English Working Group published in June 1989 make plain, (para. 4.48) that a principle aim of English teaching between the ages of five and sixteen 'is the competent use of Standard English'.

However, Honey thinks that a parallel erosion of what I am calling alternative circles is inevitable: he 'mourns their passing' (1989: 173). But they need not and should not decay. For each distinct circle of language has its individual strengths, and all have a potential for immense creativity. Choice from these alternative circles can and must be preserved in the face of deadening uniformity, in order to cross the boundaries of Humboldt's magic circles and thus extend ourselves: a man, or a woman, by learning a second language becomes two. The Kingman Report also noted that when 'children go to school for the first time, their language may differ in many respects from Standard English, depending on where they live, their parents' speech habits, and so on. This is natural and proper and a source of richness' (14). And the Secretary of State's 1989 proposals, though stressing in considerable detail the need for standard English, note (para. 4.43) that the aim 'is to add Standard English to the repertoire, not to replace other dialects or languages'. In Wales, 'all pupils will be learning both English and Welsh' in secondary schools (para. 13: 6). And though Standard English is generally the favourite for written, formal and public use, non-standard forms 'may be much more widely tolerated – and, in some cases, preferred – when the language is spoken, informal and private' (para. 4: 41). Besides, the proposals acknowledge, 'Standard English . . . varies according to style, purpose and audience' (4.10).

However, this book describes non-standard forms in contexts apart from the spoken, informal and private. It considers the more formal and public medium of dialect poetry. And it offers examples of language (both prestige and non-prestige) that are non-conformist, non-standard in the broadest sense. I aim to show their identifying features, their effects and achievements – particularly their achievements, which should make them, in their contexts, preferred rather than tolerated.

But first, in Chapter One, I have gathered together, for those who are not familiar with language studies, a number of linguistic concepts underlying my argument. Subsequent pages offer examples of language that take advantage of a capacity for creativity which – we shall argue in this first chapter – is open to us all and which inspires our variety of expression. It goes without saying that literary art has forms and conventions that distinguish it from everyday language, writing differs from speech, and the prestige standard from non-standard dialects. But all have a common, creative core. It is their shared, creative properties that are discussed in this introductory chapter.

The rest of the book is not directed specifically towards the professional linguist but to all who are interested in the semantic and aesthetic power of different kinds of English. Chapters Two and Three look at deliberate rejections of the prestige English dialect in the poetry of William Barnes, Alfred Tennyson, and Tom Leonard. They consider too the unusual language of Thomas Hardy's poetry and the inclusion of dialect in his prose. These writers demonstrate the semantic, aesthetic and political potential of dialect art, and also reflect the linguistic theories of their contemporaries.

The second half of the book focuses on creativity outside literature: there is art in the everyday. It looks at variations of language apart from the standard/non-standard English dichotomy, variations which can cut across all the major circles of cultural, social and regional difference.

Chapter Four takes as its theme the issue of gender and language difference. The danger of linguistic sexism is very real. But I do not agree with some feminists that the deliberate creation of a radically new female version is essential. We have sufficient creative potential at present. If we do not use it, the reason lies at least in part outside the systems of our language.

The final chapter concentrates on a particularly healing creativity that is open to all of us. To a large extent we construct our individuality through language, particularly through its potential for metaphor and for narration. With this in mind I consider the dialogues of therapeutic conversation and especially the way in which original 'standard', accepted formulations of perceptions may be challenged. It is possible, out of conversation, out of the stories we tell as we try to make some personal sense of our lives, to create new circles of language and of self.

Edward Thomas saw language in poetry as both 'fixed and free' (1964: 40, 'Words'). The same is true of language as a whole. It has its conventions, standards, rules, as we shall see in more detail in Chapter One. Without competence in these we could not communicate. But through them we can move between the circles of language; innovative, creative, individual.

CHAPTER ONE

A Creative Competence

Describing the Circles

In order to distinguish between the circles of language recognized in the Preface, we shall need to be able to describe a variety or style of language very precisely. We shall need some idea of likely distinguishing features to look out for and a way – a *metalanguage* in fact – of talking about these.

Present-day linguistics is essentially *descriptive*. It aims to avoid the *prescriptive* nature of the old school language lesson which taught rules of syntax and composition. Certain kinds of rules (to which we shall be returning) are essential to language, but traditional instruction in English often had more to do with the structures of classical languages than with English itself, and more to do with matters of social taste and elegant manners than with effective, creative, and powerful communication.

But if linguistics did no more than describe the language it examined – said, for example, that *Jack and Jill went up the hill* has one active past tense verb, a couple of proper nouns and a common one, a preposition and a definite article – it would be arid and useless. And of course description is merely a preliminary, albeit a vital preliminary, which paves the way for the more profitable analysis and evaluation of language. After describing the kind of language children use, the psycholinguist can analyse and evaluate the collected data in order to arrive at knowledge about language acquisition. The sociolinguist may consider the significance of these same descriptions in relation to information about the class or family groupings of the children involved. The literary critic can confirm or even inspire responses to a text through careful linguistic description, analysis and evaluation.

Yet an awareness of nouns and verbs, subjects and objects may take us only a little way towards the descriptions that help analysis and evaluation. The *monist* view of *style* assumes that content (ideas) and its expression (style) are difficult to separate and are therefore virtually one and the same thing (Leech and Short 1981: 10–41). Stylistic variation from this point of view is far more than the merely ornamental dress of thought; it is not simply a part of a two-tier *dualist* system consisting of thought distinct from its dressed-up expression. Put so baldly, the monist view appears over-simplistic but, if its implications are entertained at all, it becomes essential to describe as much as possible of a piece of language under discussion, every feature and its attendant significance. In order to do so, *models* of language more powerful than the traditional subject-predicate-object kind will be needed. The last forty years has seen the development of such models.

Moreover, these models can help to combat criticism that circles of language other than a prestige standard, in elegant style, are generally incapable of profound expression and creativity. For the careful description of the non-standard can demonstrate the potential for communicative and creative power in the unusual, the informal and the everyday. It is to the value of explanatory linguistic models, particularly in this respect, that we now turn.

Grammatical Models

Models of language, however, are only partial descriptions. After all, models in general, virtually by definition, must be selective. An architect who needs to helpfully describe – model – a house he has been commissioned to renovate, is not going to reproduce the entire building in all its detail and precise dimensions. If he did so he would have rebuilt the original! Besides, practical issues like space, time, materials and skill restrict him to a model that in scale and other respects cannot precisely match its subject. But, quite apart from such inevitable restrictions, *motivation* is a prime element in the shaping of any model. A model assembled for an architect's use will look very different from that created by, say, an interior designer working on the same project. The architect will not clutter his particular model with fabric and furnishing details, unless these affect his own work directly.

Much the same restrictions and choices apply to the linguist who is modelling the complexities of language. Therefore it may be necessary to draw on more than one linguistic model to describe every aspect of a particular circle of language. Moreover, the motivations lying behind different models are illuminating in themselves. The language models of both Michael Halliday (a distinguished English linguist who has highlighted the 'functional' and 'systemic' aspects of language) and Noam Chomsky (who, working in America from the 1950s, has revolutionized understanding of the nature of language) are particularly relevant to the issues we are concerned with here, not only because they can describe elements of non-standard language in fine detail, but also because their basic premises relate to our central interest in creativity and variety.

1) Halliday and Choice

Halliday's approach to language description is helpful in our context not only because the techniques he offers, implicit in the chapters that follow, facilitate revealing stylistic analysis. Most importantly, seeing language as an available set of systems, he demonstrates the ways in which we choose from these systems. This emphasis upon the potential for choice is clearly relevant to our central theme, for the principle of choice challenges that of standardisation. For example, we shall be discussing, in Chapter Five, the psychological implications of choices made from the transitivity system. We shall describe this Hallidayan model only in broad outline. The reader will find *Explorations in the Functions of Language* (Halliday 1973) a detailed explanation of its theory, with some examples of its application. And *An Introduction to Functional Grammar* (Halliday 1985) analyses the structures realized as a result of choices made from the systems of language in a way designed to 'make it possible to say sensible and useful things about any text, spoken or written, in modern English' (Halliday 1985: xv).

Naturally, Halliday recognizes the possibility of choice at the word level. It is up to us whether or not we call a spade a spade. But he also stresses the human ability to choose different ways of syntactically structuring language. These choices can be profoundly meaningful.

Take, for example, Robert Browning's 'My Last Duchess' (published in 1842 in *Dramatic Lyrics*). This monologue's voice is that of the Duke of Ferrara. He is exploiting both vocabulary and syntactic structure when he refers to the demise of his last Duchess. Having finished a description of what he believes to have been her smiling, flirtatious misbehaviour, the Duke chooses three active clauses, referring first to the escalation of her misdeeds, then to his reaction, and finally to a further event. He remarks:

> . . . This grew (1); I gave commands (2);
> Then all smiles stopped together (3).

We are likely to assume, given all else we know from the poem, that the Duchess is now dead. (Today, says Ferrara the Duke, she stands in her picture only 'as if' alive.) And we are likely to conclude, given his chillingly dismissive attitude, that the arrogantly evil Duke's commands resulted in her death. But the Duke does not choose to taint his lips with words that unequivocally claim responsibility for a murder. Nor does he even refer precisely to death, its moment, or its manner. Instead he chooses to refer only to the activity of smiles! *They* stopped. Neither murder itself, nor the human agent who murdered, nor the woman whose life was taken, are included in the Duke's carefully selected, evasive subject and verb. There is no sign, in this carefully packaged construction of words and syntax, of an acceptance of crime or direct culpability. It avoids responsibility for anything other than a command, a vague command which might have effected anything from a chastened – to a dead – Duchess. It makes clear only that the smiling ceased. A passive construction would have invited the Duke to say – or at least caused hearers to wonder – *by* whom the Duchess's smiles were stopped: 'Her smiles were stopped (by . . . ?) . . .' But instead the Duke selects active syntax through which he proclaims only the authority in which he delights: *I gave commands*.

The Duke is 'behaving' through language. Halliday's model sees all language as essentially *behaviour*. A bad headache may lead to a visit to the doctor, but it could also prompt language activity. 'I must ring the surgery for an appointment'; or, 'I haven't had a headache like this since the last phone bill came'. In other words, language for Halliday is *functional*. By choosing linguistic options from its functions we can behave in particular ways through language. He identifies three primary, or 'macro', functions. An utterance can carry all three at once, striking them simultaneously, as it were, like three notes in a chord.

There is the *ideational* function which, loosely, is the expression of ideas, of what Halliday calls 'content'. Another macrofunction, the *interpersonal* function, helps to set up social relations at the same time as content is being expressed. It is principally conveyed by options in the mood system through which we make statements, ask questions, deliver commands. Each of these choices, represented in linguistic structures, marks out our relationship to those hearing us. The aggressive suitor who chooses to demand *Marry me* is probably feeling more in control of a relationship than the one who politely enquires *Will you marry me?* (though we would need to know more about the utterances' tone, rhythm and accompanying paralinguistic signals to be sure). Thirdly, Halliday identifies the *textual* function, which allows language to make links with itself. It does so in a number of ways, including lexical and syntactic choices. But he takes particular note of the part played in this function by stress and intonation. These elements of sound can draw attention to the 'new' bit of information in an utterance, playing down the item already considered and moving communication on. Asked *Will you marry me?* with emphasis upon *marry*, an answer is unlikely to repeat the same stress, because the possibility of marriage is now 'given' information. A response must move on to something relevant but new; perhaps – if the enquirer is fortunate – to *I will marry you* with the emphasis upon *will*.

However, whilst we may behave through the functions of language, it must be emphasized that the correlation between a social trigger and its chosen linguistic consequence is not as uncomplicated as these simple examples, designed to make a general point, might suggest.

Sometimes, it is true, the link is virtually indivisible. A good example is that of so-called *performative* verbs. Try choosing to 'mean' or to 'behave' the making of a promise without using language, specifically some such verb as *I promise, I assure you*. The carrying out or otherwise of the promise is of course not a direct matter of words. But the making of the promise in the first place quite definitely is. Here the signifying language exactly matches that which is signified. (For a discussion of the concept of *signification* see Lyons 1977: vol. 1, 95–119.)

Yet, on other occasions, the parallel between a social intention and the language of its expression is more subtle and complex. I may make a statement: *It is my birthday next week*. But at the same time as passing on the information I may also be implying, indirectly, an instruction, and perhaps a warning: *Don't forget to buy me a present, or else . . . !* (We would need further information about the tone and context of utterance to be sure.)

On other occasions the language used has even less precise connection with what is meant. The communication is *phatic*. That is to say, I may greet you with 'Good morning. How are you?' but my query doesn't – unless I am a doctor addressing a patient – really expect a health bulletin in return. I am merely, phatically and rather ritualistically, signalling recognition and making contact.

Not only the speaker, but also the hearer needs then to be highly sensitive to all the nuances of a language user's choices, and their context, in order to recognize implied as well as directly articulated behaviour. But we do not always hear clearly. Sometimes the health bulletin will still be delivered, despite a merely phatic enquiry made not in the surgery but in the middle of the high street. Our language choices can fall on deaf ears – and with more serious consequences than mere irritation at a tediously related list of physical symptoms and operation scars. A speaker may choose from the options of a non-standard dialect – and a hearer may dismiss their unusualness, and consequently their particular meaningfulness, as unworthy of attention. Then again, a new piece of language may be created, but it need not be acknowledged. The coining of *Ms*, whilst it freed women from identification according to their marital status, did not automatically give them equality or liberation: creating utopias through our language options need not make them materialize.[1] Language is vital to the creation and expression of self and society. The link between the signifying language and the signified self and society is close and powerful. But it is not an inseparable or simple connection.

Moreover, despite a theoretical availability and freedom of choice for the language user, options are not always unrestricted. And if our language options are restricted – standardized in some way – so too is our potential to behave, to function. We shall be returning to consider the possible extent of limitations upon both hearer and speaker/writer.

For the moment, however, I want to turn from Halliday's model of language to that of Noam Chomsky. In some respects, Chomsky's very different approach is complementary to Halliday's as it too focuses upon the power and possibility of language – a potential that would appear to be innate.

2) Chomsky and Creativity

Chomsky's model of language takes as a premiss the immense linguistic creativity which he believes is part of human potential. In 1959 he reviewed and demolished B.F. Skinner's argument (1957) that language is acquired as a trained habit, reinforced by reward and punishment – rather like rats learning to perform tricks in cages. On the contrary, Chomsky believes that we can produce and understand perfectly new and even strange utterances: we do not accumulate and store up a batch of ready-made utterances from which we select when required. Moreover, our response to a particular circumstance cannot be predicted in the same way that rat behaviour in reaction to stimuli can be anticipated. Faced with a picture, a crisis, an examination question, there is no knowing precisely what language we will use in response. All of us, in theory, possess this considerable creativity – until, that is, our communicative capability is restricted in some way that is initially outside language.

Before looking at Chomsky's ideas in more detail, we should note that our potentially vast creativity contributes to our capacity for *displacement*, one of a number of vital features of human communication to which Charles Hockett (Hockett 1963 and Sebeok 1968) drew attention. (A number of these are discussed at length in Aitchison 1989.) Displacement refers to our ability to create language about something, someone, an idea, an event, which is not at that moment before our eyes. It is a feature which helps language users to write history, plan for the future, imagine through prose and poetry – and tell lies. I can impress upon you that my Uncle Basil, who emigrated to Australia in 1950, will be coming over next week for a reunion with his family – despite the fact that Basil did not emigrate, will not be travelling home, and in truth does not even exist beyond the confines of these words. As we have already suggested, there is a certain gap between the signifiers of language and the signifieds of the 'real' world.

So far as it is known, animals and other creatures do not have this facility of displacement, at least not to our considerable extent. It is true that bees, more so than other creatures, come some way towards it. Through the signals of dance movements they can report back to the hive the location of a source of pollen, found some way away. But this would seem to be all they can do. They cannot extend their creativity further, 'talking' of notions beyond the limits of pollen geography. So far as we know, they cannot mention the bad temper of the new Queen Bee in the next door hive, discuss the economics of honey production, wonder where the gardener will be going for his holidays next year, or repeat the legends of The Great Bees to their young. They cannot do so because, apart from anything else, their dance movements only refer, quite precisely, to direction (a 'round dance' indicates nectar close by, a 'waggle dance' implies it is further away). Moreover, only horizontal direction can be indicated. A bee might have difficulty directing a friend up to the rich pollen sources in a hanging basket.

Human language can achieve very much more partly because it has in large measure the feature of *duality*. That is, it is a two-tier system. It has a limited number of useful sounds (or, in the language of the deaf, a limited number of hand signs). But, from these finite 'building blocks' we can create an infinite number of words. Moreover, we are aware of *structure dependence*: we exploit the patterned, syntactic nature of language. Language is thus rather like a set of children's Lego bricks. The set includes a finite set of shapes (sounds). These can be combined together in certain limited ways – at the top, side, bottom (words and syntax). Yet, given these materials and techniques, an infinite number of structures can be designed.

A trivial example demonstrates this powerful creativity. Take just three sounds at our linguistic disposal: *t*, *a*, *c*. First, we can shuffle these into a variety of orders to form two different words: *cat*, *act*.

Next, we can extend their meaning by the addition of prefixes and suffixes. Then we can make use of our knowledge of syntax (involving the placing of words in ways which help to define their function and meaning) to further extend their range of meaning.

> He was invited to act the cat in *Puss in Boots*. In the first act this versatile young actor brought the house down. The press reacted encouragingly. If he acts as well as this in future, his acting career is assured.

Duality, in small measure at least, is not exclusive to human beings. Birds convey meaningful messages through the combined notes of their songs. But animals and other creatures do not seem to possess, and it does not seem possible to teach them to understand, our potentially potent use of structuring, where placing is meaningful in itself. Washoe, one of the chimpanzees encouraged in the 1960s to learn human language, did demonstrate some structuring and creativity (Gardner and Gardner 1969). She knew a sign (she used hand signals instead of sounds) for *water* and one for *bird*, and she then invented *waterbird* when she saw a duck. But she did not seem to know that the order in which she put her signs could also be significant. In a hurry to eat raspberries she would sometimes pull at those caring for her and sign *Go sweet*: but she was equally likely to sign *Sweet go*.

Thus it would appear that language is a vital part of our being human. Animals do not seem to have our kind and extent of language knowledge, particularly of syntactic knowledge, and therefore our considerable potential for communication and creativity.

Chomsky concentrates his language model upon this human knowledge. He models what he believes we *know* about language, not what we do with our knowledge in specific social contexts. He focuses, that is, upon what he calls language *competence*, describing in detail the kind of knowledge we have about the elements which go to make up the sentences of our immense creativity.

Most importantly, Chomsky argues that the capacity for language, for acquiring this knowledge, is to a large extent innate. Competence is not the self-conscious kind of knowledge we build up as we learn a second language at school, the lists of verb conjugations, vocabulary, and useful phrases we deliberately commit to memory. It is not even, basically, local language specific. Chomsky has in mind the kind of competence which includes a more universal knowledge. It is the kind of general understanding of language that he believes all human beings must be born with and which develops into an adult structuring of language. We shall be returning below to some details of his *Transformational Generative Model* (first explained in Chomsky

1957 and 1965) which derive from this notion of competence. It is the concept of competence, motivating his model, which is of particular interest at the moment.

Without some innate competence, Chomsky argues, without some initial understanding of what language is, small children could not begin to acquire language, working it out from the mass of sounds surrounding them. These sounds are too imprecise, too fragmented. How does a toddler, sitting in a high chair, learn a particular language from the assorted topics, the half sentences, the questions, commands, and statements hurled around him as his parents discuss the day's events at home and abroad? He can hardly learn by imitating phrases and sentences gleaned from this jumbled data. Besides, if parroting were at the root of language acquisition, then one family's child would start by copying anxious remarks about the state of her parents' joint account; another would repeat the headlines of the morning paper. But this learning of lines does not happen. A child invents utterances that s/he is unlikely ever to have heard before. S/he is much more likely to declare 'Want tractor' or 'Where Teddy go?', saying what s/he chooses to say and constructing what s/he says as creatively as possible, given the stage of language acquisition s/he has reached.

If parents or researchers do try to teach children to use language – perhaps systematically correcting errors and offering perfect utterances to copy – those children, far from forging linguistically ahead, actually seem to fall behind others who were not so deliberately instructed. But, left relatively to their own linguistic devices, so long as they can hear language around them, children the world over gain language and do so in much the same sequence of acquisition. One word utterances are followed by pairs of words, then by inflections, then by negative and interrogative structures, and finally by complex constructions, roughly – and universally – in the same sequence between the ages of one and five. (The issue of language acquisition, touched upon so briefly in these paragraphs, may be followed up in, for example Fromkin and Rodman 1988, and Aitchison 1989.)

Chomsky believes that this universal pattern of acquisition must be the result of a kind of innate language starting pack. Other linguists, despite accepting in principle the concept of an innate linguistic ability, may question the starter pack's precise composition. But, for Chomsky, it amounts to what he calls a *Language Acquisition Device* (LAD). The device is made up of three things: a sense of linguistic universals, a hypothesis-making device and an evaluation procedure. The hypothesis-making device would allow children to theorize about the rules governing the language they hear around them. The evaluation procedure would allow them to choose the most accurate of these theories. The universals are assumed to be of two kinds, substantive and formal. Substantives are the raw materials of language, such as the set of sounds possible for language: a child would reject coughs and sneezes but accept *p*, *b*, *g*, *r*, for example. In particular, Chomsky is convinced that children know in advance that such basic elements must be put together in certain ways. They are born with an innate sense of language's *formal* properties, of its dependence upon structure. We shall return later to his crucial argument in this respect, that an utterance has two structures, a surface structure and a deeper, underlying form.

All of this starting pack – whatever its precise contents – seems to be largely independent of intelligence. Even children of low IQ will generally acquire language. Besides, it is initially being acquired, in all its complexity, at an age before intelligence can in any child be sufficiently developed to be the prime factor. And bear in mind the difficulty, when intelligence is developed, of acquiring a second language at school.

In sum, therefore, it would appear that children all begin with a very similar capacity for language, and one that is potentially capable of a wide variety of creative manifestations. In theory, no language user need be restricted in communication since none need lack a basic competence, a competence which develops from childhood's pre-disposition into the adult knowledge of syntactic structures with which Chomsky's model is primarily concerned (and from which we can choose in the way that Halliday describes).

However, and most importantly for the issue of standard and non-standard language of all kinds, Chomsky does not imply that innate competence would set language in motion without encouragement. He accepts that participation in a language environment is essential in order to trigger the mechanisms of competence. Children who do not hear language around them do not begin to speak until the situation is remedied. Isabelle, who had remained in a darkened room with her deaf mute mother until the age of six, made only croaking sounds when she was eventually found in Ohio in the 1930s, but she rapidly acquired language once involved in a language community (Brown 1958: 192). Moreover, the particular social, language environment in which children find themselves will inevitably contribute to the use they make of their competence in what Chomsky terms language *performance*. It will inevitably shape, and perhaps restrain, the innate potential for creativity.

A Limited Performance

There can be no argument that performance differs. However homogeneous the innate starting pack of language, adults do not use language in one and the same way. Within English itself, quite apart from the vast number of very different languages found throughout the world, variations are considerable. There is difference from Somerset to Lancashire, from the language of the home to that of the doctor's surgery, from class to class, men to women, and so on and on through varying circles of language, varieties and styles, standard and non-standard, converging and overlapping, right down to each person's individual, idiosyncratic circle or *idiolect*. And this is to say nothing of the new Englishes, and pidgins and creoles that grew with colonies and Commonwealth.

It is a matter of context, not only the geographical context of national languages and their regional dialectal versions (which, it should be noted, are marked not simply by local accent but equally importantly by consistent variation of word and syntax). For when we put our innate language ability into practice, into performance, we may be said to have acquired what Hymes (1971) has called *communicative competence*. We have acquired not only knowledge of the language system of a particular socio-cultural community but also (with varying degrees of individual capability) the capacity to use that language in the style appropriate to a particular situation. Sometimes we choose the appropriate language for the occasion quite deliberately. Sometimes, however, it chooses us.

The words the Member of Parliament selects are not those she uses, perhaps less self-consciously, when she returns home to put the children to bed. And of course it is not only a difference of words themselves that is significant, appropriate or inappropriate according to the subject matter and context of a situation, but very likely also a difference of syntax, rhythm and intonation. The brisk imperatives – 'Come on! Put your toys away now!' – chosen by the off-duty politician, as she looks after her child, are likely to be replaced in the House by a different *register* of carefully picked emphatic declaratives and rhetorical questions as she affirms and denies her party's position.

The choices of communicative competence might be extended to include a fundamental option between the prestige standard and non-standard varieties of a language: many of us acquire a facility in both standard English and our regional dialect. In the House the politician may decide to use the prestige norms of received pronunciation and the syntactic forms normally used by those having the greatest social status. In her constituency she may well consider it good – politic – practice to adapt in some degree to the local dialect, at the very least in accent and perhaps in word and syntax too.

But the politician is, on duty at least, a highly aware user – manipulator – of language. Much of the time, he or she considers carefully the likely consequence of each chosen word, phrase, nuance, tone, rhythm. Yet those who do not make their living so self-consciously by words may 'choose' less knowingly from the available language circles. For instance, it may be perfectly clear to us, if we stop to consider, that we are using or not using the prestige norm. But how often do we think about the 'choices' we have made? Do we know, for instance, without deliberately thinking about it, when or if we are using sexist language? (This is an issue we shall return to in Chapter Four.) Do we know, without looking out for it, when we are *hearing* it?

Whilst it may be true that we – deliberately – do not choose to talk to our friends and colleagues in the way that we decide to address our accountant, our solicitor, or the policeman who has just breath-alysed us, a considerable amount of language is not so much chosen as adopted as a result of pressures outside ourselves. However, the extent to which we are controlled, determined as it were by language norms or standards, is debatable. Psychoanalysts, anthropologists and sociolinguists differ in their accounts of linguistic determinsm.

According to some, language choice is virtually non-existent. The psychoanalyst, Jacques Lacan, asserts that language acquisition runs parallel to a child's gradual awareness of its separation from it's mother's body, with a dawning realization of itself as speaker (*I*), as spoken to (*you*), and as spoken about (*s/he*). But Lacan claims that, from the first, boys and girls relate differently to language.

His thinking relates to the Freudian theory of child development, which posits a stage of 'castration complex', a stage at which the differentiation of male and female subjects is accomplished. Boys at this stage identify with the father who possesses, like themselves, the phallus. They are now separated from the mother – she is lost to them – and they overcome their sexual desire for her through fear that the father will castrate them. At the same time, boys are joined to the power of the patriarchal order, identifying with the authoritative father who can threaten castration, prohibit incest. Girls, on the other hand, acknowledge their lack of the phallus, recognize their lack of power. For Lacan it is the conception of lack and differentiation from the mother that draws children into language. Because, until s/he is aware of the possibility of possession or of loss, of something or someone to possess or to lose, s/he cannot envisage the notion of differentiation and of words standing for objects, concepts, ideas. Further, and most relevantly for our purposes, Lacan argues that language pre-exists the individual who – male or female – must slot into that pre-existing order.

> Symbols in fact envelop the life of man in a network so total that they join together, before he comes into the world, those who are going to engender him 'by flesh and blood'; so total that they bring to his birth, along with the gifts of the stars, if not with the gifts of the fairies, the shape of his destiny. . . . (Sheridan 1977: 68)

To Lacan, the existing symbolic order – all the signs of society and culture, including language – is essentially male, patriarchal. But are girls and women as inevitably restricted by this situation as it would sound? We shall discuss the point in Chapter Four. (For a very helpful discussion of Lacanian thinking, and Lacanian linguistics, see Cameron 1985.)

From a different standpoint, the work of Edward Sapir and Benjamin Lee Whorf has been taken to show that our perception is largely determined by language, for all languages differ in relation to their cultural context. According to this view, a French-speaking person will apparently not encounter quite the same world as a Chinese. The French language and the Chinese reflect two different cultures. And small children acquiring one or the other of these languages will be drawn to view their world through the ready-made perspectives of their particular tongue. This line of argument, acknowledging cultural difference and linguistic relativity, at least leaves room for the possibility of non-patriarchal cultures and non-patriarchal symbolic systems.

However, the now famous example of a multitude of Eskimo words for snow – the estimate of their special vocabulary to label it seems to range between four and forty – is not evidence to prove completely 'sealed in' language and cultural difference. It is true that, if the English had a variety of single words for different kinds of snow, their very existence would indicate that we are mentally prepared to expect and cope with a range of weather, from our usual inch or two of slush to those drifts and impacted masses which reduce the country to shivering ineptitude. But the fact that we do not have words already in our vocabularies, already structuring our thinking to prepare for unusually hard winters, does not prevent us from at least recognizing – and describing, and cursing – the unexpected onslaught if it happens. We use two or three words or phrases where the Eskimo may have a ready reckoner of individual ones to hand. Besides, languages do develop, adding new elements and shifting the implications of old. As Sapir observed, '. . . aborigines that had never seen or heard of a horse were compelled to invent or borrow a word for the animal when they made his acquaintance' (1921: 219). Therefore it would seem that the effect of cultural grouping is not unavoidable linguistic/perceptual difference. We evidently can – if we will – understand and talk, to some extent at least, about the experience of another culture and about unusual developments in our own. And language extended in this way can have powerful effect. Whorf believed, 'A change in language can transform our appreciation of the Cosmos' (1956: vii).

Still, breaking out of our linguistic/cultural circle may need considerable conscious effort. For instance, if our own symbolic system is patriarchal we have a ready reckoner of male-oriented signs which encourages its users towards a patriarchal perception. It is easier to look and speak within our standard circle of culture and of language than to break out of it. And even determined efforts to step outside are not always totally successful. Translation between languages is difficult. Anne Cluysenaar (1976: 42–9) makes the point succinctly in her analysis of C. Day Lewis's translation (1954: 299) of Paul Valéry's poem *Les Pas* (1957: 120–21). One brief example from her work will suffice here. It relates to the difference of formality between the French *tu* and *vous* forms. The poem begins with the phrase *tes pas* and ends with *vos pas*. This clear signalling of a change from intimacy to distance could not be achieved simply through the current pronoun system of English. (English 'Thy', used as an intimate contrast, would draw in, additionally, an archaic flavour of meaning, one not implied in the original phrase.)

Moreover, it is not only major cultural groupings which can contribute to the shaping of the symbolic order. Sub-groups of various kinds, including social class and the family, may impose their language variation or their style, their particular language standard as it were, upon the individual speaker. And it may be as difficult to translate and step between these circles as it is between more obviously foreign languages. But just how far, and in what significant ways, do these differences of language affect differences of cognition and communication?

Basil Bernstein's views on society and language have been familiar for some time. But his arguments are contentious and, besides, their popularization has often misleadingly oversimplified his thinking. (The work of Bernstein and his colleagues is gathered together in *Class, Codes and Control* [1971, 1972, 1973, 1975] and a very helpful critique is given by Michael Stubbs in *Language, schools and classrooms*, 1983.)

Bernstein assumes a difference in language usage between different children. This, according to his most recent thinking, is a consequence of difference in *sociolinguistic codes*, *elaborated* or *restricted*, which he believes underlie *speech variants*. These variants may also be either *elaborated* or *restricted*. The elaborated kind, apparently characterized by wide vocabulary and syntactic choices, realizes meanings which are *universalistic* in the sense that they need not be tied to a given context and offer sufficient detail to be understood by a hearer who does not share meanings with the speaker. By contrast, restricted speech variants realize *particularistic* meanings that assume shared knowledge between speaker and hearer. Thus, as someone comes into the room, a child realizing a restricted code might say of a television programme she is watching: 'It's really good. She's caught him and they're friends again.' A child realizing elaborated code, on the other hand, might call out more comprehensively: 'This is really good. Cagney's caught the man who killed the old lady and she and Mary Beth are best friends again.' The language choices the second child makes allow her language to be reasonably context free: that is, hearers would not need to be watching the television programme itself in order to understand her comment.

Bernstein has suggested that differences of class relate to differences of code. But he has not made the simple connection between class and language that has often been assumed. He has argued that both middle-class and working-class children have, usually, access to both codes. He suggests that it is the kind of family group they belong to that encourages the choice of one or the other. He supposes there are *person-centred* and also *positional* families. Positional families are so called because in these the social identities of individual family members are clearly defined and unambiguous. By contrast, person-centred families are not based upon role-defined status. Instead, they form around the personality differences existing in their individual members. In this kind of family, members would be constantly making and remaking their roles, rather than simply stepping into them. Both kinds can be found in all classes, but Bernstein implies that positional families are more typical of working-class groups. Moreover, he claims that we should expect – but not invariably find – code restriction in a positional family and elaborated code in person-centred groups. The assumption then must be that working-class children *tend* to choose restricted sociolinguistic codes and speech variants. But Bernstein does not imply the hard and fast connection between class and language that his popularizers have frequently implied. (His critics, indeed, suggest that he has discussed nothing hard and fast and that his theories and supporting data dissolve under close scrutiny [Stubbs: 1983]).

His work cannot therefore be taken – as it often has been – to prove a direct connection between language, the working class and educational difficulty. It is true that school is a place of universalistic meaning in that the knowledge it deals in is not restricted to local time and place, to already shared assumptions and knowledge. The school is a world organized around talk, talk which allows the exploration and creation of meaning through language. Elaborated speech variants may be the most efficient language for so doing. But, as we have said, Bernstein suggests that working-class children do have access to the elaborated sociolinguistic code that underlies these. The fact that they do not choose to realize it must have to do with extra-linguistic reasons. It is this point that is most interesting to us in our discussion of choice and creativity. It has to be emphasized, moreover, that Bernstein has said there is absolutely nothing in non-standard, dialect English which need prevent a child from internalizing and learning to use universalistic meanings. Dialect English may be realized in what he has called either restricted or elaborated speech variants.

Besides, it does not automatically follow that children who, for whatever reason, do not choose elaborated variants are less effective language users. Labov (1969) demonstrated that a paradigmatic Harlem speaker of non-Standard Black English actually responded to an interview with less verbiage and in consequence greater clarity and logic than an upper-middle-class college-educated Black. The latter larded his talk with elaborate modifications and qualifications in a standard English that duplicated or padded out his main argument. Moreover, the non-standard speaker in this case was discussing abstract ideas about life after death, challenging the assumption that only standard and elaborate language can cope with the abstract and hypothetical.

Quite apart from the choice of restricted or elaborated language, the use of non-standard linguistic forms does not automatically result in illogical or defective understanding. Although, as we have seen, the choice of language forms is certainly meaningful, there is no simple one-to-one correspondence between a form and its implications. Its meaning is derived from a complex of linguistic and extra-linguistic, contextual factors. Stubbs discusses (1983: 68–70) the omission of the verb *to be*, as in *this my sister*. The Russian language is only one of many that would not include the verb *to be* in this construction. Yet Russians can hardly be assumed to understand existential relationships differently from English speakers because of this – to us – unusual grammar. So if a speaker acquires non-standard, less prestigious, or even less complex forms, it cannot automatically follow that s/he is deficient in understanding or communicative capability.

Lacan, Whorf and Sapir, and Bernstein are no doubt right to assert that we tend to acquire the language circle of our group, cultural, national, family and so on. And this will certainly guide our perceptions and their communication: it may be difficult to see round the edges of our particular language. But we cannot over-simplify the nature of this guidance – or be overly pessimistic about the strength of its determinism. Nor can we assume that language alone, by and of itself, is the sole creator and controller of cognition. Bernstein himself insisted that there is more to socialization than simply the forms of its linguistic realization. Besides, as we noted above, languages do not remain fixed, frozen in a mould, dictating for all time one world view. They are by definition creative: they adapt to changing perception. New terms are coined, and old forms change their implications. Language is not of itself determinate – although, used unthinkingly or imposed upon others, it may be used deterministically.

Even so, in a special sense language is not entirely free. Certain kinds of restrictions are necessary to its very formation and use. Language control is a complex concept, involving acceptable – indeed essential – rules of the game.

Rules and Regulations: Creation and Convention

At the very beginning of this chapter we acknowledged that certain kinds of rules are essential to language. But these are not the exclusive property of prestige language varieties. Non-standard dialect, for instance, is as dependent upon the consistent application of rules – its own special rules – as standard language. Moreover, to say that language is *rule-governed* but has a potential for creativity is not a contradiction in terms. For certain kinds of rules are themselves a source of creativity. Others are frameworks within which language users can select and develop their particular circle and style of expression.

To begin with, rules of a particular kind are an essential part of Chomsky's model of language. He models language competence by describing the 'rules' which, in his special sense, we 'know' explain the composition of syntactic structures: syntactic structures are, by Chomsky's definition, rule-governed. We have already mentioned his concept of two structures of language, *deep* and *surface*. His models, introduced in 1957 and developed in 1965, describe a web of structure that we 'know' lies behind, and develops into what we generally consider to be 'well-formed' surface utterances. Chomsky describes the structures underlying uttered sentences as noun and verb phrases which, expanded and transformed, step by step, rule by rule, generate our complex surface structures. (Generation, as we shall see in Chapter Five, has to do with our knowledge of language, not its actual production.)

For example, a simple set of *phrase structure* rules could generate the phrases that make up the sentence *The gardener planted a tree*.

(1) S   →   NP + VP
(2) VP   →   V + NP
(3) NP   →   Det + N
(4) V   →   planted
(5) Det   →   the, a
(6) N   →   gardener, tree

(S indicates sentence, NP refers to Noun Phrase, VP to Verb Phrase, Det to Determiner. The arrow means 'rewrite as'.)

A 'tree diagram' interprets these rules helpfully. Its branches demonstrate a gradual expansion of the basic syntactic elements – the phrase structures – that we know make up the sentence and lead to their eventual conversion into words.

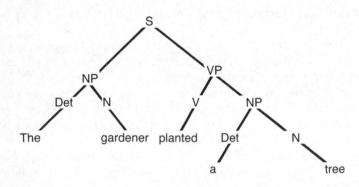

But our knowledge of syntactic structures can be much more complex than this example shows. We might also say that, given our competence, we 'know' certain structures are related to each other. For example, we know that (1) *The doctor treated the patient* has, at some deep level, the same underlying structure as (2) *The patient was treated by the doctor*. Traditionally we have called sentences like the first *active*, and have referred to sentences like the second as *passive* constructions. But in both cases we know that the doctor is the agent of the treatment – not only semantically but, crucially for Chomsky, also syntactically. His model allows us to show this structural relationship between the two. At the end of the tree diagram, before conversion into words, sentence (1) would be represented by a string of symbols like:

NP1 – Aux – V – NP2.

We can describe the passive version however, sentence (2), by saying that a *transformational rule* has been operated on sentence (1). The transformation can be formulated thus, with the symbols of sentence (1) on the left of the arrow, the symbols of sentence (2) on the right:

NP1 – Aux – V – NP2 → NP2 – Aux + be + en – V – by + NP1

(NP1 and NP2 refer to the first and second nouns in the sentence, V stands for verb, Aux refers to tense and to auxiliary verbs, and be + en (where *en* stands for the past participle) indicates the passive element.)

The symbols on the left of the arrow have been rearranged and added to, in order to turn them into a description of the structure of the passive version of the sentence. Because we recognize some link between the two sentences, the process of transforming one from the other is appropriate: it reflects our knowledge of the two structures and particularly of a relationship between them. The concept of transformation, modelling more of our knowledge about language than phrase structure rules alone can achieve effectively, made Chomsky's model of grammar – his *Transformational Generative Grammar* – a radical departure from traditional approaches.

Our 'rule-governed' syntactic understanding of language can be further demonstrated by a look at the sentence *The shooting of the hunters was terrible*. The sentence is ambiguous on the surface – ambiguous, that is, unless we have the additional explanatory knowledge that the hunters are somewhere lying murdered, or alternatively that they are bad shots (either in terms of their technique, or maybe morally having perhaps killed some preserved species). Therefore, somewhere behind its surface form, depending upon which meaning is intended, it must have one of two deep structures. That is, if the sentence refers to murdered hunters, then, back in the deep structure, these hunters were grammatical objects. In a sense, in this case, two sentences have been combined to form the sentence we hear. One was something like *Someone shot the hunters* the other something like *It was terrible*. But if, on the other hand, we have unskilled or immoral shooting in mind, then two different sentences lie behind the sentence. Here the shooters would be grammatical subject. The sentences would have been something like *The hunters shot (something). It was terrible*. We 'know' this because we can choose to understand the identical structure in one of two fundamentally different ways (see also Palmer 1971: 149–50).

The rules of a Chomskyan transformational-generative grammar are designed to generate all the sentences that we know to be part of a language. A dialect is generated by rules slightly different from those of a standard language, but they are no less consistent in their application. Indeed, it is their regular observance of phonemic, syntactic and lexical rules which distinguishes them from a merely idiosyncratic or random variation.

But a grammar should generate *only* the sentences of a language. It should not be so powerful that it allows for the creation of unacceptable sentences. Under normal circumstances it should not, for instance, generate *The food-blender smiled contentedly*, because – as a rule – inanimate nouns do not form up with animate verbs. Certain additional rules in Chomsky's model would prevent such an anomaly.

To repeat, these are rules of competence: they describe what we know to belong to the structure of English language. They do not relate to prescriptive instructions like those recently handed out by the editor of a north-country newspaper forbidding his staff to use words such as *kids*, *massive* and *giant* in their reports. And they certainly need not tie us into a strait-jacket of language. Chomsky's kind of rules relate to the knowledge of structural possibility that we have seen is fundamental to our immense language creativity.

This is a very superficial explanation of a part of Chomsky's early models (see Lyons 1985 and Aitchison 1989 for a full discussion). The 1965 formulation of his ideas developed and extended his original concepts, and subsequently he has shifted his emphasis towards a theory of the relationships between items in sentences, particularly the ways in which they 'govern' or 'bind' each other – *government-binding* theory, or GB (see Chomsky 1985 and Aitchison 1987.) Nevertheless, this brief discussion demonstrates the concept of our 'rule-governed' understanding of language and the transformational-generative model will be relevant later on, particularly in Chapter Five.

Human language may be thought of as rule-governed in other ways. There are, for example, rules of conversation, in that a conversation is by definition a conversation only if it follows certain patterns. This is not Chomsky's kind of competence but part of the *communicative* competence mentioned earlier. H.P. Grice (1975) has drawn attention to aspects of the co-operative principle which appear to be defining features of conversation. He describes what he calls *maxims of implicature*. These concern the quantity, the quality, and the relevance of the communication made, as well as the manner of its delivery. As regards quantity, we tend to make our contribution to a conversation as informative as possible (given the context of the exchange): we try to give neither too much nor too little information.

An example of a violation of the maxim of quantity is contained in the following conversational exchange.

'Have you finished mowing the grass and put the cuttings in the bag?'
'Yes, I've finished the mowing.'

The questioner could reasonably have expected a greater quantity of information in response to his query. Indeed, so obvious is it that a bit is missing (according to the conventional maxims of conversation) that he is likely to fill in the gap himself – concluding that the gardener has not finished the job and that cuttings are still scattered all over the lawn!

It can also be argued that there are rules of story-telling in the sense that narrative structure can be said, by definition, to have certain conventional elements. That is, probably only one of the following will strike us as a 'story'.

(1) I bought some herbal bubble-bath.

(2) I bought some herbal bubble-bath. I used it when I got home.

(3) I bought some herbal bubble-bath and used it when I got home. I shan't buy that brand again. It was all herbs and no bubbles.

By identifying the third example as a narrative, however minimal and brief, we no doubt feel we are merely stating the trivially obvious. But this is the point. Its very obviousness suggests that we recognize 'rules' of narrative: a certain temporal ordering is inevitable and, maybe, some sort of explanation or resolution. The second example has temporal ordering and therefore could be said to form a very simple basic narrative but it probably feels incomplete, leaving the hearer wanting to ask, 'So what?' The first example of course satisfies no defining rules of narrative. It is merely a statement.

It is perhaps most helpful therefore to think of rules not as orders but as *definitions* or *descriptions* of those structures of language which we conventionally choose in order to allow our creativity and communicative competence. In precisely what ways then can we be creative, within and because of these necessary, defining rules of language?

A Creative Competence

In theory, we need never repeat a particular sentence that we have already used or heard. We can always add more clauses to an utterance, use a different word, construct a new one. We have seen that Halliday's systemic approach to language gives us ways of describing the multiplicity of combinations of choices open to us. There is room for exercising these options within the conventions of language use; within, for instance, the essential framework of narrative structuring. We have suggested that, by definition, narrative includes the description of events with some reference to their temporal order, and probably with some kind of interpretation, direct or implied, of the relationship between a set of events. Within this frame, however, there is considerable room for manoeuvre. Imagine that the two following sentences are headings introducing a report of the same incident but printed in different newspapers. They summarize rather different stories.

(1) Local JP knocks down couple.

(2) Elderly couple knocked down by car.

Different people and different issues, although all were no doubt involved in the incident, come to the fore through the different emphases of carefully chosen words, syntax and imagery. The first sentence will probably precede a tale of scandalous violence: the JP is a protagonist to be villified. We are drawn to focus upon him/her. S/he is referred to immediately. S/he is important to us because s/he is described as local. S/he actively injured someone – and we are not distracted from his/her guilt by any language image of the couple who were knocked down. The second may well introduce a story of tragedy in which the car driver is of much less importance than the lives of the injured pair. This heading attends primarily to the victims. We are at once told they are aged and so immediately we have some image of the pair. They are much more real to us than the car involved: the vehicle is left to the end of the sentence without a qualifying adjective that might have fixed it in our minds.

Within the same narrative frame alternative perceptions have been created. The truth of the matter will depend upon which story is read and how well it matches the reader's experience of the incident as well as his/her particular interest in those involved. If the reader was not at the scene, and knows nothing of the events except through the medium of a newspaper, language will create its own truth, its own story within broad, verifiable, temporal limits.

But we can do more with language than manipulate its syntactic potential, choose from its vocabulary, or even invent new words.

Our creative competence is partly the result of our ability to use *metaphor* which, very roughly, is a use of language which produces meaning by relating one concept to another. Lakoff and Johnson (1980) demonstrate that metaphor is not restricted to the province of literature but is actually a crucial element in everyday language behaviour.

To begin with, they reject both objectivism and subjectivism as being equally inadequate accounts of a relationship between language, thought, truth and the world. They prefer an 'experiential' synthesis of the two attitudes. Anything does not, for Lakoff and Johnson, go: they do not accept a view that no reality exists outside the individual mind. On the other hand, a total faith in objectivity misses the creative individual element in perception that their preferred model of 'imaginative rationality', a synthesis of objectivity and subjectivity, acknowledges.

Metaphor plays a crucial role in this imaginative rationality. To Lakoff and Johnson it has a certain rationality in that it is grounded in objective experience. For example, a whole system of metaphors which imply a war-like element in *argument* have rationality in the sense that our experience of argument does involve us in behaviour akin to the actuality of the battlefield. English speakers say they win or lose arguments. We may demolish them by shooting them down, using a particular strategy or attacking a weak point. We, in our culture, tend not to see argument as a co-operative venture, achieving a mutually agreed conclusion. We would not, therefore, choose metaphors of the dance-floor – taking our partners for the argument, one leading the other, the other following, then each executing a few independent steps, finally coming to a halt together on the last beat of the music! Such a metaphor sounds ridiculous, irrational, because it is not within our experience. To take another example, the metaphor of time as money, understanding it as spent, wasted, used up, also relates to our actual experience in our economy of the value of time as a resource. In this sense it is 'true'.

On the other hand, response to experience is personal, subjective, imaginative in that it derives from the human subject. It is a response stemming from an individual's participation in experience, including the part played by his/her imagination in that experience. So we can choose from a variety of metaphors to describe, for instance, our subjective understanding of love. We might call it magic (*she cast a spell over him – she was bewitched, charmed, by him – the magic had gone from the relationship*). On the other hand we might speak of it in terms of health (*the relationship is in good shape, on the mend, dead – it is a sick relationship, a healthy marriage*). Or we could see it as madness (*she drives me out of my mind – he's mad about her – she raves about him*). Our choice will depend (as we shall demonstrate when we return to the subject in Chapter Five) on a combination of our experience and our own personalities. Our choice will again be 'true' to the extent that it matches our individual perception.

But metaphors can actually play a part in the construction of experience itself. For they frequently pre-exist experience, becoming familiar to us, part of our perceptual equipment. They can then restrict the user to a limited perspective, confine his/her imagination. For they tend to highlight only certain aspects of possible experience, at the same time hiding others. Consider the love metaphors again. All of them relate to experience that is possible: we can feel overtaken by magic or madness, or else feel the need to take care of someone. Still, it is something of a chicken or egg situation. For having love metaphors readily available in our habitual language may limit perception, shape behaviour and consequently dictate the experience. Their habitual use could draw us to assume we have no control over what we do about our feelings, and thus could assist the abrogation of responsibility in a relationship. Health metaphors, on the other hand, shape a very different perception of love, one which involves responsibility and control, for these see love as vulnerable but responsive to nurture. A person accepting this kind of metaphor may construct for themselves a different kind of relationship to a friend who is convinced that love is wholly uncontrollable. To a large extent, then, it would appear that love is the metaphor we choose.

On the other hand, the creation of absolutely new metaphors, and therefore new understanding and new experience, is possible. Lakoff and Johnson illustrate this potential with an intriguing anecdote. An Iranian student had not heard the phrase 'the solution of my problems' before he came to America. When he did, he thought it was a metaphor involving a bubbling liquid in the chemistry laboratory, assumed to contain all of a person's problems, with catalysts continually dissolving some of them – for the time being – and precipitating out others. It could be a comforting metaphor of problem-solving for a personality that is intent on success and afraid of failure. Indeed, it might encourage such a person to no longer see the existence of problems as personal failure. For as Lakoff and Johnson remark (1980: 143–44):

> Rather than direct your energies toward solving your problems once and for all, you would direct your energies toward finding out what catalysts will dissolve your most pressing problems for the longest time without precipitating out worse ones. The reappearance of a problem is viewed as

a natural occurrence rather than failure on your part to find 'the right way to solve it'.

The evidence here is anecdotal. But reading about it demonstrates the way in which new metaphors can create new meaning. For the Iranian's perception now becomes a consideration for us too. Once prepared to listen carefully to the implications of someone else's metaphors – we do not all share the same standard ones – our perceptions are broadened. Further, knowing that the creation of new metaphors, new understanding, is a possibility, we might experiment with the linguistic shaping of fresh ways of seeing.

Max Black (Ortony 1979: 36–40) helpfully clarifies the different ways in which language, in particular metaphor, may actually create 'new truth'. Metaphors can draw our attention to features of actuality that are ready and waiting but not yet experienced. It is like the view of Mount Everest from a point above the summit. The top always existed – but not the view of it until it had been seen. Then again, language can build on to existing actuality. Were genes in existence before they were recognized by biologists? Yes and no. Whatever they refer to always existed. Yet the 'term *gene* has its place within a man-made theory, in whose absence it would have no intelligible use'. Language can also create something totally fresh. It is like the slow-motion appearance of a galloping horse on film. Did it exist before cinematography? No, says Black – but once created on film it became part of our world, part of its truth. The bubbling solution metaphor is a similar case: now we have heard it, it is a part of our experience.

The Creative Listener

Until now we have been implicitly focusing upon the producer of language, its speaker or its writer. But naturally this is only half the story. There is also a recipient of language to be taken into account; a hearer, or else a reader, who plays a part in the creation of language meaning. The recipient will assemble the meaning of the words, syntax, rhythms and intonations heard or read. The signifiers of language do not produce single, discrete meanings but are meaningful in conjunction one with the other, and according to the context of their utterance. Additionally, response is personal, bringing into play the shaping pressures of individual experience and interpretation.

We do not patiently and attentively hear and decode each bit of language as it comes to us, as if we were blank screens, like word processors, on to which the words are printed and simultaneously understood. Instead we begin by playing a guessing game – though it is an informed game. We have to, since, apart from anything else, the speed with which spoken language bombards us is faster than we can assimilate, unless we have some preconceived sense of where we are going. So we work from certain assumptions. For instance, English speakers appear to come to language expecting it to consist of sentences patterned around a noun phrase followed by a verb, with an option to follow this by another noun phrase. We assume that normally the first noun is the actor, the second the object of the sentence. Moreover, we expect language to make sense. This sounds ridiculously vague. But there is a contrast in this respect between children's responses and adults'. To a child, unlike the adult who has experience of the world, the sentence *The rosebuds rang three times* may be no less acceptable than *The telephone rang three times*. But as the child grows, expectations change: increasing experience is brought to bear upon language meanings. If our assumptions are challenged then we ask for language to be repeated, or read the sentence over again, looking for intelligibility.

Still, even when the words and syntax of a sentence make immediate logical sense, sometimes their implications are still not clear. *There's a Porsche coming towards us*, may suggest and *I'm drawing your attention to it because I know you'd like one for your birthday*. On the other hand, the remark may be intended as a warning, perhaps suggesting the need for evasive action. The hearer will have to make decisions about the speaker's intended meaning on the basis of factors apart from the words and syntax used.

Context, of course, will normally play a large part in clarifying the significance of any utterance or text. But what context? It is not always easy to know the significance – or the extent – of the relative context. Do you, at the wheel of your decaying family saloon and faced with an oncoming Porsche, decode your passenger's words only on the basis of the immediate physical context, the state of the road perhaps and the speeding image of the oncoming car? Or do you add something from the wider context of your relationship with your passenger, maybe recalling past conversations about fantasy birthday presents? Consider both contexts at once and a crash may be imminent! Choices will have to be made and frequently these tend to be limited for the receiver by the speaker/writer. Intonation, for instance, helps to fix the intended meaning. It is hardly likely that a Porsche set on a crash course would inspire the same sort of intonational curve that a birthday present discussion might trigger.

I am going to look at the complexities of meaning-creation, particularly by the recipient of language, through examples from poetry. But the choice of examples from art is relevant to naturally occurring language as well. Art draws on the creative facility for language use and response possessed at some level by us all. By definition, of course, it uses this facility to capacity. But in consequence it is an excellent model of our potential. Joseph Brodsky remarked in his speech accepting the Nobel Prize for Literature:

> . . . it is not that art is a by-product of our species' development, but just the reverse – if what distinguishes us from other members of the animal kingdom is speech, then literature – and poetry, the highest form of locution – is, to put it bluntly, the goal of our species. (Translated from the Russian by Barry Rubin and quoted in *The Sunday Times*, 10 January 1988.)

There are of course certain distinguishing factors of art language; rhyme in poetry, for instance. There is no suggestion that we should start to speak in rhyme whilst doing the shopping and waiting for buses. Still, even these techniques develop from the competence we all share: in the case of rhyme, from our basic facility to manipulate sound patterns and to do so in meaningful ways. It is true, certainly, that the province of art is a context of its own: knowing that we are hearing/reading art language leads us to make special interpretation in certain cases. But, again, the pressure of context itself is, as we have said, just one of the influences we encounter in using and responding to any kind of language.

In the following poem Philip Larkin chooses to use standard English (1964: 44), and he does not (except, perhaps, for the one word *estateful*) select any unusual words, sounds, or syntax. Even so, there is nothing 'standard' about this poem's potential for meaningful interpretation. The reader/hearer is invited to respond to the language of the poem with flexibility and creativity. It is a flexibility and creativity that we shall bring to bear on language – prestige and non-standard dialect English, as well as other circles of speech and writing – in later chapters.

This poem displays in particular the profound meaning potential of *words*. (Later we shall also look briefly, through another poem, at the meaningfulness of sounds, rhythms, and syntax.) Here, words are not restricted to any fixed definition: the contexts in which they appear challenge and expand a narrow decoding. This is not to say they are vague, mean*ingless*. Rather, they have depth of possibility.

Afternoons

Summer is fading:
The leaves fall in ones and twos
From trees bordering

> The new recreation ground.
> In the hollows of afternoons
> Young mothers assemble
> At swing and sandpit
> Setting free their children.
>
> Behind them, at intervals
> Stand husbands in skilled trades,
> An estateful of washing,
> And the albums, lettered
> *Our Wedding*, lying
> Near the television:
> Before them, the wind
> Is ruining their courting-places
>
> That are still courting-places
> (But the lovers are all in school)
> And their children so intent on
> Finding more unripe acorns,
> Expect to be taken home.
> Their beauty has thickened.
> Something is pushing them
> To the side of their own lives.

It seems to me that the contexts of myth, of historical perspective, and of personal experience all surround and shape the implications of these stanzas – just as they might influence any use of language. In addition there are the special contexts of the poem itself, of literary convention, and of Larkin's other writing.

The poem's own context, the choice and arrangement of words within its particular structure that is, encourages a wide frame of reference. *Hollows* will always refer to some kind of dip, a scooping out: but does the word here signify a comforting hidey-hole or else an empty, lonely period of the day? It appears to be the time when mothers can be together and children can play – so probably it should be a warm time of re-creation. Yet these mothers *assemble*, and this word may recall not relaxation but a formal summons, maybe the kind of regimented gathering that takes place on a parade ground. For there is something in the newness, and in the geometric shape of the play area (bordered by trees, whose leaves fall so neatly in ones and twos) that is itself orderly, coldly restricting even. Each word's possible meanings are shaped in this way by the possible implications of others that surround them: their semanticity is a package deal. But nothing in this first stanza's particular package limits us to a final choice from the two possibilities introduced in its first sentence. The experiences of warm pleasure – or a dead end of disappointment – are both ideas to be held in mind as the lines wear on.

Then, into the second stanza, comes myth, in the sense in which Roland Barthes describes the phenomenon in *Mythologies* (originally published in 1957, an extract – *Myth Today* – is translated by Susan Sontag 1983: 109–59). In this understanding of the term, myth is an everyday feature of language meaning: it is not limited to literature in general, or fairy tales in particular. Barthes describes the language of myth as a second order of language. For, in myth, he finds the signifiers of ordinary language to be invested with a further signification, saturated with broader implications. They are not lies: myths are more like partial truths, for the user of a myth focuses only on certain aspects of a concept, an event, and so on. There is myth in this poem. For here is the album, lettered *Our Wedding*. The reader, bringing a knowledge of the 'myth' of marriage to bear upon the poem, will recognize that the pictures the album must contain, and the words of its title, do not simply refer to a set of events on a certain day. Instead they can carry with them a partial truth, by offering particular concepts of the value of marriage, domesticity, family life. This myth is in no sense fantasy. On the day of the wedding and for some time after it was very probably the truth. But Larkin invites the reader to recognize with him a challenge to the myth. For now the happy photographs and the phrase *Our Wedding* have apparently lost their original mythical significance, their original partial truth. Now, cast aside, the album appears to give the lie – it 'lies' by the television, no longer as proudly 'placed' as it very likely was in the beginning – to those original hopes that have decayed and been replaced by other languages, the consoling myths of televised fiction.

But why do husbands now stand at intervals? Here historical, cultural and personal contexts, apart from the poem's own, are likely to contribute to a reader's answer. The poem's social context at the time of writing would have focused its implications for its contemporary readers. In addition there are the implications of later readers' own contexts. On one occasion when I discussed this poem with a group, its members felt that the poem's husbands were physically and emotionally present sometimes, as and when they saw fit, offering support when they chose to, not when they did not. Some years later, a different group of students who were particularly aware, both personally and nationally, of growing unemployment, thought the poem referred to husbands who were sometimes in work, sometimes out, involved in a situation beyond their control.

The poem's own context does not seem to me to prevent either – or both – of the readings. Indeed, the invitation to weigh and balance a number of possible interpretations of the whole poem is offered to its very last lines. After all, there is a certain kind of freedom for the children implied, a certain kind of comfort for their mothers, despite the limitations Larkin suggests. And in the final couplet he invites the reader once more to define the meaning of his poem. In fact, the invitation is now more expansive than ever. The most general of signifiers, broad enough to carry a variety of significances, is used: *something*. 'Something is pushing them / To the side of their own lives.'

What? Who? I feel we are to consider only the mothers here, because 'their' seems to me to refer to the subject of the line *Their beauty is thickening*, and this could suggest the thickening waist of pregnancy, the pregnancy which leads into another phase of married life. But in my experience other readers have wanted to include the children too, the next generation that will experience the same dreary adulthood. Yet what pushes any of them to the side of their lives? Is it outside pressures, economic and social and other inadequate people? Or is there some responsibility to be born by the mothers themselves, those who cease (unlike their young offspring) to 'expect' anything of anyone, perhaps including themselves, as they cease to believe in the myth of the wedding pictures and focus instead upon the remoter images of the television screen?

The final meaning of the poem, particularly its closing couplet may be fixed for a reader if s/he feels a response guided by awareness of a further context, that of Larkin's other poems. Other literary know-ledge can also be brought to bear. For instance, a knowledge of more conventional literary metaphors and symbols comes into play with reference to 'summer' and 'afternoons'. The spring of youth, the summer of maturity, are of course, in our particular culture, conven-tionally understood in relationship to the autumn and winter of ageing and death. There is also a conventional understanding of the morning and the evening as symbols of the beginning and end of life. In this poem, the convention seems played upon and extended to separate the beginning and ending by the 'hollow' of an afternoon. Of course, we know the conventions well enough to use them outside of art as well – though the words may not be so readily understood, in this particular way, in the contexts of idle conversation at the bus stop or market.

Reading this poem demonstrates, then, the active part that a recipient of language plays in the language game. The making of meanings is a combined, creative effort, in art and in everyday language. This is as true, of course, of all kinds of unusual, non-standard language as it is of prestige standards. We will miss the implications of an unusual circle of language if we insist on stripping it of its specialness, imagining that we can better understand it by translating it back into some more standard form of English. Anne Cluysenaar (1976: 50) provides a brief example which precisely makes the point. She discusses a couplet from a Chinese poem translated by Arthur Waley (1949: 107). Before considering Cluysenaar's particular argument, we might note that she is demonstrating through these lines the meaning potential of syntax – but these two lines show how sound and rhythm can also be vital additions to the meaning potential of words. The hearer will respond to the second line's ponderous syllables and rhythms, and its falling tone, in contrast to the speed and uplift of the previous line's fewer and lighter stresses and its suggestion of rising intonation. These signals mimic and emphasize the meaning of the words – and also the implications that Cluysenaar finds lying in the couplet's carefully chosen syntactic pattern.

> Swiftly the years, beyond recall.
> Solemn the stillness of this spring morning.

Cluysenaar argues that an understanding which notes that there are no verbs in the couplet – and then mentally replaces them – misses the full potential of the lines.

> The syntax is not missing, it is being used – to better effect than if the verbs that 'should be there' had been there. . . . The adverb *swiftly* (for example) leads us to expect a verb, a verb which could still appear after *beyond recall.* . . . The second line therefore breaks in upon line 1, as if line 1 were short of time, and in its completeness it represents time stilled instead of snatched away. . . . what we have is a skilful use of syntax to mime the meaning.

All the examples of unusual language which are to follow (examples of non-standard dialect art and also other circles of language which are creative and unusual in different senses) require, like this couplet, to be accepted on their own terms. If viewed with an awareness of the subtle implications of all their creative language choices – phonemic, lexical, syntactic, rhythmic, and so on – they should not be dismissed as essentially inferior versions of some standard form of language. Their impact, aesthetic, semantic, psychological may, with the help of metalanguage, be fairly assessed and appreciated. And entering their special circles can be admission to fresh perspectives and fresh possibilities.

Note

1. *Ms* was included in the Supplement to the Oxford English Dictionary in 1976. Its earliest appearance cited there is 1952: an American business manual advised its use if there was doubt about marital status. The OED's first examples of its appearance with a feminist, political gloss, however, are from the *Daily Telegraph* and the *New Yorker*, both in 1970.

CHAPTER TWO

The Language of Men, Poets and Linguists

The particular, in the poetry and prose of this chapter, is resonant with the universal. The individual voices of men and of women, past and present, urban and rural, are influenced by the linguistic philosophies of their age. And in these philosophies meet politics, art and science.

We shall hear (moulded to a greater or lesser extent by literary convention) *idiolect*, the language of personal idiosyncrasy, fuse with *dialect*, the language of class and regional group. A dialect is not an offspring from standard English: standard language is yet another variety of English, each version having its own special and synchronically consistent lexicon, phonology and syntax. But whilst synchronic consistency is a defining feature, dialects have of course altered and developed diachronically. It would appear that all have equal semantic and communicative potential in their combined phonological, lexical, and syntactical systems. But we spoke earlier of 'circles' of language. This potential will develop according to the changing needs of its users' cultural and social circles.

Nineteenth-century writers at home and abroad, whether or not they imaged a 'circle' of language, perceived psychological and sociological implications in the making of art from dialect. In France, Frédéric Mistral, together with the Félibrige group formed by him in the early part of the century, had worked with Provençal dialect, believing in the importance of its local expression of local character, despite accusations of a regionalism prejudicial to the unity of France. And in America, James Whitcomb Riley insisted upon language appropriate to personality: 'never – on penalty of *death!* – must any word not in the vocabulary of the unlettered be used. Their vocabulary must do their thinking, in its place' (Phelp 1930: 179). In southern England, the philologist William Barnes approved (as we shall see in the following chapter) of the Arabic proverb that 'a man by learning a second language becomes two' (Barnes 1841: 22) and wrote much of his own poetry in local Dorset dialect. It is in this sort of climate that Alfred Tennyson and Thomas Hardy, whom we shall be considering first in this chapter, chose on occasion to write in non-standard English.

But nineteenth-century interest in speech variation was not confined to the literary world. It was accompanied by the attentions of scientists, grammarians, educationalists and sociologists. Actually, the systematic study of dialects had already begun. John Ray, Fellow of the Royal Society, published his *Collection of English Words not generally used* in 1674, and the late eighteenth century saw attempts at dialect dictionaries. But then, in 1873, the English Dialect Society was founded by Professor Skeat, and *English Dialects* (1911), drew on the society's researches. The society also contributed to Dr Joseph Wright's *English Dialect Dictionary*, which appeared between 1898 and 1905.

Behind this accelerating interest in dialect was a particular nineteenth-century approach to language: comparative philology, backed by increasingly empirical and rationalist approaches to scientific study. In 1786 Sir William Jones had delivered a paper to the Royal Asiatic Society in Calcutta, suggesting that Sanskrit shared a common source with Greek, Latin, and the Germanic languages. The tantalizing possibility of discovering the origin of all languages intrigued the nineteenth-century imagination. Moreover, a number of early linguists were Sanskrit scholars, and amongst them was Friedrich von Schlegel who encouraged comparative grammatical studies to establish the structures of variations. The subsequent works of Rasmus Rask and also Jacob Grimm in comparative Indo-European linguistics were pioneering attempts in continental philology. It was Benjamin Thorp and John Mitchell Kemble who, having studied with these men in Europe, introduced the new doctrines and methods into England. Their approach led on to Richard Trench's *On The Study of Words*, published in 1851 and reprinted many times. In 1842, the Philological Society of London had its origins in a meeting convened by Edwin Guest, and the Society initiated the compilation of the Oxford English Dictionary which adopted philological methodology in defining words on historical principles.

Interest in comparative, historical philology links logically with Victorian imperialism and the era's preoccupation with evolution. Richard Trench insisted 'If we would know what a man really is, we must know his "antecedents" . . . This is quite as true about words. If we would know what they now are, we must know what they have been' (Trench 1873: 194). But pessimistic reactions to the century's developments, particularly in industrial and educational changes, also played their part in the focus, literary and non-literary, on dialect. In 1870 W.A. Wright, calling for the foundation of a dialect society, remarked that 'In a few years it will be too late. Railroads and certificated teachers are doing their work' (Aldis Wright 1870: 271). Yet although the railway played its part in the new mobility that helped to break down local communities, increased travel must also have increased awareness of speech variants. A.J. Ellis, who compiled a book entitled *On Early English Pronunciation* (1869–74), actually employed a book-keeper in the Manchester, Sheffield and Lincoln-shire Railway offices to gather phonetic records of local speech heard as he travelled up and down the country on railway business!

The value placed upon threatened dialects might stem from a romantic desire to preserve the past, and from a glorification of the unsophisticated in the 'noble savage' tradition, together with an increasing awareness of the plight of the poor. Yet Professor Skeat, justifying *English Dialects*, spoke particularly of the potential he had found in dialect words to enrich standard English. He talked of 'dialect regeneration' and said 'we shall often do well to borrow from our dialects many terms that are still fresh and racy, and instinct with a full significance' (Skeat 1911: 4). He was speaking then not so much of preserving group identities, but of sharing and blending, across the country, the most 'significant' lexical items, old and new. It is an eclectic approach – drawing from a variety of linguistic circles, past and present – that appears to have influenced Hardy's writing. Tennyson, however, and William Barnes too, each chose, with the meticulous accuracy of philological science, to concentrate upon one particular (in their case rural) English variety.

Skeat also appears to have been referring particularly to rural forms of speech and in recommending these he seems to have been affirming a value in rural life. Tennyson's literary approach was more complex, but Barnes's work was similarly affirmative. The new urban dialects, however – although Hardy drew from every conceivable variety of language – were not so admired. A.J. Ellis, whilst referring to the particular language of a certain manufacturing community, remarked that the 'real dialect' was to be heard only in the surrounding villages. Well, urbanisms lacked, semantically, the pastoral purity and beauty which literary convention had idealized, and besides they connected with the new and disturbing working class. Moreover, the music halls contributed a sense of the comic to urban dialects: their rapid expansion and consequent demand for performers meant that they became stages for indigenous performers, entertaining in their local language variations. Nevertheless, city speech was preserved without mockery in industrial ballads that expressed a solidarity in the new social groups. And the sociologist, Henry Mayhew, chose to record some of his case histories in the Cockney speech of the people he was investigating. The accurate rendering of non-standard speech, particularly as an indicator of personality, was being clearly recognized in and beyond the literary world.

In fact, attempts to render dialect speech had been made in literature from Chaucer onwards, but these tended to be approximations only.[1] From the late eighteenth century however – from Robert Burns, through Tennyson, Barnes, Hardy, Emily Brontë, George Eliot and Charles Dickens – came an upsurge in literary dialect usage, a largely rural usage that frequently shared the new philology's concern with precision and accuracy.[2] Cockney writing was also responding to the new preoccupation with precision and acknowledging diachronic changes in the language. Henry Mayhew's sociological record of Londoners' own stories, although it stressed idioms and slang terms which appear to have been authentic, used an older phonology of literary convention. But Andrew W. Tuer's *Old London Street Cries* which came out in 1885 used a newer dialect and Anstey's Cockney writing in *Punch*, mid-century, also appears to have been fairly modern. So do Barry Pain's 'Tompkins' verses in the *Daily Chronicle*. And Bernard Shaw claimed that the speech he used in *Captain Brassbound's Conversion* was 'up to date'. He was well aware of a distinction, for he wrote,

> When I came to London in 1876, the Sam Weller dialect had passed away so completely that I should have given it up as a literary fiction if I had not discovered it surviving in a Middlesex village and heard of it from an Essex one. (Matthews 1938: 62)

Not that any of this received wholehearted approval. Even acceptance of Wordsworth's highly selective 'language of men', 'purified indeed from what appear to be its real defects, from all lasting and rational causes of dislike or disgust' (Preface to the 1800 edition of *Lyrical Ballads*) had not been instantaneous. An early reaction to Wordsworth in the *New London Review* – despite the fact that his poetry merited the description 'language of men' more through its contrast with the conventions of markedly poetic diction than through its close rendering of any one particular speech form in daily, local use – objected firmly to his 'simple' style.

> We may distinguish a *simple* style from a style of *simplicity*. By a simple style we may suppose a colloquial diction, debased by inelegance, and gross by familiarity. Simplicity is a manner of expression, facile, pure, and always elegant. (Sampson 1984: 54)

As for much more precise renderings of dialect, the *Hampshire Advertiser*, some years later (August 1846), was only happy to include one example of dialect poetry by the Dorset William Barnes in its pages: 'We cannot so far prefer our native 'Doric', to what we must with all *deference* call *good English*, as to give more than one specimen of the modern West Saxon.'

Nearly a century afterwards, in July 1934, similar value judgements may well lie behind the wording of the following question on a finals English paper examining trainee teachers at Goldsmith's College, University of London: 'How far have the changes which have taken place in our language been due to the influence of uneducated speakers?' And more than fifty years on again, as we saw in the Preface, a belief in a 'superior' kind of language – the prestige standard – still persists. The non-standard language that we shall look at in this chapter is therefore not certain of a sympathetic response. The language that men and women really use is not always readily heard.

But matters are changing. The National Curriculum Council recommended in its *Consultation Report* published in March 1989, that children between the ages of five and eleven should be helped to recognize different kinds of English. Moreover, this should be achieved with a conscious awareness of the process. 'Children should be encouraged to discuss language. They should be given extensive opportunities . . . to acquire the necessary appropriate linguistic terminology which will make that discussion well directed' (p. 47). In speaking and listening, five to eleven year olds should be introduced to regional variation in vocabulary, and especially to the differences between spoken Standard English and dialects. But this is not intended to lead to blanket condemnation of the non-standard: children should understand the *appropriateness* of their own use of language (p. 41). As for writing, 'universal competence in Standard English' (p. 46) is seen as essential. Nevertheless, whilst children should learn to write in Standard English they should 'understand' how it has come to be the written form most frequently used and choose it themselves specifically 'where the context demands it' (p. 35). As we saw in the Preface, the Secretary of State's latest proposals pertaining to children aged five to sixteen stressed the teaching of Standard English first and foremost – but allows that dialects have their place.

A number of schools have been including non-standard writing in their curriculum for some time. The *Guardian* (11 April 1989: 21) describes experiments in Lancashire where the class is encouraged to consider why the writer chose dialect and 'how different the story or poem would have been if it had been written in standard English'.

This year (1989) a General Certificate of Secondary Education examination, for sixteen year olds, included a question on one of the Lincolnshire poems of Alfred Tennyson. It is these Lincolnshire monologues with which we shall begin, monologues which try to render the local speech with a precision resembling that of dialectology. Then we shall turn to Thomas Hardy's language and its links with the interests of philology, before looking briefly at twentieth century linguistic concerns and their reflection in Tom Leonard's Glasgow writing.

Alfred Tennyson: The Lincolnshire Monologues

Between 1861 and 1892 Tennyson wrote and published seven Lincolnshire monologues: 'Northern Farmer, Old Style'; 'Northern Farmer, New Style'; 'The Northern Cobbler; The Village Wife'; 'The Spinster's Sweet-Arts'; 'Owd Roä; 'The Church-Warden and the Curate'.[3] Each of these expresses the unvarnished feelings of a local character. And – appropriately enough if, as we have been suggesting, local language can signify local personality – each character appears to speak out in unvarnished local language. Lincolnshire words, sounds and syntax combine, with accuracy apparently worthy of a philologist, to produce rich and colourful lines like this stanza from 'Northern Farmer, Old Style' (1123: 29–32).[4] Here an old man asks his young nurse if she remembers the waste land where a ghost had once sounded like a bittern – until he had 'grubbed' the spirit up and moved it out along with the weeds.

> D'ya moind the waäste, my lass? naw, naw, tha was not born then;
> Theer wur a boggle in it, I often 'eärd 'um mysen;
> Moäst loike a butter-bump, fur I 'eärd 'um about an' about,
> But I stubb'd 'um oop wi' the lot, an' raäved an' rembled 'um out.

Tennyson himself claimed linguistic authenticity for these poems. He said 'The Church-Warden and the Curate' was written 'in the dialect which was current in my youth at Spilsby and in the country about it' (Ricks 1969: 1433). And he had had the opportunity to familiarize himself with the language when, as a boy distressed by the difficulties of his home life, where his Rector father was ill, depressed and sometimes violent, he had spent time with local labouring families. Moreover, Joseph Wright (mentioned above in our brief survey of nineteenth century dialect interest) must have taken the poems to be dialectally accurate. In his *English Dialect Dictionary* (1898–1905) five of them – all except 'The Village Wife' and 'The

Church-Warden and the Curate' – are given as Lincolnshire source material. Also, Tennyson read a number of his poems to A.J. Ellis, who compiled *On Early English Pronunciation* (1889). Ellis made several suggestions for amendments towards greater accuracy and some of these seem to have been taken up in revised versions of the poems. For instance, as Philip M. Tilling explains in his very informative linguistic discussion of the poems (Wakelin 1972: 90), the first edition of 'Northern Farmer, Old Style' has *yaäl* 'ale' and *yeäd* 'head', but these appear in subsequent editions and elsewhere as *aäl* and *eäd*. The accurate description of authentic sound, word and grammar does seem then, as it was for the philologists and dialect-ologists of his day, to have been a main aim for Tennyson. He was not offering the kind of suggestive approximation that we shall find in Thomas Hardy's work. All in all, he would appear to have matched very closely the variety of English described by Ellis as the 'Mid Lincolnshire Form'.

Still, Phillip Tilling finds dialectal inaccuracies in the poems, particular in their phonemes. Indeed, Tennyson himself acknowledged the difficulty of indicating sound on paper, but he trusted that his audience would make up any deficiency. Beside 'The Northern Cobbler' (Ricks 1969: 1256) he noted:

> The vowels *aï*, pronounced separately though in the closest conjunction, best render the sound of the long *i* and *y* in this dialect. But since such words as *craïin'*, *daïin*, *whaï*, *aï* (I), etc. look awkward except in a page of express phonetics, I have thought it better to leave this simple *i* and *y*, and to trust my readers will give them the broader pronunciation.

But Tilling is not confident that readers can compensate for this kind of deliberate mistake. In fact, he suggests that imperfections of this sort actually make the poems inaccessible. He argues:

> . . . the poems, though they contain much that seems to be genuine, cannot really be said to give an entirely reliable impression of the Lincolnshire dialect heard by Tennyson in his youth. His attempts to indicate the quality of particular sounds by use of a diaeresis and by unusual letter combinations were not consistently applied and Tennyson clearly found it difficult to describe some of the sounds he heard. . . . It is a pity that these poems . . . should be largely inaccessible to the general reader because of an unsuccessful attempt by the poet to indicate the precise nature of the sounds of his native dialect. (Wakelin 1972: 107–8).

Yet though dialectal inaccuracy may make the Lincolnshire poems of limited help to the dialectologist, does this deficiency really matter to Tilling's 'general' reader? Do we require philological perfection?

After all, however accurate the language, it could be inaccessible to any standard English speaker unwilling to tussle with unfamiliar sounds and syntax. The same might be said of any non-standard writing.[5] But minor phonetic or grammatical inaccuracy is surely not, of itself, likely to bother a sympathetic reader who, in any case, has little knowledge of the original model.

Besides, Tennyson may have bent the local rules from literary choice. Tilling is prepared to excuse some inconsistent spelling – *maäybe/mebbe* – on the grounds of their appearance in different syntactic contexts. But it is also possible that Tennyson chose one or other form in response to metrical pressure. For the longer vowel of *maäybe* would disrupt the rhythm of the following two lines from 'The Village Wife' (1272: 69–70):

> 'Coom! coom! feyther,' 'e says, 'why shouldn't thy booöks be sowd?
> I hears es soom o' thy booöks mebbe worth their weight i' gowd.'

On the other hand, the longer vowel permits the slight emphasis and intonational curve that helps to signal irony – or else puzzlement – when the new-style farmer remembers from long ago the original attractions of his plain but enticingly wealthy bride.

> Maäybe she warn't a beauty: – I niver giv it a thowt –
> But warn' she as good to cuddle an' kiss as a lass as 'ant nowt? (1189: 23–4)

But still, given a willingness to come to terms with their unfamiliar English, what precisely can the carefully chosen non-standard language of these poems – in spite, or perhaps in part because of its occasional idiosyncrasies – offer to the ordinary reader? Does the dialect help to produce poetry which, given its local themes, is beyond the scope of standard English?

First, W.D. Shaw suggests that 'the Lincolnshire dialect allows [the poet] to escape Victorian norms of refinement and decorum. Tennyson can enjoy the raciness and vigor without being held responsible for the harshness or uncouthness of a dialect . . .' (Shaw 1976: 70). There is certainly unusual vigour in these poems. But I shall be arguing that, far from avoiding responsibility for dialectal roughness, Tennyson openly selects and exploits a so-called 'uncouth' register – a register that is available in Lincolnshire dialect just as it would be in any regional variety: harshness is not simply an inevitable and incidental consequence of using a dialect, nor elegance the prerogative of standard speech. Besides, there is more to these monologues than mere raciness.

In any event, apparently not all his readers found their non-standard speech excused the poems' unusual themes and lack of refinement. They held Tennyson firmly responsible for some sort of lapse in his art for he remarked:

> The worst of folk is that they are unable to understand the poet's mind. People who criticise me seem to be lacking in a sense of humour, you know. A man without humour is a fool. Some of the best things I have written are those Lincolnshire sketches, the 'Northern Farmers', but it needs humour to understand them. (Campion 1969: vii)[6]

Well, though his contemporary William Barnes, the Dorset dialect poet, was certainly no fool, it was perhaps a lack of humour that led him to criticize Tennyson's Lincolnshire work on the ground that, to write the poems as he did, he could not have 'loved' the local labouring family.[7] The implication is that in contrast to Barnes who, as we shall see in the following chapter, generally tries to give dignity to his rural personalities, Tennyson mocks and does not respect his characters. But the criticism is misleading.

It is true that Tennyson does not pick his characters' prettiest sides. The tone of most of his speakers is querulous or carping. A village wife gossips maliciously to a kitchen maid. A middle-aged new landowner castigates a son who puts love before profit. A spinster vents irritation and contempt as she grumbles away at her cats. And a dying old farmer demands his forbidden ale, damning his doctor and nurse.

> Wheer 'asta beän saw long and meä liggin' 'ere aloän?
> Noorse? thourt nowt o' a noorse: whoy, Doctor's abeän an' agoän:
> Says that I moänt 'a naw moor aäle: but I beänt a fool:
> Git ma my aäle, fur I beänt a-gawin' to breäk my rule.
> ('Northern Farmer, Old Style' (1123: 1–4))

It is not surprising that Barnes, hearing this old farmer's delight in drink, together with an open admission of responsibility for an illegitimate child and an arguably shallow religion, might feel Tennyson was unloving. For Barnes believed, as we shall see in Chapter Three, that in art only the 'best' of rural people – those aspects he considered to be 'good and loveworthy' – should be recorded for the sake of their own self-image.

But Tennyson clearly had other motives and Edward Campion takes a different and, I think, more helpful view of his work.

> Tennyson's Lincolnshire characters are brilliantly portrayed. He has no illusions and he sees people as they are, faults and all. Few of them are lovable but he treats them benignly, enjoying their foibles with an understanding born of a close association with the labourers in his childhood. (Campion 1969: viii).

There is no doubt that Tennyson enjoyed his Lincolnshire people. H.D. Rawnsley, whose mother was a cousin of Lady Tennyson, first met him in 1884. He recalled that on one occasion at dinner,

> . . . the poet had been almost silent, but a change came over him, and humour and good sayings and capital stories of old Lincolnshire days, and quaint Linconshire sayings, kept the whole table alive. I did not know till that evening what a splendid mimic Tennyson was. He altered his voice from the deep-toned bass of the master of the farm to the shrill treble and cracked voice of the farmer's dame, and capped story after story with infinite zest. . . . [Later] we heard the poet read not what we chose, though he gave us choice in most courteous manner, but what he would. (Page 1983: 62)

The choice included 'The Northern Farmer, Old Style' and 'The Spinster's Sweet-Arts'. In these and every other Lincolnshire poem Tennyson enjoys and treats his local people with understanding. He finds their funny side, but he does not trivialize. In fact, the poems frequently deal with situations that had troubled Tennyson's own life. Drink, which had broken his despondent and ill father, is rejected in 'The Northern Cobbler', though the old Northern Farmer enjoyed it to the end of his irascible life. And social snobbery and 'marriage-hindering Mammon', which Tennyson had witnessed in Arthur Hallam's relationship with Emily Tennyson, and came up against in his own friendship with Rosa Baring, lies behind the father/son dispute of 'The Northern Farmer, New Style'. Moreover, the half-imaginary Lincolnshire personalities who deal with these situations may in any case be more lovable that even Campion admits.

For none of them is uncomplicated. They are all human and their human weaknesses are explicable and mostly forgiveable. A father, who slept while his house burned and endangered his child, had fallen asleep in his chair not from selfish laziness but distracted by thinking 'o' the good owd times 'at was goan', and weary of worrying about the repeal of the Corn Laws:

> Fur I thowt if the Staäte was a gawin' to let in furriners' wheät,
> Howiver was British farmers to stan' ageän o' their feeät.
>
> Howiver was I fur to find my rent an' to paäy my men?
> ('Owd Roä' [1379: 45–7])

As for the gossip ('The Village Wife; or The Entail' (1272)), her tongue is bitter and sharp and she cannot wait to tittle-tattle to the newcomers at the Hall about the daughters of the family they have just replaced.

An' Hetty wur weak i' the hattics, wi'out ony harm i' the legs,
An' the fever 'ed baäked Jinny's eäd as bald as one o' them heggs,
An' Nelly wur up fro' the craädle as big i' the mouth as a cow,
An' saw she mun hammergrate, lass, or she weänt git a maäte onyhow!
(101–4)

(hammergrate=emigrate)

But her own life has been hard and it is little wonder that her relationship with the old Squire's girls had been ambivalent. She explains to the maid who has been sent down from the Hall for eggs:

Sit thysen down fur a bit: hev a glass o' cowslip wine!
I liked the owd Squire an' 'is gells as thaw they was gells o' mine,
Fur then we was all es one, the Squire an' 'is darters an' me,
Hall but Miss Annie, the heldest, I niver not took to she:
But Nelly, the last of the cletch, I liked 'er the fust on 'em all,
Fur hoffens we talkt o' my darter as died o'the fever at fall:
An' I thowt 'twur the will o' the Lord, but Miss Annie she said it
     wur draäins.
Fur she hedn't naw coomfut in 'er, an' arn'd naw thanks fur 'er
     paäins.
Eh! thebbe all wi' the Lord my childer, I han't gotten none! (5–13)

Still, Tennyson himself makes no open judgements as authorial voice. He neither obviously approves nor directly condemns his speakers. The monologue form allows him to avoid taking sides. And their circles of local and personal language, dialect and idiolect, combine to express all that his characters apparently choose to reveal of themselves and their lives.

Only of course it is not they, but Tennyson, who does the choosing as they tell their tales. 'Owd Roä' was based upon a newspaper article Tennyson had read, about a dog saving a child from a burning house. But, as he said, 'The details in this story are, of course, mine' (Ricks 1969: 1379). Other poems grew out of Lincolnshire remarks that Tennyson had heard at first or second hand. He presumably found them memorable because each succinctly encapsulates a life style or a motivating force behind a type of personality. 'The Village Wife' grew out of a sentence attributed to the Tennysons' own cook: 'If you raäked out hell wi' a small-tooth coämb you wouldn't find their likes' (Campion 1969: v). The words are assumed to sum up unhappy family relationships when Tennyson was a boy, and he did claim particular authenticity for his poem's image of this woman: 'The village wife herself is the only portrait that is drawn from life in the Lincolnshire poems' (Ricks: 1272). Other characters may be half-imaginary, but 'The Northern Farmer, Old

Style' recalls at least the legendary dying words of a farm-bailiff. These were repeated to Tennyson by a great uncle (Ricks: 1124): 'God A'mighty little knows what He's about, a-taking me. An' Squire will be so mad an' all.' Tennyson, as we shall see below, builds a poem up and around the sentence's comical pride and arrogance. 'Northern Farmer, New Style', however, presents a totally different character. It too was inspired by a sentence repeated to Tennyson, this time a remark credited to a wealthy Lincolnshire man (Ricks 1969: 1189): 'When I canters my 'erse along the ramper [highway] I 'ears proputty, proputty, proputty.'

These last two monologues can be seen as complementary, examples of the paired poems that Tennyson called 'pendants' (like 'The Charge of the Light Brigade' and 'The Charge of the Heavy Brigade', or 'Locksley Hall' and 'Locksley Hall Sixty Years After'). The contrast between the two Lincolnshire poems allows Tennyson to describe two kinds of men, two perspectives, and leave the reader to compare and contrast.

In between cursing doctor and nurse, and demanding the drink they have forbidden him, words – similar to the ones Tennyson had been told – express the old style farmer's exasperated puzzlement: what can God be thinking about, taking one as dependable as he?

> Do godamoighty know what a's doing a-taäkin' o' meä?
> I beänt wonn as saws 'ere a beän an yonder a peä;
> An' Squoire 'ull be sa mad an' all – a' dear a' dear!
> And I 'a managed for Squoire coom Michaelmas thutty year.
> (1123: 45–8)

He is proud of the work he has done all his life. Self-satisfied and smug might be nearer the mark: he is convinced the 'quolity' smile when he passes by, saying to themselves, 'What a man!' For he has turned waste land into crops, looked after eight hundred of the squire's acres, and acquired some land of his own. He cannot imagine who can take over. After all, in his opinion Jones hasn't 'a 'aäpoth o' sense', and Robins never 'rembles' (picks up) the stones from the fields. The old man's greatest fear is that it will be 'the Divil's oän teäm' – the steam cultivators – which will come in his stead, 'huzzin' an' maäzin' the blessèd feälds'. Men, on the other hand, have never intimidated him. He has never been a respector of persons – other than himself. He is sceptical of the parson's authority, based as it seems to be on less contact with the real world than his own: 'I weänt saäy men be loiars, . . . But 'e reäds wonn sarmin a weeäk, an' I 'a stubbed Thurnaby waäste.' And as for changing the habits of a lifetime and missing his ale: 'I weänt breäk rules fur Doctor, a knaws naw moor nor a floy'.

This old man has always made his own rules, with arrogant disregard for other people except perhaps the Squire. But if he wished for any defence – unlikely possibility! – it is there in the sheer vigour and independence of words that testify to a life lived to the full. And then there is the contrast with the newcomer.

In the 'Northern Farmer, New Style' (1189), instead of a worker largely dependent upon the Squire and serving him faithfully, like the old man, the new farmer is a considerable landowner in his own right. And he believes his son, Sam, should build up capital the way he did: by marrying into wealth. But Sam has plans of his own, including an impoverished bride. So his father castigates him with a version of the famous 'proputty' sentence.

> Dosn't thou 'ear my 'erses' legs, as they canters awaäy?
> Proputty, proputty, proputty – that's what I 'ears 'em saäy.
> Proputty, proputty, proputty – Sam, thou's an ass for thy paäins:
> Theer's moor sense i' one o' 'is legs nor in all thy braäins. (1–4)

The two monologues stand alone, but Tennyson's careful use of the dialect underlines the distance and contrast between his two, half-imaginary, farm men. For he is not merely signalling the local identity of a geographical area by employing its local speech: he is also indicating time and its passage. For 'Old Style' uses the old form of *a*, or *a'* for *he*. 'New Style', on the other hand, uses the more modern *he*, abbreviating it to *'e*. The two men represent different ways of life, evolved over time. The commercial, new-monied style of the later man would have been incomprehensible to the old-style farmer.

There is another telling contrast between the two poems. In each there is a 'bad 'un'. And in each case the bad one is a woman. For the new farmer it is his son's beloved: her sin is that she will bring no dowry. Her inadequacy, in the speaker's opinion, is a direct consequence of the sins of her parson father. For he came to the parish saddled with debts that he had run up at the University, and he then compounded his error by marrying for love and not for money. Moreover, where there is poverty there must, in this successful farmer's view, have been laziness: 'Fur work mun 'a gone to the gittin' whiniver munny was got'. Victorian notions of self-help and the work ethic justify this man in his own eyes. In his opinion, only the poor – which his son is likely to be, if he marries badly – are forced to steal. But he has no sympathy for the plight of 'them as niver knaws wheer a meäl's to be 'ad./Taäke my word for it, Sammy, the poor in a loomp is bad'. His own father, on the other hand, had worked himself to death and so he died 'a good' un, e' did'.

Well, the old-style farmer would have agreed that work was commendable. Hadn't he worked hard all his life? But he had worked mostly for the squire, not directly for himself. And he is not concerned with piling up money, only with paying his tithe and other debts. So, for the old style farmer the 'bad 'un' is the seductive Bessy Marris. The parson, come to hear the dying man's sins, has raised the problem of her child (1123).

> Bessy Marris's barne! tha know she laäid it to meä.
> Mowt a beän, mayhap, for she wur a bad un, sheä. (21–2)

But the old man is confident he has nothing to blame himself for . . .

> 'Siver, I kep 'um, I kep 'um, my lass, tha mun understond;
> I done moy duty boy 'um as I 'a done boy the lond. (23–4)

Besides, according to his lights he had been loyal to Squire and Church. And when his wife died he had gone to church, even if it was only to hear the parson

> . . . a bummin' awaäy loike a buzzard-clock ower my 'eäd,
> An' I niver knawed whot a meäned but I thowt a'ad summat to saäy,
> An' I thowt a said whot a owt to 'a said an' I coomed awaäy. (18–20)

Little wonder if, as Tennyson observed, some of his contemporary readers were not amused. They may not have been happy to hear the respectable Victorian ethics of hard work, thrift, sexual morality and religious observance travestied in an unattractive but energetic and self-congratulating way. The dying old farmer has been industrious all his life – but he makes no apology for having enjoyed his drink and his women. And the new landowner has also worked admirably hard – but he is undeniably greedy, selfish, and exploitative. A questionable kind of progress! Nor do these dialect poems offer a comfortable and easy categorization of women. They do not encourage the Victorian tendency to separate women into two camps: whores or angels. Bessy Marris's illegitimate child is at least as much the hedonistic old farmer's sin as hers. And then there is the confirmed Spinster and her 'sweet-arts'. Like all good Victorian women, she loves her hearth and home. But a lord and master sharing them is unthinkable. For she has noticed that men tend to be dirty, drunken and grasping. How could a woman promise to love and obey

. . . a man coomin' in wi' a hiccup at ony hour o' the night!
An' the taäble staäined wi' 'is aäle, an' the mud o' 'is boots o' the stairs,
An' the stink o' 'is pipe i' the 'ouse, an' the mark o' is eäd o' the chairs!
('The Spinster's Sweet-Arts' [1327: 98–100])

Instead of marrying she has kept cats for company and named them after her rejected suitors, Robby, and Steevie, and the Tommies. She has loved and cared for these. But, as she says, *she* has 'mastered *them*'. She owns her own house, has her own maid, and she is respected as she goes calling in the village, doing good works. In short, despite occasional regrets for lost love, in her opinion she is '. . . a graäter Laädy nor 'er i' the mansion theer,/Hes 'es hallus to hax of a man how much to spare or to spend' (110–11). Tennyson's readers might not have agreed: in any case, this spinster's non-standard language would have disqualified her claim.

But Tennyson makes no concessions to the syntax and sounds of gentility in any of his dialect poems. His normally mellifluous tones are nowhere to be heard. On the contrary, he seems to have chosen sounds and rhythms which would intensify the monologues' tough honesty. The lines are mostly end-stopped, rhyming couplets. They are long, generally with six fairly evenly spaced main stresses, the last falling heavily, together with a tone nucleus, on the rhyme which is usually short and sharp and on a single-syllabled word. They tend to be broken internally between chunky, pithy phrases, but these intensify a dogged rhythmic beat by matching rather than cutting across its pattern.

'What's i' that bottle a-stanning theer?' I'll tell tha. Gin.
But if thou wants thy grog, tha mun goä fur it down to the inn.
Naay – fur I be maäin-glad, but thaw tha was iver sa dry,
Thou gits naw gin fro' the bottle theer, an' I'll tell tha why.
('The Northern Cobbler' [1256: 7–10])

The melodic Tennyson is not here. This is perhaps why C.H. Sisson is misled into implying (1965: 44) that his Lincolnshire verse is not so well managed as William Barnes's Dorset poetry, whose flowing blend of conversational rhythm with metre Sissons particularly admires. But of course, unlike Barnes's harmonious and beautiful personae, Tennyson's personalities are not necessarily attractive and contented, and his prosody perfectly accommodates their vigorous, emphatic and sometimes ugly talk.

It is not that Lincolnshire dialect will not mould to the usual mellifluousness of Tennyson's writing, or that Dorset language is naturally more tuneful and languorous. We shall see that Barnes deliberately emphasized Dorset's musical potential. But, like any language, including standard English, even Dorset could sound harsh and Barnes let it do so very occasionally, when his theme was in no way romantic and idyllic. Instead of emphasizing rounded and long vowels, he stressed and clustered harsher consonants:

> There's thik wold hag, Moll Brown, look zee, jus' past!
> I wish the ugly sly wold witch
> Would tumble over into ditch.
> ('A Witch' [Jones 1962: 224])

The Lincolnshire poems are always rough and pithy. Listen to the spinster explaining her distaste for children.

> But I niver not wished fur childer, I hevn't na likin fur brats;
> Pretty anew when ya dresses 'em oop, an' they goäs fur a walk,
> Or sits wi' their 'ands afoor 'em, an' doesn't not 'inder the talk!
> But their bottles o' pap, an' their mucky bibs, an' the clats an' the clouts,
> An' their mashin their toys to pieäces an' maäkin' ma deäf wi' their shouts, (1327: 84–8)

The image leaves no room for a sentimentalized Victorian picture of contented – and clean – family life. And the language, rhythm and sound, forces its dirt and disruption upon the ear. There is no escape for the reader from the plosives and harsh consonant combinations all metrically hammered home, in 'But their bottles o' pap, an' their mucky bibs, an' the clats and the clouts'.

Nor can the Village Wife's scorn for the Squire be missed, as her tongue spits out its distasteful description – not even by a refined and standard speaking reader who does not readily understand the vocabulary but must sense an unvarnished truth in its uncompromising consonants.

> While 'e sit like a graät glimmer-gowk wi' 'is glasses athurt 'is noäse,
> An' is noäse sa grufted wi' snuff es it couldn't be scroobed awaäy . . .
> (1272: 38–9)

In 'escaping Victorian norms of refinement and decorum' (Shaw 1976: 70), these poems are not, as we have heard Tennyson himself observe ('it needs humour to understand them' [Campion 1969: vii]), for humourless people. For if there is a joke at someone's expense, it is not confined to the monologue speakers: it may well be on the reader and pretentious human nature. For the poems' relevance, despite the dialect which speaks out for particular individuals, in a particular place and century, is not exclusively tied to the circle of Lincolnshire rural people. The weaknesses – and strengths – all these personalities display are not idiosyncratic but broadly human, unrestricted to a certain place or time. Greed, self-indulgence, vulgarity, spite, and cunning are hardly the distasteful sins of the few. And nothing of these is hidden behind the smooth conventions of standard talk. The harsh and strident vigour of Tennyson's careful use of dialect refuses to be ignored. The laughter will need to be generous.

Nevertheless, despite a wider relevance, the personalities who speak out in these poems are, as we have established, using reasonably accurate local speech, with a correctness no doubt inspired by the philological precision and desire to preserve disintegrating languages that is a reflection of the Victorian age. Thomas Hardy's response to the linguistic preoccupations of his day was rather different.

Hardy's 'irregular' language: symptom and symbol of linguistic evolution

From his own day to the present, Hardy has been severely censured for clumsy, quaint, or verbose style.[8] Occasionally his critics may be right: it would be surprising if a prolific writer did not err on occasion and, besides, the demands of Victorian publishing, including serialization and editorial directives, no doubt took their toll. But, in the main, Hardy's unusual language can be defended as an apt and conscious choice. Besides, it has a significance relating to the philological and evolutionary concerns of his time.

Philip Larkin was right then to applaud the precision of Hardy's, so called, 'odd' words: 'He might say, "I lipped her", when he means "I kissed her", but after all, that brings in the question of lips and that is how kissing's done' (Larkin 1968). Moreover, despite T.S. Eliot's judgement (1934: 54–5) that Hardy was 'indifferent . . . to the prescripts of good writing', his use of words and syntax was rarely careless. In fact, far from being indifferent, Hardy consciously studied language. He wrote in his diary: 'Read again Addison, Macaulay, Newman, Sterne, Defoe, Lamb, Gibbon, Burke, *Times* leaders, etc., in a study of style' (F.E. Hardy 1962: 105).

Besides, he subjected both his prose and poetry, even after initial publication, to constant revision. And, interestingly for our purposes, many of these revisions have a tendency to veer further away from, rather than towards, the conventionally acceptable. The result, in Paul Zietlow's estimation (1974: 30), is an increased 'richness of meaning' achieved by alteration towards a greater 'boldness of language' in a 'cruder, tougher diction and syntax'. Zietlow cites changes to 'The Casterbridge Captains' including the following:

> Transcendent triumph in return
> No longer lit his brain
> [His heart no longer knew]

Zietlow suggests that the original (bracketed) line lacks the 'bite of the word "brain" '. But there is still more to be said. The change also transforms 'triumph' from object (of 'knew') into subject. So now, instead of bland participation in an ergative construction, triumph is yoked in active agency to the dynamically transitive verb 'lit'. Besides, the new verb adds to the alliterated 'transcendent triumph' a further *t*, more emphatic than the final consonant of the original *heart*.

Given this evident striving, through independent, original language, for a greater and greater 'closeness of phrase to his vision' (the phrase is Hardy's own, but originally used in praise of his friend William Barnes's poetic achievement [Hardy 1908: ix]) it follows that Hardy's conception of 'style' would be in some way monistic, in the sense we discussed earlier (Chapter One). He defined style, in his essay 'The Profitable Reading of Fiction' (Orel 1967: 122–3), thus:

> Style, as far as the word is meant to express something more than literary finish, can only be treatment, and treatment depends upon the mental attitude. . . . A writer who is not a mere imitator looks upon the world with his personal eye, and in his peculiar mood; thence grows up in his style, in the full sense of the term . . .

It is appropriate then, as Samuel Hynes has argued, that Hardy's style should be 'built upon tensions and disparities', for Hardy's own personal eye, his own particular mental attitude, is focused upon 'man's ignorance, and his inability to reduce the universe to significant order' (Hynes 1956: 60). The neatness and predictability of conventional style would be a hopelessly inappropriate semiotic.

It is therefore not surprising that Hardy admired an 'irregularity' in architectural style, an irregularity which 'he carried on into his verse' (F.E. Hardy 1962: 301). But Hardy's writing is not only 'irregular' in the sense of 'inexact rhymes and rhythms' in his poems (F.E. Hardy: 105). It is, in addition, in the poems and in the prose, an irregular, unconventional, lexical and syntactic hybrid. And this synthesis of language, taken from past and present, is a signal of a particular kind of human tension and disparity: it is both symbolic and symptomatic of Hardy's sense of human and linguistic development.

Ralph Elliott (1984) identifies three intermingled strands in Hardy's language: the professional, the scholarly and the rustic. We might add, fourthly, the language of change. Together, these strands form what Hardy calls 'treatment', or style.

He acquired the first ('professional') strand of language partly from his architectural apprenticeship, adding to his vocabulary words like *architrave* and *ashlar, pilaster* and *cornice, mullion* and *transom*. But it is augmented, as Elliot demonstrates, by his knowledge of technology, science, botany, music, painting, and foreign languages (*telegraph-needles, animalcula, metallic cymballing, perspective, elevation, pari passu*, and the like). Such a lexicon harnesses his art to the objective world and, moreover, to the larger world beyond Wessex so that, as Norman Page suggests, 'Hardy may consciously have undertaken a genuine and worthwhile expansion of the range of language susceptible of being utilized in a work of fiction' (Page 1980: 159–60).

The second strand of Hardy's language, the 'scholarly' strand which is fully exemplified in Chapter IV of Elliott's *Thomas Hardy's English* (1984), stems from his voracious reading. It resurrects the ancient and blends it with the modern, uniting classical and mythological allusion, and words and phrases from the Bible, with echoes from Shakespeare, Milton, Addison, Tennyson, Mill, and so on.

The third aspect of Hardy's language originates in his own Dorsetshire background. He wrote that 'he knew the dialect, but did not speak it – it was not spoken in his mother' house, but only when necessary to the cottagers, and by his father to his workmen . . .' (Page 1980: 153). This slighting reference to rural speech – it was spoken 'only when necessary' – must stem from Hardy's tendency to conceal his humble origins, rather than from any personal distaste for the dialect. True, its local words were 'those terrible marks of the beast to the truly genteel', tell-tale marks threatening Elizabeth Jane's upward mobility in *The Mayor of Casterbridge*, but even here Hardy describes them as 'pretty and picturesque' (Hardy 1978: 200). Besides, he endorsed more than a prettiness in local language by compiling and introducing an edition of William Barnes's Dorset dialect poetry. Here he confirmed the expressive potential of the dialect by remarking in the foreword that it spoke out for the labourer and also achieved an 'expression of [Barnes's] own mind and experience' (Hardy 1908: 11). It appears to serve both of these purposes in Hardy's own writing, giving voice to some of his local characters and also contributing to his authorial, personal voice.

But, unlike William Barnes's close rendering of the Dorset speech, which we shall consider in the following chapter, Hardy's dialect is impressionistic and selective. His method is of a piece with his concept of art:

Art is a changing of the actual proportions and order of things, so as to bring out more forcibly than might otherwise be done that feature in them which appeals most strongly to the idiosyncrasy of the artist. . . . to show more clearly the features that matter in those realities, which, if merely copied or reported inventorially, might possibly be observed, but would more probably be overlooked. (F.E. Hardy 1962: 228–9).

And so, when the people of the Blackmore Vale speak for Hardy, they merely use an occasional local word – *mommet, apple-blooth* – and from time to time introduce a hint of local syntax – *wer, bain't*. In the following extract from *Tess of the d'Urbervilles*, John Durbey-field merely drops a consonant – *f* – and that not consistently (*of, o'*): 'I don't like my children going and making themselves beholden to strange kin. . . . I'm the head of the noblest branch o' the family . . .' (Hardy 1974: 65). Barnes, on the other hand, would very likely have made the local man declare: 'I don't lik my childern a-gwain an' meäken theirselves beholden to streänge kin . . . I'm the head o' the noblest branch o' the family.' But then, unlike Barnes, Hardy wrote less for local readership and more for a wider audience with a wider perspective. As Donald Wesling remarks (1979: 19):

> Hardy, wanting a larger innovation than Barnes', determined to combine dialectal and standard registers so that each would be the implicit comment on the other. That way dialect would become a graph of class in a novel written about the countryside for a readership in the city.

There are a number of varieties in Tess, each signifying a point on the graph. There is the Dorset dialect of the ancient Marlott village, and the similar speech of Talbothay's dairy. There is the standard English of the bookish and middle-class Clares, and a slick version bent to his purpose by Alec d'Urberville, new man of the new world. And there are also combinations of dialect and standard English, sometimes spoken by Tess at the very beginning of her story. At this time she is heard to use 'the dialect at home, more or less; ordinary English abroad and to persons of quality' (Hardy 1974: 48). But, even when speaking 'ordinary' English 'abroad' it seems (or so Hardy tells us, though he does not choose to signify it phonetically) her accent was local, 'the characteristic intonation of that dialect for this district being the voicing approximately rendered by the syllable UR, probably as rich an utterance as any to be found in human speech' (Hardy 1974: 42). The reason for Tess's hybrid speech is the education she is receiving from the London-trained mistress teaching at the local National School. Tess is at a point of transition, between a dying tradition and the wider world.

But later of course, she acquires yet another teacher. Tess catches, with his approval, her husband Angel Clare's 'manner and habits, his speech and phrases, his likings and his aversions' (Hardy 1974: 245).

And so, when Alec d'Urberville comes into her life for the second time, after her disastrous marriage to Angel, he wonders, 'How is it that you speak so fluently now? Who has taught you such good English?'. 'I have,' replies Tess, 'learnt things in my troubles.'

She has learnt, but not enough. It is true that 'between the mother, with her fast-perishing lumber of superstitions, folk-lore, dialect, and orally transmitted ballads, and the daughter with her trained National teachings and Standard knowledge under an infinitely Revised Code, there was a gap of two hundred years' (Hardy 1974: 50). But Tess's London-trained mistress has not prepared her pupil for the new world's trickery, grafted in the self-made Alec d'Urberville on to the deceit of an age-old patriarchy. And, as Tess despairs, Joan Durbeyfield did not warn her daughter of the 'danger in men-folk. . . . Ladies know what to fend hand against, because they read novels that tell them of these tricks; but I never had the chance o' learning in that way, and you did not help me!' (Hardy 1974: 117). Tess has learnt that Marlott's tradition can no longer protect her, but she has insufficient new knowledge to survive the changed world, language and all, in which she finds herself.

Yet Angel Clare is equally dislocated. He had been convinced that, unlike his brothers – steeped in book learning – he understood and experienced 'life as it really was lived'. So he was amused at Felix and Cuthbert's fear, from the 'tone' of his letters and conversation laced, after a season at Crick's dairy alongside Tess, with her dialect words like 'a drop of pretty tipple', that he was 'somehow losing intellectual grasp' (Hardy 1974: 200–2). But both he and his brothers are wrong: despite the gloss of new ways, Angel remains embroiled in the formulae of old understandings, useless in his changed existence. Tess is right to claim: 'It is in your own mind what you are angry at, Angel; it is not in me. O, it is not in me, and I am not that deceitful woman you think me' (Hardy 1974: 274).

Thus, in the case of *Tess*, dialect has contributed, as it does in other Hardy novels, to the signalling of contrasts and changes in character and culture. It serves a similar 'labelling' purpose in some of the poems. The dialect of 'Bride-Night Fire' (Hardy's first published poem, which appeared in the *Gentleman's Magazine*, November 1875) marks the poem as a folk-tale, telling the story of a local woman forced to marry her father's choice but, on her wedding night, saved by her true love from a fire in which the groom perishes. Dialect here stresses only the localness of the tale: class, and town and country contrasts and developments, are not signalled. But, they are the ironic subject of 'The Ruined Maid', in which Amelia has found, to the amazement of an old country friend, a certain fortune in the evil city (158).[9]

'O 'Melia, my dear, this does everything crown!
Who could have supposed I should meet you in Town?
And whence such fair garments, such prosperi-ty?' –
'O didn't you know I'd been ruined?' said she. . . .

– 'At home in the barton you said "thee" and "thou",
And "thik oown", and "theäs oon", and "t'other"; but now
Your talking quite fits 'ee for high compa-ny!' –
'Some polish is gained with one's ruin,' said she. . . .

– 'I wish I had feathers, a fine sweeping gown,
And a delicate face, and could strut about Town!' –
'My dear – a raw country girl, such as you be,
Cannot quite expect that. You ain't ruined,' said she.[10]

However, in addition to the signifying of individuals and of regional groups, Hardy also used the dialect within his own authorial voice. It forms part of his idiolect. In both prose and poetry, his personal voice combines the resources of all his various language strands. The following extract, again from *Tess*, blends local words with an example from Hardy's more technical vocabulary, to which we referred earlier.

The swede-field in which she and her companion were set hacking was a stretch of a hundred odd acres, in one patch, on the highest ground of the farm, rising above stony lanchets or lynchets – the outcrop of siliceous veins in the chalk formation . . . (Hardy 1974: 331)

The qualifying, technical explanation of lynchets is perhaps part of Hardy's coyness about his own personal use of the dialect. On the other hand, he may simply be indulging his interest – and that of his Victorian readers – in the popular nineteenth-century study of geology. Frequently, as in the following example from *Desperate Remedies*, he pointedly yokes standard/technical and dialectal varieties together, demonstrating his knowledge of both: '. . . a large bed of flints called locally a "lanch" or "lanchet"' (Hardy 1965: 199). But sometimes, as in 'My Cicely' (51), a dialect term slips unremarked among the standard words to form one voice.

And still sadly onward I followed
That Highway the Icen,
Which trails its pale riband down Wessex
By lynchet and lea.

However, this strand of dialect – Hardy's third kind of language – together with a smattering of revived archaisms, like *clave, with-*

holden, *glode*, *upclomb*, is, in its preservation of dying speech, the very antithesis of the rich inventiveness that might be called Hardy's fourth kind of language.

This fourth strand, its invigorating creativity energizing the conventional poetic diction of the present at the same time as giving new life to ancient language, invites a particular interpretation of Hardy's stylistic motivations. His style – his 'treatment' – is certainly symbolic of tensions and disparities, as Hynes has pointed out. But these disparities are of a certain kind. Hardy's eclecticism stems in part from a sense of language as a dynamic and developing force – a force generated from a rich, valuable and still living linguistic past. He told William Archer (Elliot 1984: 20):

> I have no sympathy with the criticism which would treat English as a dead language – a thing crystallized at an arbitrarily selected stage of its existence, and bidden to forget that it has a past and deny that it has a future. Purism, whether in grammar or in vocabulary, almost always means ignorance.[11]

As Dennis Taylor points out: 'Hardy's anomalous vocabulary reflects his sense that current language is a compound of many kinds of language at many stages of evolution' (Taylor 1978: 14).

The mingling of ancient with new is a practice Hardy had witnessed in his friend and mentor, William Barnes. Hardy commemorates the older man (whom he first met whilst an apprenticed architect, working next door to Barnes's private school in Dorchester) in a number of poems, including 'The Collector Cleans His Pictures' (573) and 'The Last Signal' (412). Both have echoes of the older English that Barnes himself had favoured. And the rhyme scheme of 'Last Signal', including as it does a particular kind of internal rhyme, is reminiscent of the ancient verse forms in which Barnes honoured the ancient lineage of the Blackmore families peopling his poems. But in each case Hardy blends the old with a creativity that is not the invention of brand new lexical items, of the Lewis Carroll *bandersnatch* and *slithy toves* variety. Instead it stems from the addition of affixes to an existing stem, or else, using an old established literary process to fashion the new, the compounding of two lexemes. Barnes himself used and heartily approved these methods of creativity, since they seemed to him to preserve a language's purity whilst 'increasing strength' and encouraging 'vigour and growth' from its own 'growing limbs' (Barnes 1854: 50).

The economic and emotive compounding, by Hardy, of two separate noun images into one, new, nominal (reminiscent of Anglo Saxon kennings) is exemplified by the following:

> . . . ducks preen out in changing weathers
> Upon the shifting *ripple-tips*.
> ('The Torn Letter' [313])

> Grieved I, when, as the *hope-hour* stroked its sum,
> You did not come.
> ('A Broken Appointment' [136])

Hardy is also creative in a way that Barnes was unlikely to have approved. Barnes wanted above all else to preserve a language's 'purity', allowing it to develop only from its own origins. So, despite the unrealistic nature of his aim (given the constantly changing and overlapping boundaries of languages and their varieties) he would personally have rejected imaginative, innovative syntax as a perversion. Hardy, however, did not balk at inventive syntactic change through the invigorating creation of nouns from verbs. He coined, for example

> Twenty years have gone with their *livers* and *diers*
> ('The Sunshade' [490])

> Blankly I walked there a double decade after,
>   When *thwarts* had flung their toils in front of me.
> ('The Voice of Things' [427])

Moreover, affixing, in Hardy's case, achieves the particularly energizing conversion of nouns and adjectives into verbs, or into modifying adjectives with a verbal effect.

> . . . the far farewell music thins and fails,
> And the broad bottoms rip the bearing brine –
> All *smalling* slowly to the gray sea-line –
> ('Departure' [86])

> She is shut, she is shut
>   From friendship's spell
>   In the *jailing* shell
>   Of her tiny cell.
> ('Lament' [344])

All in all then, we have in Hardy's blending of numerous language strands, conventional and unconventional, old and new, a diachronic conception of language. His conscious awareness of language as a developing, elemental thread, interlacing time and cultures, is demonstrated in 'The Pity of It' (562), written in April 1915. Its first two stanzas hear in dying rural Dorset speech echoes of another land.

I walked in loamy Wessex lanes, afar
From rail-track and from highway, and I heard
In field and farmstead many an ancient word
Of local lineage like 'Thu bist', 'Er war',

'Ich woll', 'Er sholl', and by-talk similar,
Nigh as they speak who in this month's moon gird
At England's very loins, thereunto spurred
By gangs whose glory threats and slaughters are.

But Hardy's language synthesis does not produce the 'sad hash' that he feared resulted from local Dorset children's mixing of dialect with their new National School speech. Theirs turned out, in his opinion (expressed in *The Dorsetshire Labourer*, 1883), to be 'a composite language without rule or harmony' (Morrison, 1970). But Hardy's composite language, blending past, unstable present and future, is both a symbol and a symptom of his fundamental concerns. It is a use of language only to be expected given a preoccupation, throughout his work, with the tensions of change, loss, evolution and memory. And he appears to draw on every one of his linguistic resources and time-spanning visions, juxtaposing one with another, not through carelessness, as T.S. Eliot implied, but through his search for the right word – that word which will most precisely express his perception of the present with its dependence upon the past and its influence upon the future. It would seem, as Ralph Elliot argues, that his eclectic style "was one of the principal weapons he chose to "make war upon this bloody tyrant Time'" (1984: 218).

Not that Hardy necessarily expected his composite language to provide, in its synthesis, a totally satisfactory description and rationalisation of a changing and chaotic world. Dennis Taylor writes:

His self-understanding is endlessly forestalled, deferred. Words continue to diversify and point back to a receding point of origin which is real but unrecoverable. . . . The secret of words which bind the mind is lost because the past keeps changing, leaving us in 'Riddles of years ago' as in 'Neutral Tones'. (Taylor 1978: 14)

In the same way, the nineteenth century philological desire to recover the origin of all language was inevitably foredoomed. Even so, as Taylor goes on, 'For Hardy the real language of men, once made into poetry, must reflect the fact that our thoughts are mediated through words which represent multiple classes and stages. . . . In a sense our minds are strung out over the centuries' (1978: 14–15). Hardy's use of linguistic variety contributes thus to what David Wright calls a kind of 'living' language, so that one reads him and 'ends by knowing, almost as a participant, what the nineteenth century was like to be alive in; one sees it, smells it, hears it, feels it' (Wright 1978: 21). As it happens, Wright is referring in this case specifically to the poems, but his comment is apt across the range of Hardy's work. We have, through his irregular language, a sense of Victorian life – but the blend of several strands of language, forging the distinctive idiolect of his authorial voice, describes and symbolizes Hardy's special sense of an era balanced and evolving between the past and the future.

Before we move on to the final example of dialect art in this chapter, we need to up-date the outline of linguistic interests and practices with which we began. Then we can look in its context at the recent work of Tom Leonard, written in a Glasgow dialect.

The old search for the origin of all languages has lost its fascination in the twentieth century. But the scientific methodology, which was developed and applied to language study in the last century, has gained in precision and widened its linguistic application. The meticulously careful study of all aspects of language, including sound, word, syntax and semantics, has intensified.

And the related science of semiology – investigating signs – has come to the fore. If language is seen as a sign system, then the study of syntax is concerned with the relationship between its signs; the study of semantics considers the link between signs and that to which they relate; and pragmatics considers signs in relation to their interpreters.

The value of linguistic and semiotic sciences to other disciplines, as they develop in depth and scope, is now clearly recognized. Their insights and practices are increasingly applied in a wide variety of fields including sociology, psychology, anthropology, historical study and so on. Language is recognized as a pivotal aspect of human behaviour.

Moreover, Edward Sapir and Benjamin Lee Whorf's arguments for linguistic relativity (to which we referred briefly in Chapter One and which, roughly, suggest that people's views of reality are in large measure related to the language mould into which they are cast) have extended nineteenth-century understanding of the psychological and sociological importance that language variety has in relation to different groups. Awareness of variety – if not its welcome acceptance – has magnified generally. No one, linguist or layman, can miss the fact that, as we become an increasingly multi-cultural nation, English is now spoken in this country in a vast number of ways. Black English communities, for example, use varieties of English ranging from that heard in the immediate locality of native

English speakers to a very unusual English evolved from Caribbean creoles.

A major thrust in linguistics was of course inspired by Noam Chomsky, whose work we mentioned in Chapter One. Innateness and the concept of rule government are two major tenets of his thinking, and he makes a clear distinction between competence – what we know about language – and the performance of language. Still, the notion of rule government, and an awareness that human beings share some basic, universal innate linguistic competence, do not give impetus to prescriptive attitudes to language. That is, they do not play into the hands of those who would still, just as in the last century, reject non-standard varieties of English on the grounds that they do not follow the rules, are incorrect, and in some sense a travesty of human capability. For it is these very rules, and innate capacities, that permit individual creativity. Hence, the resources of linguistic science are brought to bear not only in relation to the shared language traits of a wide variety of groups (cultural, national, regional, familial, etc.), but also to describe the distinctive language behaviour of individuals.

'Description' is a key word for twentieth-century linguistics. Its models of language are not prescriptive, designed to reflect some authority's sense of correct usage or good taste. They merely describe what is actually done with and through language. Though 'merely' is a misnomer. Given the considerable advances in the capacities of linguistics, description can be infinitely delicate, recognizing, as we have said, variations in the kind, use and significance of signs in every respect, in syntax, semantics and pragmatics – and thus acknowledging the profound capacities of all varieties of language.

The poetry we shall now hear is written in a certain variety and style of English. Broadly, it belongs to working-class Glasgow. But it also displays variation between independent voices. And, resonant throughout the poems is the voice of the poet himself, Tom Leonard, expressing his personal awareness of the importance of language to individual human behaviour. He does so with twentieth century linguistic developments consciously in mind – and particularly with his sense that some of their insights have not yet reached those who still insist on a prescriptive attitude to standard English.

One Human Being Speaking to Another: Tom Leonard's Glasgow Poetry

Tom Leonard's dialect is urban speech; Glasgow talk. It is the language of his upbringing and, unlike Thomas Hardy, he makes no attempt to mask his familiarity with non-standard speech. On the contrary, he celebrates it. His attitude is clearly explained in an article and interviews in *Edinburgh Review* (1987), and also in three essays included with a collection of his poems in *Intimate voices: 1965–1983* (Leonard 1984).[12] It is a point of view stated openly in some of his poems, and implied in all his Glasgow work. Essentially, Leonard rejects class-ridden society's acquisitive attitude towards standard language. Instead he embraces the speech of individual and local personality: as he says (1984: 36) –

> *Poetry*
>
> the pee as in pulchritude,
> oh pronounced ough
> as in bough
>
> the ee rather poised
> (pronounced ih as in wit)
> then a languid high tea . . .
>
> pause: then the coda –
> ray pronounced rih
> with the left eyebrow raised
> – what a gracious bouquet!
>
> Poetry
> Poughit. rih.
>
> That was my education
> – and nothing to do with me.

He explains the motivation behind his first six poems in Glasgow dialect, written in the late 1960s.

> I was very angry when I wrote them. . . . I was absolutely sick to death of what I took to be kind of cuddly toy representations of Glasgow speech on the page. I remember the phrase that was going through my head was *we exist*, and these fucking people don't recognise that we exist. (1987: 68)

That anger is resonant in 'Good Style', the last of the six (1984: 14). It is released in the sneering and spitting rhythms of the good (in the sense of actually used and deeply felt) style which 'they' misrepresent and prettify.

Good Style

helluva hard tay read theez init
stull
if yi canny unnirston thim jiss clear aff then
gaawn
get tay fuck ootma road
ahmaz goodiz thi lota yiz so ah um
ah no whit ahm dayn
tellnyi
jiss try enny a yir fly patir wi me
stick thi bootnyi good style
so ah wull

For Leonard the problem is, essentially, a matter of 'them and us'. It is a question of division between classes, and also between two kinds of poets. As regards class (we shall be returning to the two kinds of poetry later), Leonard argues that those who talk in standard English with RP accent believe speakers of other varieties of English 'are' their language.[13] So, dismiss that other language as inferior, and in effect one has also dismissed, cancelled out, the people who speak it. It is a standpoint that Leonard himself must accept – but in a very different way – for it explains his protective fury at the misrepresent-ation of Glasgow speech. (His attitude would equate with our earlier discussion of circles of language.)

But, when it comes to themselves, Leonard thinks that standard speakers consider they are separate from their speech, owning the precious 'possession' of a language that they judge to be formally correct. It is an object, to be 'bought', since he believes it to be obtainable primarily by those monied classes whose cheque-books buy them entry to the institutions (including schools, and the universities, especially the arts faculties) where, he argues, it is taught and perpetuated. And it is a particular kind of object, an instrument, through which owner-users may further their social power and acquisition of yet more property. Moreover, it follows from its presumed correctness of form that this language must seem, to those who possess it, to be an instrument disseminating correctness of knowledge, Truth and also Beauty.

That supposed insult 'the language of the gutter' puts forward a revealing metaphor for society. The working-class rubbish, with all its bad pronunciation and dreadful swear words, is only really fit for draining away out of sight; the really great artists though, will recycle even this, to provide some 'comic relief' to offset the noble emotions up top. (Leonard: 1984: 65)

. . . the regional and the working-class languages, whatever else they're capable of, certainly aren't capable, the shoddy little things, of great Art. (Leonard 1984: 96).

In poetry, Leonard's kind of poetry (and we have said that he defines two kinds of poets, two kinds of writing, his own and a contrasting craft), he puts it like this (1984: 86):

> *Unrelated Incidents (1)*
>
> its thi lang-
> wij a thi
> guhtr thaht hi
> said its thi
> langwij a
> thi guhtr
>
> awright fur
> funny stuff
> ur
> Stanley Bax-
> ter ur but
> luv n science
> n thaht naw
>
> thi langwij
> a thi
> intillect hi
> said thi lang-
> wij a thi intill
> ects Inglish
>
> then whin thi
> doors slid
> oapn hi raised
> his hat geen
> mi a fare-
> well nod flung
> oot his right
>
> fit boldly n
> fell eight
> storeys
> doon thi
> empty
> lift-shaft

The poem's unpopular point may be rejected, its lines safely dismissed as a bit of slap-stick comedy in faintly bad taste. But it cannot be misunderstood: Leonard's kind of writing makes itself *felt*. The man in the lift, grandly acclaiming, in half-baked phrase, 'luv n science n thaht' and pompously raising his hat, shows himself to be a cliché-touting, convention-following fool. So it is a pleasure to laugh, at him, when he drops to the bottom of the lift-shaft. But, if clearly heard, it may be a discomfiting laugh. For the fall is real: the language induces a reflex action. The poem makes the reader go down with the fool: for a syllable is removed from the last lines and the bottom falls rapidly out of the poem. If we readers are ourselves pretentious pedlars of standard English, the laugh – of the wholehearted Glaswegian speaker – is disconcertingly on us.

Leonard's personae tend to utter language that is a direct response to their immediate moment. And the reader is drawn into the experience of this moment. For the poems are 'descriptive' not 'prescriptive'. Leonard borrows the terms 'descriptive' and 'prescriptive' (Leonard 1987: 68) from twentieth century linguistic science. A 'description' seems to mean, as it does in linguistics, a careful model of actual speech. Though, unlike Tennyson, Leonard is not looking to achieve fairly precise phonetic accuracy or text-sentence syntactic perfection. At least, he does not want to draw self-conscious attention to these matters. 'I wouldn't want someone to look at the page and think "Oh, how wonderfully this chap has caught the sound!" ' (Leonard 1988: 68). His poem must not be looked on as a curiosity, then, but as a shared event. He does not want anything to stand between the speaker and the hearer. Nothing should distract from a poem's main focus: the *intimacy of its voice*, be that voice angry, weary, spiteful, bewildered, teasing, loving. It should be 'like one human being speaking to another' (Leonard 1987: 71) and it is this quality which gives the title to a volume of his work: *Intimate Voices* (Leonard 1984).

It follows therefore that obviously crafted literary devices are intrusive for Leonard.

> . . . simile, metaphor, all those devices by which you pulled up flowers by the roots and stuck them in your poems as if they'd been growing there all their lives, those devices won't work so easily any more. They won't, because it's dawned on us that language itself is an object in the world – the world is not an object in *it*. (Leonard 1984: 102)

Intimacy is achieved for Leonard through 'kinetics'. In an analysis of the American poet William Carlos Williams's 'The Locust Tree in Flower', Leonard admires the 'kinetics of its thought', the movements of the poem's rhythms and lexical juxtapositions shaping, being its meaning (Leonard 1984: 99–102). The process is akin to Leonard's own syllabic play of the lift-shaft incident. Moreover, many of Leonard's poems seem kinetically effective through their description of tone units. Units of tone in the natural voice are separated by pauses, sometimes infinitesimal. Within each of these natural boundaries there will be one tone nucleus, a shift of tone. In 'Cold, Isn't It' (1984: 11), Leonard groups words – their sounds suggested by a contortion of standard English – into clumps, each of which roughly suggests a natural tone unit. In addition, each unit carries, in this instance, one main stress. The orthography therefore encourages a particular hearing of the poem, a particular hearing of its voice (and these poems do ask to be *heard*, not merely silently read). Punctuation is not needed to understand the writer's intentions and, unlike e.e. cummings's work, there is little ambiguity, intended or accidental, in its absence.

Cold, isn't it

wirraw init thigithir misyz
geezyir kross

But Leonard does not hear only one Glasgow voice intimately. He aims, he says, for fluidity of register. And therefore his kinetics suggest not only the spiteful voice of 'Unrelated Incidents, (1)', or the furious invective of 'Good Style'. There is also the shared misery of 'Cold, isn't it', and the unequivocal love that we shall hear voiced in 'A Summer's Day'. There is, too, the exasperated frustration of the mother of 'The Dropout' (1984: 51). Here, all of the lines are complete in themselves, mostly with one major stress, their stabbing questions or complaining assertions hammered out one after the other, tonal curves rising and falling with remorseless, uninterruptable indignation, till three shorter lines, with falling tones, lead into the last and longest, its measured length closing the matter once and for all. A reader must feel their target's inability to get a word in edgeways.

The Dropout

scrimpt nscraipt furryi
urryi grateful
no wan bit

speylt useless yi urr
twistid izza coarkscrew
cawz rowz inan empty hooss

> yir father nivirid yoor chance
> pick n choozyir joab
> a steady pey
>
> well jis take a lookit yirsell
> naithur wurk nur wahnt
> aw aye
>
> yir cliver
> damm clivir
> but yi huvny a clue whutyir dayn

And then there is the poor, bewildered and very funny voice of feminism's victim. Its kinetics, balancing one idiotic over-simplification with another, are a cry from the heart.

> its awright fur you hen
> at least your oppresst
> yi know wherr yi urr
>
> no mahtr whuts wrang way yi
> yi kin looknthi mirrur
> nsayti yir sell
>
> I am a wummin
> naw
> I am a persn
> who ztreatid izza wummin
> bi thaht basturd therr
> niz imperialist cock
>
> but ah luknthi mirrur
> na sayti ma sell
> ahv goat a cock
> a canny help thaht
>
> I am a man
> naw
> I am a persn
> who happnz tay be a man
> but ahm no iz bad iz summa thim
>
> its no thi same
>
> (From 'Ghostie Men' [1984: 106])

He has my sympathies! Well, a feeling response is inevitable in the presence of such feeling language.

In fact, a group of people with whom I discussed the poem – not all of them standard speakers by any means, but none of them as it happened Glaswegian – actually recoiled with feeling at Leonard's first six, most angry, Glasgow poems. They felt a viciousness they disliked, and felt it intimately. But as we have just noted, anger is by no means the only emotion expressed in his poems. Leonard, moreover, defines two kinds of poetry. The distinction he finds between his own and another approach, for him explains and justifies this weight of strong emotion of whatever sort, in his own poetry. For he contrasts his feeling language with a second kind of poetry, a poetry that lacks intimacy and which he therefore disparages as much as he detests 'bought' language. This is the poetry of the distanced 'professional', a poet who is 'a spectator at someone else's experience'.

> The 'professional' exists through a language that acquits him of present personal involvement: he is in control, through his craft. The ardently opinionated, the ardent in all forms, the raisers of voices, the thumpers on the table, the 'swearers', the passionate, those who burst into tears – these are all absent [from his/her poetry].
> (Leonard 1987: 41)

Of these poets Leonard would not say, as he can of a certain eighteenth century Scottish poet (James Maxwell), thunderous anger and all: 'He was healthy. His mind was in his language' (Leonard 1987: 46). It is as if the persona, in so-called professional poetry, 'is the Patient, while the writer has become the Doctor, the-man-who-sees. . . . This patriarchal image of the poet as detached diagnostic judge still dominates the influential literary scenes' (Leonard 1987: 40–41). But if a 'professional' poet believes himself/herself to be objective, Leonard insists s/he is mistaken. S/he may not wish to acknowledge a subjective influence upon a work, but its presence is inevitable, just as standard speakers may think they possess an object/language, but do not appreciate that they (like non-standard speakers) *are* in some sense their language. No, admit it or not, this kind of writer is merely, in Leonard's view, quasi-objective.

Yet 'part of the semiotic of [this kind of poem], part of the subliminal message is that it is objective' (Leonard 1988: 66). And so Leonard himself, preferring the intimate voice, must shun a doctor/patient relationship. It is for this reason that he avoids punctuating his dialect in a way which could suggest deficiency. The local language is a law unto itself. So there will be no apostrophes implying that a letter/sound is 'missing' from the language, no suggestion that an 'h' has been 'dropped'. He believes that to do otherwise is to patronize by communicating with the reader over a persona's head. Complex literary metaphor is rejected too, not merely because it is intrusive in the way we have mentioned already, but also because it is 'a way of avoiding, a way of getting under cover' (Leonard 1987: 65). Not that Leonard shuns ambiguities. These are acceptable to him so long as the writer is not evasive through them, but is totally committed to his personae. He justifies in this way the inclusion of a pun on 'insane' in 'The Good Thief' (1984: 9). 'I felt it OK to use that as that's a kind of friendly aside that maybe this whole thing is insane, the author on the page talking to the reader like the man talking to Christ' (Leonard 1987: 69). Presumably he would justify, in a similar manner, his decision to use a title, and a standard English title at that, to draw a point from this poem that takes it beyond the transcription of voice.

> ### The Good Thief
>
> heh jimmy
> yawright ih
> stull wayiz urryi
> ih
>
> heh jimmy
> ma right insane yirra pape
> ma right insane yirwanny us jimmy
> see it nyir eyes
> wanny uz
>
> heh
>
> heh jimmy
> lookslik wirgonny miss thi gemm
> gonny miss thi GEMM jimmy
> nearly three a cloke thinoo
>
> dork init
> good jobe theyve gote thi lights

Yet, friendly asides or not, the readers I mentioned above were critical again, this time in a different way. They felt excluded by the poem's local reference, unable to share in its intimacy, and certainly we needed Leonard's own notes (which I have included in a footnote 14) to explain its reference to local sectarianism, a reference that runs moreover through many of his poems. But whilst Leonard is personally all for relevance to the reader, he makes the point that universal appropriateness and shared perception is well-nigh impossible to achieve.

. . . if you're a woman cleaner working nightshift at four bob an hour or something ridiculous, saying 'Hello' to your husband as you come in in the morning and he goes out, your lifestyle won't be made all that more satisfying by sitting down and comparing him to 'a summer's day'. (Leonard 1984: 69)

The title of the following poem suggests it may be Leonard's alternative offering, a local voice that could, in similar circumstances, be more rewarding than a Shakespearian sonnet.

> *A Summer's Day*
>
> yir eyes ur
> eh
> a mean yir
>
> pirrit this way
> ah a thingk yir
> byewtifl like ehm
>
> fact
> fact a thingk yir
> ach a luvyi thahts
>
> thahts
> jist thi wey it iz like
> thahts ehm
> aw ther iz ti say (1984: 41)

Which is certainly not to imply that the lift-shaft victim's 'luv n science n thaht' are beyond the dialect speaker's interest, comprehension or language. But 'all there is to say' is more than adequately meaningful here.

On the other hand, Leonard is not rejecting standard English *per se*, or saying

. . . "Keats, and that" is simply a load of elitist rubbish, or that all teachers and university lecturers are simply willing estate agents in the property market of "intelligence". It's the system that uses people in this way that I'm trying to get at, the system that ensures that "culture", like everything else, is blasphemed into something to do with ownership, something to do with defining oneself – according to one's cultural tastes – on the hierarchy of power and status. (Leonard 1984: 70)

Presumably, then, Leonard would not necessarily want dialect work to figure in a university literature course. If obtaining a degree means obtaining culture, yet another object to be possessed, then any regional and working class writing on its syllabus may also become property – and the object of a take-over bid.

So it is best that one of Leonard's voices, rather than academic talk, should have the last word. It says it all. For it works through the kinetics it speaks for. And its patronizing lady linguist can only have 'lost' her accent if she believed, with the acquisitive classes, that language is an object to be owned. But abandoning a language, as she has done, is from Leonard's point of view abandoning a self. So a mobile society, in this context, is a contradiction in terms. It seems that the lady linguist has moved herself, her original self, nowhere at all: she has bought a new language and in consequence fundamentally changed.

> ah knew a linguist wance
> wanst ah knew a linguist
>
> shi used tay git oanty mi
> ah wish I could talk like you
> ahv lost my accent
>
> thi crux iz says ah
> shiftin ma register
> tay speak tay a linguist
>
> would you swear tay swerr
> and not abjure
> the extra-semantic kinetics
> uv thi fuckin poor
>
> ach
> mobile society
> mobile ma arse
> (From 'Ghostie Men', 1984: 113)

We have looked briefly, then, at three poets who write the language of men and women and who do so aware, more or less self-consciously, of the concepts of linguistic science. In the next chapter we shall hear the dialect poetry of a man who was a professional philologist.

Notes

1. Chaucer included some northern dialect in the Reeve's Tale, Spenser used an impression of dialect, mainly northern and archaic, in his

Shepherd's Calendar, Shakespeare's Fluellen approximates a Welsh variation and there is some south-western speech in King Lear. But I am most concerned here with literature paralleling interest in philology and adopting some of its methodological precision. Even Robert Bloomfield, who had used some Norfolk dialect in poems like his ballad 'The Horkey', displayed only an approximation of the provincial dialect through the occasional local word and the occasional suggestion of non-standard sound. The following extract from the ballad indicates Bloomfield's own italics and footnotes as they appeared in 1806 in his collection *Wild Flowers: or, Pastoral and Local Poetry* (Lawson 1971: 321).

> Sue round the *neathouse** squalling ran,
> Where Simon scarcely dare;
> He stopt, – for he's a fearful man –
> 'By gom there's *suffen*† there!'
> And off set John, with all his might,
> To chase me down the yard,
> Till I was nearly *gran'd*†† outright;
> He hugg'd so woundly hard.

> * Cow-house
> † Something
> †† Strangled

2. Skeat's *English Dialects* includes a number of examples of less familiar dialect work that attempt a consistent rendering of apparently local phonemes, words and syntax. There is an extract, purporting to be in Norfolk speech, from *Erratics by a Sailor* printed in 1800. Rabin is describing Ursula, the collar-maker's daughter.

> She's a fate mawther, but ollas in dibles wi' the knacker and thackster; she is ollas aating o' thapes and dodmans. The fogger sa, she has the black sap; but the grosher sa, she have an ill dent.

And Skeat includes a Wiltshire poem, written in 1853, by J. Yonge Akerman, beginning:

> A harnet zet in a hollur tree –
> A proper spiteful twoad washe;
> And a merily zung while he did zet
> His stinge as shearp as a bagganet;
> Oh, who so vine and bowld as I?
> I vers not bee, nor wapse, nor vly!

Other examples, from rather later in the nineteenth century, include apparently faithful representations of Sussex, Shropshire, Yorkshire and Cheshire variations of English.

3. 'Northern Farmer, Old Style' was published in 1864 in *Enoch Arden and Other Poems*. 'Northern Farmer, New Style' appeared in *The Holy Grail*, 1869. 'The Northern Cobbler' and 'The Village Wife' were published in *Ballads and Other Poems* in 1880. 'The Spinster's Sweet-Arts' appeared in 1885 in *Tireias and Other Poems*. 'Owd Roä' was published in *Demeter and Other Poems*, 1889. 'The Church-warden and the Curate' was written in 1890 and published posthumously in 1892 in *The Death of Oneone*.

4. All the extracts from Tennyson's poems are quoted, giving initial page reference and line numbers from Christopher Ricks's edition, 1969.

5. Besides, the standard English-using reader should never be too ready to assume his/her own pronunciation of standard syntax, even when this is RP. Charles Tennyson pointed out that

> . . . all through his long life [Tennyson] continued to speak with a "Lincolnshire accent". . . . [he] habitually used the advanced open vowel in words like "dance" and "blanch". For example, the Southern pronunciation ruins such lines as:–
>
> > "But follow; let the torrent dance thee down
> > To find him in the valley"
> > *The Princess*, Canto VII
>
> "Roar'd as when the roaring breakers boom and blanch on the precipices" *Boadicea*. . . .
>
> Speak them in good Lincolnshire and London English and compare the results. (Campion 1969: II-III)

6. Christopher Ricks notes that a 'grim humour . . . was always part of Tennyson's character and conversation' but he seldom allowed it into his poems'. "St Simeon Stylites" and "The Vision of Sin" are important exceptions in the 1830s, and late in his life he was to recover it creatively in his dialect poems . . .' (Ricks 1972: 18)

7. William Allingham recorded in his diary a number of meetings he had witnessed between Barnes and Tennyson. In his opinion the two liked each other. But they had their differences. Allingham wrote on 1 November 1865, Tennyson 'likes Barnes, he says, "but he is not accustomed to strong views theologic" ' (Page 1983: 54).

8. For example, Henry James, reviewing *Far from the Madding Crowd* in *The Nation*, New York, 24 December 1874; Andrew Lang, reviewing *Tess of the d'Urbervilles*, in *New Review* February 1892; Virginia Woolf, 'The Novels of Thomas Hardy', *The Second Common Reader*, 1932; F.R. Leavis, 'Hardy the Poet', *Southern Review*, Summer 1940; Cleanth Brook, 'The Language of Poetry: Some Problem Cases', *Archiv fur Studium der Neuren Sprachen*, 1967.

9. All extracts from Hardy's poems are quoted, giving initial page reference, from James Gibson's edition 1976.

10. Hardy manages the conversational tones of non-standard and standard speech to marvellous effect here. The poem's final line is beautifully ironic. Its first four words suddenly slow the poem's flow, particularly because the introductory iambic foot which shapes every other line is abandoned here and the first syllable is stressed, a stress which immediately implies a highly superior – city – tone followed by a city drawl. Then hoity-toity languor is delightfully counterpointed, after a significant pause, by the final utterance of the country-girl-made-good as she falls back into the dialectal negative verb inside a brisk punch line.

11. It is unlikely that Hardy had Barnes in mind. We shall see, in Chapter Three, that Barnes's concept of purity was rather different.

12. The three essays are 'The Proof of the Mince Pie'; 'Honest'; and 'The Locust Tree in Flower and Why it had Difficulty Flowering in Britain'. 'The Proof of the Mince Pie' first appeared in *Scottish International*, 1973. 'The Locust Tree in Flower and Why it had Difficulty Flowering in Britain', which includes a functional analysis of William Carlos Williams's 'The Locust Tree in Flower', was first published in *Poetry Information*, 16, Winter 1976–7.

13. Leonard notes that the received pronounciation of Edinburgh will differ from that of Oxford 'in its retention or elision of 'r' in a word, for example' (1984: 95).

14. Leonard notes (1973: 3): 'The author was brought up to believe that Christ died on the cross promptly at three p.m. on Good Friday. Three p.m. is also usually the time at which football matches start. In Glasgow, Catholics generally support Glasgow Celtic, while Protestants usually support Glasgow Rangers. The Good Thief is therefore assumed to be a Celtic supporter, who addresses Christ shortly before 3 o'clock, as darkness descends on the earth. The reason for assuming that the Good Thief was a Celtic supporter is because Christ said to him, "This night thou shalt be with me in Paradise" – and "paradise" is the nickname for Celtic's football ground'.

CHAPTER THREE

A Poetry of their Own?

The nineteenth century dialect poet, William Barnes, has been described as a 'fierce revolutionary' (Jacobs 1959: 156) and the term might seem appropriate since he appeared to champion through poetry not the conventional language of art – a standard prestigious English, together with universal themes – but a local Dorset dialect and the local Blackmore people who spoke it.

On the other hand, he has also been suspected of misrepresenting and misleading this local audience by using their particular speech to brainwash them with a vision of idyllic possibilities that he must have known were wholly impractical within the harsh conditions of rural existence.

I think neither assessment is accurate. Instead, I see Barnes as his son Miles described him: a man of 'passive courage' (Hinchy 1966: 66). For he seems to me to have created, through dialect, a kind of vision which was meant neither as an incitement to change, nor as a lying, evasive pastoral fantasy. It was intended rather as an encouraging and supportive model, an image of a richness which might lie beneath – and make bearable – the harsh exterior of Dorset labouring life. At the same time, Barnes's vision quietly faces a threat to these riches from an encroaching, changing world. It has been suggested and I agree, that his work was probably intended as a constructive kind of *myth*. Above all, it is a fine poetry which has sometimes been sadly underestimated, the challenge of its non-standard language avoided simply because it is different.[1]

Sir, I shook hands with you in my heart . . .

> *Sound o' Water*
> I born in town! oh no, my dawn
> O' life broke here beside theäse lawn;

Not where pent aïr do roll along,
In darkness drough the wall-bound drong,
An' never bring the goo-coo's zong,
Nor sweets o' blossoms in the hedge,
Or bendèn rush, or sheenèn zedge,
        Or sounds o' flowèn water.

The aïr that I've a-breath'd did sheäke
The draps o' rain upon the breäke,
An' bear aloft the swingen lark,
An' huffle roun' the elem's bark,
In boughy grove, an' woody park,
An' brought us down the dewy dells,
The high-wound zongs o' nightengeäles,
        An' sounds o' flowèn water.

An' when the zun, wi' vi'ry rim,
'S a-zinkèn low, an' wearèn dim,
Here I, a'most too tired too stand,
Do leäve my work that's under hand
In pathless wood or oben land,
To rest 'ithin my thatchèn oves,
Wi' ruslèn win's in leafy groves,
        An' sounds o' flowèn water. (270)[2]

Barnes himself was born near Sturminster Newton, in Dorset, in 1801. Like the poem's speaker, he lived on the land, at least as a child. In his early years he knew hardship. His mother died when he was very young. Thereafter he lived partly at his father's smallholding and, in the care of his aunts, at his uncle's nearby farm. Both his father and uncle encountered severe financial problems, but eventually Barnes left the land and made his own way. Using the ability which he had begun to display at the local Dame school and Sturminster Endowed School, he started work as a clerk in a local solicitor's office. At the same time he began a rigorous programme of self-education. Ultimately he became something of a polymath. He was a fine and innovative headmaster of a private school[3] (he would become friend and mentor to Thomas Hardy, who joined the architect's office next door to Barnes's Dorchester school), a philologist, a vicar, and a journalist writing on subjects as diverse as architecture, Christian marriage, and tribal art. He was also a pioneer of local adult education to which he contributed history, language, and science lectures – and, in addition, readings of his poems in the Vale of Blackmore dialect.

Earlier, Barnes had written in a 'poetic', standard English. In this

conventionally literary language he tended to produce only man-
nered, self-conscious stanzas like the first verse of 'The Farewell'
(Jones 1962: 28), which appeared in *Poetical Pieces*, printed in
Dorchester in 1820, probably at Barnes's own expense.

> Adieu, 'tis for ever I bid thee adieu,
>   Thou dear spot of my first youthful love;
> Thy moss-coated tow'r fast recedes from my view,
>   On the verge of thy precincts I move.

In his last years he would write again in standard English, an
important reversal which I shall be discussing.

But the initial transition, from his earliest standard English experiments into dialect, was a stimulus to Barnes's art. It gave him an
opportunity to experiment with the conversational diction and
labouring social situations that freed him from conventionality of
language and thought, and which encouraged him to focus on fresh
material outside himself.

However, Barnes always feared that standard-speaking audiences
would be ill-equipped to appreciate his rural themes. He suspected
that those who had 'had their lots cast in town-occupations of a
highly civilized community . . . could not sympathise with the rustic
mind' and therefore could not credit that the 'wisdom and goodness'
which he intended to be the abiding focus of all his rural poems could
be found in the rural family: the town-dweller seemed to Barnes
convinced that 'every change from the plough towards the desk and
from the desk towards the couch of empty handed idleness is an
onward step towards happiness and intellectual and moral excellence'
(Barnes 1847: 49). Perhaps this would be Barnes's personal answer to
those who now suspect his work is a disservice to the Blackmore folk
for whom he wrote and whose 'plight' they believe he concealed.

At any rate, whatever outsiders have felt about the dialect poems,
the locals for whom they were originally written were proud and
delighted to hear them as Barnes trudged the countryside to read
aloud at one Working Man's Club or another. Thomas Hardy
remarked,

> The effect indeed of his recitations upon an audience well acquainted with
> the nuances of the dialect – impossible to impart to outsiders by any kind
> of translation – can hardly be imagined by readers of his lines acquainted
> only with English in its customary form. (Hardy 1886: 502)

And Lucy Baxter, Barnes's own daughter, wrote (under the name of
Leader Scott) of a gathering at the Dorchester Town Hall,

It seemed . . . that the crowd of human beings was a magic harp on which (Barnes) played, bringing forth at his will the emotions he chose. If this seems exaggerated, let it be remembered that it was the first time a Dorset audience had heard its feeling, language, and daily life portrayed in its own common speech, and the effect was all the greater from the newness of the emotion. (Scott 1887: 167)

Barnes himself would not have been surprised. He believed that it was only by using their own local, vital language that poetry could reach the hearts of those who figured in it. And certainly, by aiming to offer his poetry through the signifiers not of standard English but of the dialect, Barnes intended, literally, to speak out on behalf of its Blackmore user. He wanted the local labouring families to have 'a poetry of their own'; a poetry that was 'sound, high-toned' (Barnes 1841b). But in precisely what respects was his work 'their own'? Did the requirement to be 'sound, and high-toned' in any way affect ownership? How right was Lucy Baxter to claim that her father portrayed his audiences' life and language?

John Lyons explains that a local language may be locally 'owned' in the following sense.

In so far as the more specific semiotic needs of one society differ from those of another, languages will tend to differ from one another in their grammatical and lexical structure. At its most trivial . . . this implies that a language will not provide a lexeme denoting any object or class of objects which the society using the language never has occasion to refer to. More generally, it means . . . that the grammatical and lexical structure of different languages will tend to reflect the specific interests and attitudes of the cultures in which they operate. What it does not mean, however, is that every grammatical and lexical distinction must be correlated with some important differences in the patterns of thought of the society using the language. One cannot legitimately draw inferences about differences of world-view solely on the basis of differences of linguistic structure: the cultural and linguistic differences must be independently identifiable before they can be correlated. (Lyons 1977: 249–250)

Barnes believed that his poetry *did* correlate with local culture. He explained his beliefs about language in a number of articles and in a 'Dissertation' preceding *Poems of Rural Life, in the Dorset Dialect* (1844 and 1847). Rather like von Humboldt, Whorf and Sapir (mentioned in the Preface and Chapter One) he thought that local language was expressive of local personality. Therefore, in his view, each circle of language must be preserved by those born to it, all borrowing from other languages outside the circle must be resisted by its users, and creativity must be encouraged from within a dialect's own ample resources. He thus, as he explained in his 'Dissertation', preferred to speak of a *riding-bag* rather than a portmanteau, and a *build-cutter* rather than a sculptor. He was trying in this way to preserve what he thought was the 'purity' of a language, to establish and use its original form. For he was convinced of a rightness in what he took to be 'God's first creative or forming will', untainted by the alterations of man's 'falsehood of ornament' (Barnes 1861). To Barnes, original languages must have been the indirect products of God's first forming will, not because he saw grammars as innate linguistic structures (in the modern Chomskyan sense), but because he believed they arose in 'conformity' with a man's particular God-given environment (Barnes 1854: Preface).

Of course his faith in possible purity is based on a fallacy. As his contemporary, Professor Skeat, explained in a discussion of dialects from the eighth century onwards, 'the purity of the dialects from contamination with foreign influences is merely comparative, not absolute' (Skeat 1911: 83). Even Barnes's Blackmore dialect speakers would be familiar with the word *sugar*, yet it is a descendant of Sanskrit; *tea* is Chinese.

Furthermore, there is little evidence that can now be drawn upon to prove that Barnes's phonetic orthography does convey a precise rendering of Blackmore speech as it was actually pronounced, or that the syntax he uses was exactly the local form, or that his lexicon was perfectly authentic.[4] However, he was a respected philologist and, as a teacher, insisted upon precision and accuracy. It therefore seems likely that he recorded at least what he *believed* he heard.

And this is what is most important in an assessment of Barnes's art: not his actual achievement of accuracy, but his intention to be accurate and his belief, in company with contemporary opinion, that he had succeeded. Gerard Manley Hopkins insisted that in some sense, through the dialect poetry, 'Dorset life and Dorset landscape had taken flesh and tongue' (Abbott 1938: 220–22). Barnes's contemporary Dorset readers evidently agreed. There were those delighted audiences, witnessed by Hardy and by Barnes's daughter. And Barnes had a letter in 1869 from a Blackmore woman now living and working in London. She wrote that as she read his poetry, 'Sir, I shook hands with you in my heart, and I laughed and cried by turns. The old home of my youth and all my dear ones now mouldering in the earth came back to my mind' (Barnes's papers in Dorset County Museum: Vol 4, 42).

Besides, a contemporary city reviewer believed that the poetry gave, to oppressive and ignorant upper classes, a much-needed true picture of the poor.

If the landlords and upper classes generally may thus be led to a more intimate acquaintance with [the poor] and their feelings and habits, and to a more sincere sympathy with their wants and hopes, and for their homely and household prejudices, which are far too frequently violated and despised, we are convinced that Mr Barnes will feel that his poems have aided in a work, whose success he would value far above any fame or emolument that may accrue to himself. (Scott 1887: 82–3)

Yet, despite these testimonies, it is indisputable that only *part* of Dorset life and speech are expressed by Barnes. His vision is selective, so that our 'intimate acquaintance' is invited with only certain aspects of the labouring family. H.J. Massingham was correct to claim that 'all the graciousness and greeness and floweriness of the Dorset pastures is in Barnes', but it was not strictly accurate to add that 'all that lives upon them' is also there (Massingham 1942: 408). For Barnes 'stage-managed' his setting and the people of his landscape, carefully selecting his characters, their dialogue and their backdrop, in order to create a special, mythical – though not precisely, as we shall see, evasive or fantastic – image: an image which contemporaries were eager to accept as accurate. Barnes's poetry was no doubt honestly intended to be representative and supportive of Blackmore people, and was accepted as such, but it was, as I shall explain, 'theirs' only in a very particular and limited way.

A Poetry of Their Own . . .

The language choices – from sound, rhythm, word, syntax and so on – made in Barnes's poems, contribute to a sense that this is local poetry.

For instance, our sense that we are reading poetry belonging to a particular, living community, is helped by use of those rhythms and intonational patterns which can suggest natural, spontaneous talk. C.H. Sisson writes that Barnes's work has 'the very inflection of ordinary speech, and where else would you look for that in the verse written in England in 1844?' (Sisson 1965: 44). Sometimes we are witness to a dialogue, sometimes an eavesdropper on a speaker's monologue as he or she talks to a silent figure, sometimes we are part of an audience listening to a story.

Take for example 'Polly be-en Upzides wi Tom' (66). The poem is in the form of an anecdote, a highly appropriate form for such local poetry, because the story-teller, and the custom of listening to 'teäles a twold', were of course integral features of the community, as Barnes himself explained in a contribution to *Hone's Year Book* about 'harvest home' (Scott 1887: 7). The first lines of many of his poems immediately establish the suggestion of a gossipy raconteur. Polly's poem begins with the remark 'Ah! yesterday, d'ye know . . . .'.

Then Polly proceeds to tell how she stuffed Tom's discarded smock-frock pockets with stones and sewed together its sleeves and collar so that he could not put it on again. Tom's reaction is predictable.

> Then in a veag away he flung
> His frock, an' after me he sprung,
> An' mutter'd out sich dreats, an' wrung
>   His vist up sich a size!
> But I, a-runnèn, turn'd an' drow'd
> Some doust, a-pick'd up vrom the road,
> Back at en wi' the wind, that blow'd
>   It right into his eyes.

There is – as well there might be, since the stones were sharp and 'their edges gi'ed en sich a cut' – a furious Tom implied in the first four lines here, but then a touch of Polly's delighted and stealthy cunning creeps into the second four. The fury is implied by the five major natural stresses, all of them coinciding with metrical stress and, apparently, with tone nucleii[5] – veag, frock, sprung, dreats, size – and reinforced by the hard-sounding consonants g, k, d, t, together with the alliterated f and v. A sense of tension, mounting tension, is partly conveyed because 'an' after me he sprung' seems to have much the same intonation pattern and appears the same length of utterance as the following phrase 'an' mutter'd out such dreats'. The next two tone groups, separated with a boundary after 'up', also appear to be of similar length, but have a shorter, and perhaps therefore more agitated-sounding pattern than the previous one. It seems that cunning interrupts remembered anger, however, because the fifth line slows the fury down, by the introduction of two early caesuras, each preceded by a slight stress and probably a rise-fall intonation, followed by the even measure of a delicate stealth that is helped by the alliterated d and t of the clause 'turn'd an' drow'd some doust'.

In this kind of way we are encouraged to imagine a persona in most of Barnes's work. And the choice of local dialect for that person's conversation, or story telling, immediately suggests that Barnes's poetry speaks through its personae on behalf of Blackmore people: it belongs to them.

Moreover, he concentrates on registers and literary forms which, I suggest, he believed to be appropriate to his rural speakers. For example, he did not include the church hymn amongst his dialect writing. Yet hymns do appear in his standard English work, much of which still appears to represent the labouring voice and rural environment but which also covers a wider variety of themes. It cannot be that Barnes felt the words of the church were defiled in the dialect, for he translated the Song of Solomon into Blackmore speech.[6] It is more likely that he usually avoided in his dialect work any structure which could be seen as particularly and inappropriately – given the generally everyday, working register of his dialect writing – literary. Such an explanation would also account for the omission of the sonnet, a highly wrought literary form, from the dialect poems, whilst it is still used in his standard English work.

Furthermore, a concentration upon an everyday, rural, labouring register may also be a reason for Barnes's sparing use of particularly complex or conventionally literary metaphor in his dialectal work. He never slighted rural intelligence. But he did contrast – and contrast favourably – rural knowledge with that of conventional and formal education. In his opinion (mentioned in an address to Sherborne School, and reported in the *Dorset County Chronicle*, 1 July 1880) rural families possessed 'a great body of knowledge, Folklore . . . which in the rating of the people's knowledge is often slighted . . . With children we think world-knowledge should be gathered before book-learning'. Book-learning would no doubt include the reading of literary poetry (as against the hearing of folksong), and perhaps Barnes made a distinction between the literary-linguistic competence of the rural family and that of the more formally educated. For some of his standard verses have a rather more metaphysical, speculative nature, and some like 'Rooks and Swallows' (Jones 1962: 744) draw on more literary signifiers and syntax than do his dialect poems.

> *I sat me* where an ash tree's head
> From *o'er* a bankside reached around,
> With outcast shade that overspread
> Some grass, and *eke* some stubbled ground,
> While hedges up the hillock's brows
> Held out their now *befruited* boughs. (italics mine)

The dialect verse, however, contents itself with straightforward observation, or perhaps clear simile. Statements are open: they do not require the reader to delve into a memory of literary signification or to evoke complex symbolic implications. So that when Barnes declares ('The Weather-Beäten Tree' [94]): 'True love's the ivy that do twine Unwith'rèn roun' his mossy rine,' he does not depend upon some implicit and complex response to the sign, understood by his audience either automatically or through some metaphorical process of comparison and creation. Imagery is clearly explained for his reader, as it is when the ivy figures again in another poem, 'The Ivy' (83).

Upon theäse knap I'd sooner be
The ivy that do climb the tree,
Than bloom the gaÿest rwose a-tied
An trimm'd upon the house's zide.
The rwose mid be the maïdens' pride,
    But still the ivy's wild an' free;
An' what is all that life can gi'e
    'Ithout a free light heart, John?

knap hillock

There is of course no reason why Dorset dialect could not produce literary metaphor, since like any language (as we discussed in Chapter One) it works daily through symbolic language. But, in his poetry, Barnes chose not to make particularly complex and literary use of his countrymen's capacity for symbolism, presumably preferring to concentrate upon what he took to be the everyday.

He habitually worked within an everyday – but definitely not rough and ready – register, and chose from an everyday lexicon. Now, as Lyons indicates, the lexicon of a language belongs to its users in so far as it reflects their way of life. Of course, the mere unusualness of local words naturally lends local 'flavour' and ownership to a poem immediately. But, in order to appreciate the full sense and specialness of local terms, the unfamiliar reader will need to understand them more fully, stepping within their circle, as it were, in order to grasp more than merely their superficial semiotic of strangeness.

The Dorset word *drong*, used in 'The Sound o' Water' (270, quoted in full earlier), is a good example of the point. To be fully understood it is necessary to know that in Barnes's area the word could refer to two ideas. On the one hand it could refer to a *throng*; on the other, it could mean a *narrow way*. Its selection is therefore particularly appropriate to convey the feeling of imprisoned claustrophobia, of pressure, that people who are accustomed to field-work, out in the open, might experience if trapped in close, crowded, city lanes.

I born in town! oh no, my dawn
O' life broke here beside theäse lawn;
Not where pent aïr do roll along,
In darkness drough the wall-bound drong . . .

But, in addition, these lines are still completely misunderstood and trivialized if it is automatically assumed – as well it might be by the standard English reader – that *lawn* means a smooth, well cared for, sweep of garden grass. In fact, for Barnes's community, the word meant unploughed land in a field. Therefore the poem is not contrasting an unreally dainty cottage life with grim Victorian urban streets, but instead compares the freedom of a vital – and tough – rural life with the restrictions of a city working existence. A standard English reader of today might well underestimate this important distinction.

It would be similarly easy for a reader – familiar with, and reading according to, standard and conventional literary devices – to confuse the significance of the pronoun *he* in Barnes's work. Barnes explained in his 'Dissertation' (1847: 35) that the pronoun was used unselfconsciously, in local everyday speech, to refer to many inanimate nouns. He is not then, in the following extract from 'Leädy-Day, an' Ridden House' (5), using a careful literary technique, a self-conscious literary personification, as he describes the house movers loading up a wagon with their goods, their bedsteads, chairs, kettle, saucepans and also their

> . . . fryèn-pan, vor aggs to slide
> In butter round his hissèn zide,
> An' gridire's even bars, to bear
> The drippèn steäke above the gleäre
> O' brightly-glowèn coals. An' then
> All up o' top o' them ageän
> The woaken bwoard, where we did eat
> Our croust o' bread or bit o' meat, –
> An, when the bwoard wer up, we tied
> Upon the reäves, along the zide,
> The woaken stools, his glossy meätes . . .

Ernst Cassirer (1946) suggests that this kind of syntactic personalization need not have arisen from a community's belief in animism. The syntactic construction can itself encourage the perception. But whatever its origin, pronominalization in these respects appears to add a resonance of vitality which would otherwise have been difficult to convey: that is, it makes clear, in an almost totemic way, the importance to the rural labouring family of certain objects, plants and creatures. And, since it is emphatically not, in Barnes's work, a standard literary device, a convention belonging to a less spontaneous arrangement of speech, nothing of that importance is transferred from actuality to draw attention to itself as an art form. There is no ignoring the domestic necessity of the household equipment, carefully carried – and therefore in the poem, very carefully listed – from one house to another, at moving time on Lady Day.

Nor is there any possibility of underestimating the importance of the elm tree in 'Vellen O' the Tree' (16). It had been a special tree,

Where the mowers did goo to their drink, an' did lie
In the sheäde ov his head, when the zun at his heighth
Had a-drove em vrom mowèn, wi' het an' wi' drîth,
Where the haÿ-meäkers put all their picks an their reäkes,
An' did squot down to snabble their cheese an' their ceäkes,

'He', until the day of his felling, had been a practical, protecting comfort to the workers for years.

But then, all local objects and places seemed to Barnes vitally important to the community, in that he believed them to be endowed in some sense with personality, with life, with an energy derived from the past, from the vitality of long-gone people and their work. Such energy makes for 'hallowed pleäces'. So, returning after a long absence to Woodcombe Farm one Christmas, the speaker finds 'the geärden's wall-bound square,/Hallow'd by times o' strollèn there,' ('Hallow'd Pleäces' [240]). The stone bench in the porch is also 'Hallow'd by times o' youthvul fun', and the old blue gate is 'Hallow'd by times o' passen drough'.

Marks of previous generation's industry – 'our fathers' works' – are particularly hallowed.

Zoo now mid nwone ov us vorget
The pattern our vorefathers zet;
But each be fäïn to underteäke
Zome work to meäke vor others gaïn,
That we mid leäve mwore good to sheäre,
Less ills to bear, less souls to grieve . . .
('Our Fathers' Works' [224])

Most importantly, I am sure that it is in this sense that Barnes viewed his poetry: his own contribution, work accomplished for the benefit of his neighbours and, expressing their local culture in their local speech, living on as their vital memorial. To this extent at least his work belongs to Blackmore people.

This being so, and given Barnes's belief that local language is so intrinsically expressive of local personality, it is something of a puzzle, which I cannot satisfactorily explain, that Barnes actually translated some of his dialect work into standard English. It is the more puzzling because he said himself that 'the spirit of an author always evaporates in the process of translation' (Dorset County Museum Papers, vol. 21, p. 34).

Equally puzzling is a remark by Geoffrey Grigson (1950: 12), who generally much admired Barnes's linguistic skill.

Barnes does translate, and without a great loss. . . . Indeed, a lack of knowledge of the euphony of Dorset dialect does not, to my ear, make it impossible to enjoy Barnes's poems clearly and intensely. These are two lines I keep among the furniture of memory, and keep in this form:

> *The cuckoo over white-waved seas*
> *Do come to sing in thy green trees.*

Barnes wrote:

> *The gookoo over white-weäv'd seas*
> *Do come to zing in thy green trees.*

The translation I make, more or less without meaning to, is much nearer Barnes's writing than, shall I say, Barnes's, or anyone else's reading of the Idylls of Theocritus was ever near to the original sound of Theocritus.

This comparative judgement may well be accurate. But Grigson's translation is not, in my view, near enough. The lost diphthong and voiced z helped in the original to lengthen the lines very slightly and to encourage a flowing rise-fall intonation: they are tiny features, and they make only slight differences, yet they are important differences which may help to make a mere statement of fact (which is virtually all Grigson is left with) one of more vital imagery, with a mimetic hint of movement and sound.

However, translation of Barnes's work from dialect to standard English has even more significance in so far as it may affect its lexicon and syntax as well as its sound. A small but crucial semantic difference is the result in 'Home's a Nest' (Jones 1962: 884) of syntactic alteration from the original 'Hwome's a Nest' (Jones 1962: 506). The Dorset present tense requires the auxiliary *do*. In order to maintain two parts to the verb – and thus to preserve his original rhythms – Barnes has replaced the Dorset *do grow* with a wholly different and, I think, unsuitable standard English alternative: *are bred*.

> Hwome's a nest,
> Where our childern do grow to vulvill
> Not our own, but our Father's good will.

> Home's a nest,
> Where our children are bred to fulfill
> Not our own, but our Father's good will.

The original's sense of gradual and personally achieved growth is lost and replaced by the forcefully deterministic verb *to breed*. It is not merely a matter of the lexicon but also of syntax. For the original was an active verb, expressing thus the children's own part in their

maturing: the latter is a passive construction implying their malle-
ability in the agency of their community's shaping hand. This
changed implication could not have been Barnes's considered preference, given that the rest of his Blackmore canon admires personal,
individual, growth through industry and the experiences, light and
dark, of life, and given that his poetry respects the place of the
individual (albeit, as I shall explain, his/her specially co-operative
place) within the circle of the community.

On the whole then, translation from Barnes's dialect into standard
English is not really viable because it damages the subtle balance of an
art which Grigson elsewhere called an 'art of wholes' (Grigson 1953:
12) and which allowed the achievement of what Hardy termed 'a
closeness of phrase to vision' (1908: ix). It detracts from a poetry
which is the Blackmore people's *own*, speaking out on their behalf –
at least in so far as it uses features of their particular circle of language.

Still, I have said that although Barnes's work appears to be a poetry
that is the Blackmore people's 'own', its linguistic performance is
ultimately stage-managed by Barnes himself, through his personal
perspective of rural life, a perspective formed from a somewhat
detached and special vantage point to produce poems which in his
estimation were, as we have already noted, 'sound and high-toned'
(Barnes 1841b).

... Sound and High-toned

It is true that the 'I' who speaks the dialect poems, companionably
addressing a friendly audience, proclaims himself, by voice and
activity, to be a labourer.

> Ah! yesterday, you know, we carr'd
> The piece o' corn in Zidelèn Plot,
> An' work'd about it pretty hard,
> An' vound the weather pretty hot.
> ('A-haulèn o' the Corn' [77])

This man is probably not then a schoolmaster, a vicar, a philologist.
He would appear not to be Barnes.

Besides, the dialect was no longer genuinely Barnes's own. He had
used it at home but seems to have stopped after he became a
solicitor's clerk and at least by the time he became headmaster of
middle-class pupils. Bernard Jones, editor of the only complete
edition of Barnes's work, observes (Jones 1962: 10):

. . . those who remember or remembered his voice recall that the sound of
the letter *r* was lightly trilled. This must have been noticeable, for several
people carried it in mind for over sixty years. As a young man around
Sturminster Barnes must have spoken with the Vale accent, but among
the Latinizations of solicitorial English his speech must have moved
towards the polite manner of the day, and the latter, as spoken by the
cream of Dorchester society, was probably his ideal in early manhood.
His accent certainly did not upset Miss Miles [the daughter of a local
excise supervisor, who became his wife]. Thereafter he must have busied
himself teaching standard English to his many pupils.

Naturally. As Hardy remarks in *The Mayor of Casterbridge* (1978:
200), first published in 1886, dialect was considered by those aspiring
to education for higher society to be 'the mark of the beast'. Barnes
did not, obviously, share this view – but he had to have pupils to
teach. Besides, he would have recognized the need for his pupils to
learn standard English in order for them to survive and progress in
the world beyond Dorchester.

The important point in relation to his poetry, however, is that
Barnes's conscious decision to write in Blackmore speech, through
personae appearing to be members of the local community, may
actually direct attention away from the fact that he personally – the
creator of the poems – was no longer of the people. Though he told
local audiences that he was 'like themselves, a working man, so he
cheered them on in the path they had chosen of cultivating their
minds and refining their tastes' (Keane 1978: 14), yet by the time of
writing he was a learned professional, himself an observer rather than
a member of the community which inspired his poetry. And, rather
than necessarily expressing the viewpoint of that community, the
poems certainly appear to confirm the attitudes of Barnes's own
authorial voice, the voice behind the mask of the Dorset speaker,
attitudes which he expressed more directly in his prose writing and
which include an appreciation of beauty, industry, the family, and a
strong faith in the Church (for example Barnes 1849, 1859, 1861,
1866). Needless to say, his personae may well have shared these
views, but it is evident, as Hardy said (Hardy 1908: xi), that Barnes
'often used the dramatic form of peasant speakers as a pretext for the
expression of his own mind and experience'. The fact that Barnes was
not a working man precisely 'like themselves' must account for the
particular shaping of his image of these working people.

It was a conscious shaping. A note in his papers, now kept in the
Dorset County Museum, is entitled 'Poetry' and sub-titled 'Teaching': 'Steering and guiding the soul to setting forth the good and
loveworthy that men's minds would more readily take and hold it'
(Levy 1960: 17).

His poetry was to be written in a manner, then, which Barnes himself considered to be 'sound and high-toned'. But it would not be true to say that it served only a public and didactic purpose. Often his work appears a release for personal emotion: love, sadness, anxiety (for example 'Woak Hill' (347) seems to concern the loss of his wife Julia). But in particular Barnes wrote, as he said (Barnes 1841b), in order to 'light up [rustic life's] more lovely features, foster its better feelings and tastes and touch its soul with the sweet pastoral spirit'. And every feature of his poetry is designed to reveal these riches – as he saw them.

It was not simply that his chosen lexicon was, though everyday, certainly not rough and ready: even the phonemes of Barnes's poetry were intended to contribute to his evocation of sound and high-toned lovely features. Lyons does not refer (above) to sound as a local semiotic. However, Barnes argued that certain Blackmore sound features – including rounded and elongated vowels and 'burry' consonants – gave the dialect a special 'mellowness', by which he apparently meant a rich, languorous tone. And he went so far as to connect this mellow tone with the local personality. The language's sleepy warmth seemed to Barnes, as he said in his 'Dissertation' (1847: 48), 'a good vehicle for the softer feelings, as well as for the broader humour' which he identified in local life. 'Broader' seems to have meant something like 'gentler', and it is true that gentleness and a simple humour are prevalent in the dialect poems, but whether such characteristics were genuinely paramount in Barnes's locality is of course a separate issue.

Bernard Jones suggests that the dialect of Barnes's chosen region did sound more melodious than the relatively staccato tones of nearby Dorchester (Jones 1962: 17). But it will be recalled that Lyons draws attention to the need to identify linguistic and cultural features separately before assuming that they are connected, and that an aspect of language is necessarily a cultural semiotic. If Barnes's own argument is carried to its logical limits, his belief that mellow tone is the result of mellow people should imply the startling sociological conclusion that Dorchester folk – living only just down the road from the Blackmore people of the poems – are generally and significantly different in character, perhaps even sharper in personality, than their Blackmore neighbours. But Barnes seems to have overlooked – or preferred to ignore – the fact that, whilst local idiosyncrasies of speech may give a general impression of local character, local personality may well appear with modifications! Presumably Hardy's Arabella of *Jude the Obscure* (first published in 1896), had she been born amongst the community of Barnes's poems, would have been blessed with tones whose mellowness would hardly have matched her aggressive nature.

Nevertheless, whatever the common-sense objections to Barnes's supposition, the fact remains that he imaged a rather 'mellow' people through 'mellow' sounding speech: his language matches his vision in every respect. I am not suggesting that he falsified the sounds he heard, but that he chose to emphasize certain ones.

For example, Barnes's orthography substitutes z for standard s (*zummer*) implying that this Blackmore consonant tended to vibrate more – was, that is, more 'voiced' – than its standard English equivalent. A number of diphthongs are also indicated, unusual to standard ears. For example, *shake* is given as *sheäke*. Clusters of consonants tend to be separated by a vowel (*elem* for *elm*), thus lengthening and maybe softening the sound.

It is these and similar kinds of sound features which lead Alan Hertz to find a 'honeyed' quality in the language of the well-known 'My Orcha'd in Linden Lea' (186).

> 'Ithin the woodlands, flow'ry gleäded,
>   By the woak tree's mossy moot,
> The sheenèn grass-bleädes, timber-sheäded,
>   Now do quiver under voot;
> An' birds do whissle over head,
> An' water's bubblèn in its bed,
> An' there vor me the apple tree
> Do leän down low in Linden Lea.

Hertz writes (1985: 113):

> This opening is a masterpiece of orchestration. The honeyed slowness of the first three lines, with their lingering diphthongs and double consonants, and the patterned alliteration of *w* and *b* in lines 5 and 7 evoke a sweetly harmonious world. The internal rhyme of line 7 neatly integrates '*me*', the speaker, into this all-encompassing euphony.

It is only to be expected that Barnes should allow the 'honeyed' sound to predominate in his verse, whether or not it marked naturally occurring local speech. He feared that city readers would automatically equate a rough-sounding dialect with the 'boorish' (1847: 49) personalities they expected to find in the countryside: they might forget that standard English could itself sound mellow or harsh, depending upon its presentation. He could not afford to risk such a reaction: he wanted, as we have noted, to proclaim only Blackmore's more 'lovely features'.

It seems significant in this respect that his orthography and the construction of some of his lines actually altered from edition to edition – altered towards a greater mellowness. For example, in its first publication in 1844 the fifth and sixth lines of 'The Spring' read, 'An' we can hear birds zing, and zee Upon the boughs the buds o' spring, –'. But by 1847 (second edition) the fifth line had become the more flowing 'When birds da zing, an' we can zee . . .'. The line seems softer because of the greater length between the two uses of z and because of the presence of an extra w fricative. But there is a further change still to come. By 1879 the line has *do* instead of the 1847 version's *da*. At the end of the 1879 collection, Barnes notes (461) that 'the *o*, when not under a strain of voice, is . . . as *e* in "the man" or as *e* in the French *le*'. It could, therefore, encourage a slightly smoother flow between the words 'birds do zing' than the previous version.

Barnes's personal – and deliberately chosen – use of local phonemes contributes then to his own particular perspective on local performance. Sir Arthur Quiller-Couch objected that, far from seeking to represent the labouring family, the publication of the poems in 'hieroglyphics [indicating regional phonemes] imply a scholar's patronage' (1934: 190). But the use of 'hieroglyphics' was never intended as a learned mystification: the diaeresis, to which Quiller-Couch is presumably referring, was essential in order to make clear the precise nature of the vowels Barnes wished to be heard. The potential for a mellowness exists in the dialect. Mellow sounds seem to emphasize a contented personality and a rich world. Therefore, in his emphasis upon the idyllic, Barnes would inevitably choose to stress and draw attention to this quality of sound.

However, the meaning potential of any aspect of language, including its phonemes, naturally depends to some degree upon the relationship of that feature with other aspects of the grammar. Now, many of the differences between Dorset syntax and standard English syntax lead to an expansion of a standard English expression, through the addition of prefixes and extra particles of the verb. So the Dorset speaker does not say 'the air I breathed shook', but rather, in Barnes's poetry, 'the aïr that I've a-breath'd did sheäke' ('Sound o' Water' [270]). This syntactic lengthening can contribute to the slowing of the rhythm in Dorset speech and also to the amount of stress which falls in certain parts of the utterance. As a result, syntax can itself be partly responsible for Barnes's implication that his dialect sounds more 'mellow' than standard English, since in this example and many others a slow rhythm draws attention to long and rounded vowel sounds, here in *breath'd* and in the diphthong of *sheäke*. (The Blackmore version of the standard verb ending, and adjective, *ing* is *en*. This also alters rhythm and sound. It appears less harsh and often permits a smoother transition on to the following word, as it does in 'Our Be' thplace' quoted below.)

Additional auxiliaries do not merely slow rhythm down in Dorset speech. The use of *did* also has a semantic implication which is important to the mellow idyll of Barnes's work. He explains (1847: 39) that this auxiliary was used in Blackmore only to indicate the *continuous* past tense, not to refer to individual, single occurrences in the past. Therefore many of Barnes's reflections take on a timelessness, a sense of comforting continuity, that contributes to his construction of an everlasting idyll. When he writes about 'Our Be'thplace' (229) then, he refers not to an occasional remembered day but to a long-lasting state of contented affairs.

> A lwonesome grove o' woak did rise,
> To screen our house, where smoke did rise,
> A-twistèn blue, while yeet the zun
> Did langthen on our childhood's fun;
> An' there, wi' all the sheäpes an' sounds
> O' life, among the timber'd grounds,
> The birds upon their boughs did zing,
> An' milkmaïds by their cows did zing,
> Wi' merry sounds, that softly died
> A-ringèn down the valley zide.

From the perspective of standard English it is easy to misread the implications of this habitual Dorset syntax, and to underestimate Barnes's deliberately skilful choosing from the dialect's potential in order to produce the 'sound and high-toned' poetry for which he aimed. In order to achieve this aim the poetry must also, thematically, be full of 'wisdom and goodness' (1844: Preface).

. . . full of Wisdom and Goodness.

We have seen that features of Barnes's chosen language could help to emphasize his vision of wisdom and goodness. As for the details of his perception, he offers above all an image of security. The poems present a close-knit, co-operative community, secure in an efficiently cultivated landscape, where time moves in comfortingly repeated cycles, and where faith in God, and in His intention that man and woman shall achieve an earthly fulfilment – through happy family life and through work – is paramount. This was the 'good and loveworthy' way of living that Barnes wished to teach through his poetry.

He concentrated upon marriage and the family: the family united in a vital, active co-operation of work and play is Barnes's epitome of wisdom and goodness. Although it is one husband's 'set time vor to goo/To the grist-mill out at Sherbrook under Bere,' his main concern is to arrange that his wife and children should meet him on the way home.

> You can saunter, if I'm leätish by the clock,
> To some greygles vor the childern on the ridge,
> Or can loiter in the tree-lewth, on the rock
> Where the stream-foam is a-shot down by the bridge;
> The while Joe's line an' his hook
> Mid catch minnows in the brook,
>
> > *greygles* wild hyacinths
>
> ('Come an' Meet me wi' the Childern on the Road' (Jones 1962: 532))

Though mother and father are both individuals, defined by their separate work and their separate parenthood, it is their roles in combination which Barnes emphasizes most in his poetry of a co-operative community. In 'A Father out, an' Mother hwome' (238) a little girl is 'bless'd wi' more than zome' because she has both parents and is secure between them, carrying to her father at work in the wood the 'welcome bit of food' her mother has prepared for him at home.

Work is not only a bond between Barnes's married couples. It also draws the children into the family effort. Though they play uninhibitedly –

> No city primness train'd our feet
> To strut in childhood through the street,
> But freedom let them loose to tread
> The yellow cowslip's downcast head . . .
> ('Rustic Childhood' [Jones 1962: 643])

– they too are rapidly learning co-operative endeavour. As soon as they are old enough, the young ones are helping their parents. And even before this they are playing at work.

> . . . the little bwoys
> Do stride an' fling their eärms all woys,
> Wi' busy picks, an' proud young looks
> A'meäkèn up their tiny pooks.
>
> > *pook* cone of hay
>
> (Hay-meäken [51])

Barnes's concept of work recalls Samuel Smile's belief in self-help. ('Help from without is often enfeebling in its effects, but help from within invariably invigorates' [Smiles 1859: 1–2]). Thus 'Work an' Wait' (547) describes the efforts of a man to create, through work, the prospect of a future for himself. From clay he has made bricks, from dried grass he has made thatch: together these construct a home to which he can bring his bride. The cart which he has made from 'liven timber', and the ploughshare he has honed from rock, will make it possible for him, in time, to make a living for himself and his wife.

There is a close correspondence, too, between Barnes's opinion of work and that of Thomas Carlyle, who wrote in *Past and Present* (1843) that 'there is a perennial nobleness, and even sacredness in work'. Barnes's milk-maid, Poll ('The Milk-maïd o' the Farm' [13]), does not stay up late or get up late; she works hard and long. As a result she seems ennobled, 'so happy out in farm' as she walks with 'steätly tread, her pail carried on her head' as if she wore a goolden crown'.

But Barnes's view of the nobility and value of work limited his artistic vision of its realities. He seems to have believed that God would distribute tasks appropriately according to capability. So maids can sing cheerfully as they do in 'The Sky A' clearen' (61) whilst they

> Still draw their white-stemmed reäkes among
> The long-back'd weäles an' new-meäde pooks,
> By brown-stemm'd trees an' cloty brooks;
> But have noo call to spweil their looks
>   By work, that God could never meäke
>   Their weaker han's to underteäke . . .

In Barnes's work there is no Tess of the d'Urbervilles, struggling just over the Vale in the turnip fields.[7] His people and the natural world are closely integrated and nature does not make co-operation difficult between the two. Barnes describes little that is wild, and there is no sense of the tradition of the sublime. Perhaps his vision simply replicates the actual Vale of Blackmore and its lush dairyland peace. But Barnes, believing in a God-given fitness to be found in all things – 'fitness of water to irrigate growth, and to run for all lips to the sea; fitness of land to take and send onward the stream' (1861: 133) – looked always for harmony, and generally found what he sought, achieved by man's God-fearing care and control. 'The Zilver-weed' (409) gently regrets the rushing feet of young children that beat down the small plant, and notes with pleasure that, now the family has grown up and moved on, nature recovers.

> But now the zilver leaves do show
>   To zummer day their goolden crown,
> Wi' noo swift shoe-zoles' litty blow,
>   In merry plaÿ to beät em down.

Yet though the silver-weed may now live unhindered, there is also, regrettably, no caring hand left to cherish the roses.

> An' where vor years zome busy hand
> Did traïn the rwoses wide an' high;
> Now woone by woone the trees do die,
> An' vew of all the row do stand.

Barnes's love of caring control is reflected in his perception of time as in part controlled by man. As we have seen, he believed that man-made objects and buildings on the landscape are 'hallowed pleäces', carrying with them the imprint of communities past, their work and personalities stamped on the present, endorsing tradition and living on through change. The building described in 'The New House' (Jones 1962: 497) is therefore altogether too new.

> An' noo mesh is eet a-spread
> O'er his zide in patchy green,
> An' noo ivy have a-clung
> To his wall, wi' leafy stem . . .

The house has not had time to acquire character, feel or stories of its own to tell. For Barnes it is hospitality and friendship which exerts some of the most valuable and lasting influences upon a building, as it will, in time, upon the new house. He urges friends to call so that – 'Wi' your looks, an' words, an' smiles,/We shall veel the mwore at hwome.'

He is comforted, too, by the security he finds in his sense of cyclical time experienced by nature and by man. Time is partly told by the natural manifestations of the seasons. Green boughs, daisy beds and swallows signal the arrival of spring, but they also carry with them the promise of another return next year. These seasonal cycles are matched by the cycles of successive generations. The church marks their progress. In 'Lydlinch Bells' (260) Barnes describes past, present and future generations, linked together.

> Their sons did pull the bells that rung
> Their mothers' weddèn peals avore
> The while their fathers led em young
> An' blushèn from the churches door,
> An' still did cheem, wi' happy sound,
> As time did bring the Zundays round . . .

The church in Barnes's vision is in no way a restricting damper on community vitality. On the contrary, it offers relief from the week's 'ceäre an' tweil ('The Church an' Happy Zunday' [140]). It is a focal point for local society:

> Tis good to zee woone's naïghbours come
> Out drough the churchyard, vlockèn hwome,
> As woone do nod, an' woone do smile . . .

In the sight of different generations, meeting after a service, there is promise and evidence of everlasting growth and vitality, of a good life on earth.

But it is not a peace of mind that comes from an easy life. Barnes accepts that existence can be hard – indeed, 'The Weather-beäten Tree' (94) implies its hardships may be God-sent.

> . . . our heads do slowly bend
> Below the trials God do zend,
> Like shiv'rèn bennets, beäre to all
> The drevèn winds o' dark'nèn fall.

bennets flower stalks of grass

Yet Barnes could accept pain because he believed it to be an intentional part of God's plan. He did not believe that shadows on the landscape were God's punishment, but rather a necessary experience if human beings were to appreciate His contrasting light. After all, light in combination with dark may make a balanced harmony, and Barnes, ever searching for controlled pattern and plan, wrote that pain comes to

> . . . meäke us zee, if tis His will,
> That He can bring us good vrom ill:
> As after winter He do bring,
> In his good time, the zunny spring,
> An' leaves, an' young vo'k vull o' glee
> A-dancèn roun' the woaken tree.

Barnes constantly emphasized these benefits he found on earth. He saw the natural world, in all its manifestations including the seasons, as the product of God – though in no sense a manifestation of God himself. He would no doubt have accepted the argument of Paley's *Natural Theology* (1802), which he probably read whilst studying for the ministry at Cambridge, that God and His creative power are confirmed by the very existence of infinite intricacies in the objects of the natural world. Therefore those intricacies must be honoured and treasured – and carefully described in his poetry, if his work is to honour God and fulfill his objectives of preserving 'wisdom and goodness' and of showing readers and hearers those good and loveworthy 'sources of nature within their own sphere of being' which he believed were 'frequently overlooked' (1847: 49–50).

But Barnes's work is not wholly insular, restricted to his perception of a rich and secure Vale of Blackmore. The poems do acknowledge a challenging outside world. Yet, on the whole, they absorb and nullify its dangers within the overwhelming security of their vision and their form.

Preservation, not Protest

Barnes's perceptions of a sunlit and colourful landscape are constantly and contentedly linked with memories of life that had gone.

> 'Tis Spring, 'tis Maÿ, as Maÿ woonce shed
> His glowèn light above thy head –
> When thy green boughs, wi' bloomy tips,
> Did sheäde my childern's laughen lips;
> A-screenèn vrom the noonday gleäre
> Their rwosy cheäks an' glossy heäir;
> The while their mother's needle sped,
> Too quick vor zight, the snow-white thread.
> ('The Lilac' [255])

It is partly for this reason that his poems can seem anachronistic, bathing his images of rural life in a light that shone from a more stable past. He persistently recalls memories of childhood, of early married life. He seems to be indulging a conscious practice, a deliberate lightening of the present through memories of the past.

> Though time do dreve me on, my mind
> Do turn in love to thee behind,
> The seäme's a bulrush that's a-shook
> By wind a-blowèn up the brook:
> The curlèn stream would dreve en down,
> But plaÿsome aïr do turn en roun'.
> An' meäke en seem to bend wi' love
> To zunny hollows up above.
> ('Woodley' [39])

In this way Barnes leaves himself open to a charge, from John Barrell, that he is 'too hopelessly nostalgic' (Barrell and Bull 1982: 431). And it is indisputable that Barnes's memory was sometimes at odds with the impressions of others, more directly involved in rural life than he. Thus he found the old squire's traditionally paternalistic labour-relations perfectly acceptable. 'He that's vur above' will repay his labourers, stooping 'wi' kindly smile' to 'reward their love' (Herrenston' [340]). There is no suggestion, in any of the poems describing the celebratory feasts given by farmers after work and enjoyed by their labourers, that Barnes would have understood Stephen Duck's feeling (1736) of deception when faced with his master's 'reward'.

> A Table plentifully spread we find
> And jugs of huming Ale to cheer the Mind,
> Which he, too gen'rous, pushes round so fast,
> We think no Toils to come, nor mind the past.
> But the next Morning soon reveals the Cheat,
> When the same Toils we must again repeat . . .
> ('The Thresher's Labour')

But although Barnes cherished the old order, wanting to preserve the spirit of 'wisdom and goodness' that he personally found there in culture, community, and family, he did acknowledge to some extent the inevitable pressure of change. The very setting of a majority of the poems in the past tense at least means that there is no attempt to pretend that their usually idyllic vision is of the present. Besides, many of the poems quite openly contrast a marvellously contented past with a present which is marked by loss. Loss is a continual theme. Barnes himself knew personal loss, of parents, child, wife, and friends. And he acknowledged too the loss of the old ways in the face of the new. 'The Happy Days When I wer Young' (115) freely admits that times have changed.

> O valley dear! I wish that I
> 'D a-liv'd in former times, to die
> Wi' all the happy souls that trod
> Thy turf in peäce, an' died to God;
> Or gone wi' them that laugh'd an' zung
> In happy days when I wer young!

Moreover, sometimes he was directly critical of the changing order. It is not entirely true that, as E.M. Forster suggested, Barnes was a 'Yes-man' (Forster, 1951: 209). He attacked, for example, the *new* farmer, the landowner of the changing economy. In Barnes' opinion, the new man thought only of his own financial gain, ploughing up every available bit of land.

> Vor 'tis meäke money, Thomas, an' teäke money,
>   What's zwold an' bought
> Is all that is worthy o' thought.
> ('The Leäne' [265])

As a result land is lost where flowers can grow, geese can graze, and children can play. Deprived children 'wull have a thin musheroom feäce,/Wi' their bodies so sumple as dough.' Furthermore, the new economists jealously safeguard their 'own' and take freedoms and sources of living away from the land worker of the older organic community.

> An' the goocoo wull soon be committed to cage
>   Vor a trespass in zomebody's tree.
> Vor 'tis lockèn up, Thomas, an' blockèn up,
>   Stranger or brother,
> Man mussen come nigh woone another.

Another man's land may now be crossed only in pursuit of the hounds.

Barnes also offered some solutions to rural deprivation, particularly in his prose writings. In 1849, for example, he published a number of articles entitled *Humilis Domus*, 'on the abodes, life and social conditions of the poor, especially in Dorsetshire'. Chris Wrigley believes that in these 'Barnes's views came close towards arguing the right to work' (Wrigley, 1977: 21), and he certainly pleaded for the self-respect and general well-being of the working-man. He argued in *Views of Labour and Gold* that 'a weekly half holiday would be a boon for the health and happiness of a degenerating class of labourers' (1859: 88). To some extent Barnes's poetry also urges reforms. 'The Lotments' (28) advocates 'letting bits o' groun' out to the poor'. 'Two Farms in Woone' (102) condemns the lack of opportunity, caused by engrossing, which prevents a young labourer from climbing the rural community's economic and social ladder. And though 'Rusticus Res Politicas Anidmadvertens. The New Poor Laws' (Jones 1962: 487) outlines the view that the Poor Law Amendment Act of 1834 justly punishes those who have lacked the initiative and foresight to save against hard times, it also emphasizes and abhors the degradation of those who suffer by it and recommends the reward of effort.

> Thiese laes mid do some good; but volk mast show
> Esteem var goodness if they'd zee it grow.
> A farmer woulden git much vrom his zeeds
> If they wer left to struggle wi' the weeds.

More generally however, particularly in the poetry, the keynote of Barnes's acknowledgement of change was *coping*: in the main, his personae absorb challenge rather than revolt against it. Given his stated aims for his poetry – a production of sound, high-toned work which might demonstrate and preserve wisdom and goodness and the riches of rural life – this is hardly surprising. Indeed, Barnes himself claimed that he never wrote poems with what he called a 'drift', evidently meaning an aggressive message of political propaganda (Jones 1962: xiii). I think it is this which accounts for Miles Barnes's assessment of his father as a man of 'passive courage' advocating endurance, rather than inspiring challenge and the active amelioration of painful change.

So the new also figures in the poems. In 'John Bloom in Lon'on' (453) a 'worthy miller' is eager to visit the Crystal Palace because he is impressed by what he has heard of its display of inventions. He enjoys too the modern train which carries him swiftly up to the city. This is an allegory of a fat man though, and when he arrives in the city, well fed and contented from his 'worthy' Dorset life, he finds himself unable to squeeze into a tiny London cab – and, surely, by implication into the strictures of city life. The general tone of the poem, however, humorous and contentedly confident of Bloom's superiority, deflects any biting criticism of urban life.

> The steps went down wi' rottlèn slap,
>   The zwingèn door went open wide:
> Wide? no; vor when the worthy chap
>   Stepp'd up to teäke his pleäce inside,
> Breast-foremost, he wer twice too wide
> Vor thik there door. An' then he tried
> To edge in woone an' tother zide.
> ' 'Twon't do,' the drever cried;
> 'Can't goo,' good Bloom replied;
> 'That you should bring theäse vooty thing!'
> Cried worthy Bloom the miller.

vooty unhandily little

In a similar way, although Barnes does acknowledge the social, political disruption of changes like enclosure, engrossment and emigration, his reactions tend to be accepting and traditionally conservative. So Robert, seeing his emigrating friend prepare for Dieman's Land, sighs –

> Ah! we must stay till GOD is plieased to tiake us;
> If we do our best he woon't forsiake us.
> Good bye, and if I shou'dent zee ye agaen,
> GOD bless you, Richat, drough your life.
> ('Rusticus Emigrans. Emigration' [Jones 1962: 482])

There is also acceptance (this time of enclosure) in 'The Common A-took in' (100), an acceptance which might come more easily to

Barnes, successful schoolmaster-writer of the poem, than to its imaginary labouring personae. Enclosure is happening and, the poem seems to suggest, it cannot be helped: there are ways of compensating, but if they are not available, then the workhouse is the only solution.

> THOMAS . . .I wer twold back tother day,
>   That they be got into a way
>   O' lettèn bits o' groun' out to the poor.
>
> JOHN Well, I do hope 'tis true, I'm sure;
>   An' I do hope that they will do it here,
>   Or I must goo to workhouse, I do fear.

But John does not protest at his loss of free land and the possibility of the workhouse. Instead, he dwells upon the remembered joy of the once open fields, children jumping and skipping, searching for birds nests and strawberries, and room enough for everyone's cows and geese. It is the kind of 'positive' and 'constructive' offsetting of misery that Barnes would have approved, given his faith in nature and his religious conviction.

> An' many times when I do vind
> Things all goo wrong, an' vo'k unkind,
> To zee the happy veedèn herds,
> An' hear the zingèn o' the birds,
> Do soothe my sorrow mwore than words;
>   Vor I do zee that 'tis our sin
>   Do meäke woone's soul so dark 'ithin,
>   When God would gi'e woone zunsheen.
> ('The Spring' [3])

Of course the very form of the eclogue, presenting two speakers and therefore, potentially, two sides to a question, can contribute to the dilution of criticism and protest. And its form can itself be a semiotic, in this case of balance and compromise. Barnes, perhaps unconsciously, also used form in another way which appears to be a semiotic of his general psychology and philosophy. That is, control, plan and pattern are used and symbolized in the complex, ordered metrical and rhyme schemes of his verse. It is appropriate too, given Barnes's belief in the past, that these are frequently ancient forms. Thus he used, for instance, the Welsh *cymmeriad*, (concentration upon a key word), *cynghanedd* (echoing of syllables within a line) and *awdlau* (same word repeated at the end of each line of a stanza), as well as the Persian *ghazal* (chain-rhyme running throughout a poem, together with assonance) and Hebrew parallelism.

Form also contributed to Barnes's aim for preservation, this time certainly consciously. He believed that the intricate patterns of his poetry, of metre and rhyme, could act as 'wordlocks', just as they had in the Bardic poetry he admired, helping the speaker and hearer or reader to notice and memorise the content of a poem (Barnes: 1867).

Above all it is Barnes's choice of the dialect itself which serves as a kind of preservative. Hardy wrote (1908: viii)

> It may appear strange to some, as it did to friends, in his lifetime, that a man of insight who had the spirit of poesy in him should have persisted year after year in writing in a fast-perishing language . . .

But Barnes was a philologist, in the nineteenth-century tradition discussed in Chapter Two. And he approved of an Arabic proverb that 'a man by learning a second language becomes two' (1841: 22a). To preserve a language, through art, would be to preserve – with what we have heard his son, Miles, call a 'passive courage' – the people who spoke it.

Sudden Irregularities . . . as if Feeling Rebelled

Nevertheless, however much he needed security, however much he wanted to preserve the authority of the old order, Barnes was not entirely confined by control and pattern. Hardy observed (1908: x) that he neither became 'a slave to the passion of form' nor wasted 'all his substance whittling at its shape' so that 'by a felicitous instinct he does at times break into sudden irregularities in the midst of his subtle rhythms and measures, as if feeling rebelled against further drill'.

We have heard the way in which this flexibility helped to suggest genuine speech. But Barnes's creativity also manifested itself in other ways. His linguistic philosophy (which he explained in a number of prose works including the 'Dissertation' preceding his 1844 edition of the poems, his *Philological Grammar* of 1854, and *An Outline of English Speechcraft*, 1878) permitted – encouraged even – the coinage of words, when no term in current local performance seemed particularly apt. But these coinages had to be built out of the existing language, putting existing morphemes into new combinations, rather than borrowed from others. He deeply regretted what he took to be a loss of the original 'purity' of English (to which we referred above) through the addition of Latin, Greek and French modifications. 'I cannot believe', he said, 'that the word "port-feuille" expresses (to an Englishman) the use of the thing better than the word "papercase". Besides, foreign modifications complicated the process of developing what we would today call English *competence* (in the sense discussed in Chapter One): English had become for Barnes a language 'fit only for learned people to converse with each other in, being no longer one in which the more learned can easily teach the less so' (1830: 501–3).

Oddly, the article in which Barnes made these remarks makes him guilty of the sin he is criticizing: he has actually signed it *Dilettante*! But elsewhere he put his convictions into practice. His poetry is rife with compounds. These often have a mannered, eighteenth-century flavour about them as they carefully qualify nouns: *long-tongued*, *springy-vooted*, *yellow-banded*, and *high-ear'd* identify a dog, a bee, and a horse. But there is a warmth and aptness in many of his compounds which give them a fresher spontaneity. Thus, children greet their father when he returns, miserably cold from his day's work, and whilst one rubs his face warm, he recalls that *another hot-slipper'd my veet* ('Fatherhood' [208]).

The image is delightful. It is perhaps not surprising that Palgrave insisted that Barnes's poetry put 'pictorial expressiveness back into the literary language' (1887: 820). Hardy compared the poems to the Dutch school of painting, a school whose 'beauty and truth of colour and action' Barnes himself admired (1861: 137). The poems are full of clear colour – snow-white lace, a hot white batch of bread, blushing red robinhoods (red campion), golden clote (water lilies), rosy hedges, raven curls – and just as light seems to both heighten and mellow the images of, say, Vermeer, so too it contributes to a warmth, clarity and energy in Barnes's images. Throughout the poems there is reference to the 'sheen' of light – on glossy hair, in loving eyes, on polished furniture affectionately cared for year after year. In consequence his poems do sometimes elicit a specialness from the objects they concern. Tom Paulin draws attention to 'The Wold Clock' (1975: 188). It is, he says 'both Dutch and Visionary', transforming the ordinary objects 'into something quite extraordinary' (Paulin 1975: 188).

> The wold clock's feäce is still in pleäce,
> Wi' hands a-stealen round . . .
>
> Who now do wind his chaïn, a-twin'd
> As he do run his hours,
> Or meäke a gloss to sheen across
> His door, wi' goolden flow'rs . . .
> (Jones 1962: 548)

Here again the masculine pronoun is attached to an inanimate object (the clock). Gerard Manley Hopkins believed that Barnes's precise and consistent use of Dorset dialect, in this kind of way, 'narrows his field' but conceded that it also 'heightens his effect' (Abbott 1935: 85–9). It is true that Barnes is undoubtedly limited to the Dorset competence and approximate performance of a labouring rural community, but in some ways it is this very limitation which allowed his dialect poetry the warmth and special vitality of localness. And, as we have seen, he was not slavishly restricted to its unimaginative reconstruction.

But did Barnes go far enough in his creativity? Coventry Patmore (Champneys 1900: 258) remarked, in a letter to Edmund Gosse dated 6 September 1886, that Barnes 'has done a small thing well, while his contemporaries have mostly been engaged in doing big things ill'. He certainly did well, in the sense that he fulfilled his self-appointed task of writing sound and high-toned poetry, preserving the local dialect and his image of its people with skill and imagination. Was this achievement so very small?

A Small Thing Well Done

Illustrating various aspects of Barnes's ideas and style has meant that no single poem, and its achievement, has been looked at in entirety. So I want to draw to a close with a brief look at an example which includes many, if not all, of the identifying features of his work. 'A Wife A-prais'd' (293) has the kind of intricate rhyme scheme (here internal as well as end rhyme) that Barnes favoured because of its wordlock and satisfying pattern. There is also the echo of an incremental refrain. These occur in many of the poems and, since they are typical of the traditional folk-song, they are an appropriate element of form for local poetry that was frequently read aloud to local audiences. There is also the description of clear, bright colour, equally reminiscent of folk poetry and an element in the 'Dutch' quality of Barnes's images. The first stanza displays a marked Dorset lexicon and contains an example of that continuous past tense which contributes to a sense of perpetual idyll. The vowels are particularly rounded and their 'mellowness' seems to help to slow the rhythm and to appropriately match the lazy persistence of endless sunshine and cooing pigeons. There is the usual reference to the satisfaction of work. But there is also pain, in the form of pressure from outside the husband and wife's own circle. It is an element not untypical of the poems but here, as elsewhere, it is almost obliterated by the warmth and tenderness which – for wife, friends and children – pervades all of Barnes's work. He declared that he wrote nothing without love, and believed that it was love – of man and of God – which transformed the combination of light and dark experience into 'good and loveworthy' life.

A Wife A-praïs'd

'Twer Maÿ, but ev'ry leaf wer dry
All day below a sheenèn sky;
The zun did glow wi' yollow gleäre,
An' cowslips blow wi' yollow gleäre,
Wi' graegles' bells a-droopèn low,
An' bremble boughs a-stoopèn low;
While culvers in the trees did coo
   Above the vallèn dew.

An' there, wi' heäir o' glossy black,
Bezide your neck an' down your back,
You rambled gaÿ a-bloomèn feäir,
By boughs o' maÿ a bloomèn feäir,
An' while the birds did twitter nigh,
An' water weäves did glitter nigh,
You gather'd cowslips in the lew,
   Below the vallèn dew.

An' now, while you've a-been my bride
As years o' flow'rs ha' bloom'd an' died,
Your smilèn feäce ha' been my jaÿ;
Your soul o' greäce ha' been my jaÿ;
An' wi' my evenèn rest a-come,
An' zunsheen to the west a-come,
I'm glad to teäke my road to you
   Vrom fields o' vallèn dew.

An' when the raïn do wet the maÿ,
A-bloomèn where we woonce did straÿ,
An' win' do blow along so vast,
An' streams do flow along so vast;
Ageän the storms so rough abroad,
An' angry tongues so gruff abroad,
The love that I do meet vrom you
   Is lik' the vallèn dew.

An' you be sprack's a bee on wing,
In search ov honey in the Spring:
The dawn-red sky do meet ye up;
The birds vu'st cry do meet ye up;
An' wi' your feäce a-smilèn on,
An' busy hands a-tweilèn on,
You'll vind zome useful work to do
   Until the vallèn dew.

It is with this kind of writing that Barnes achieved a kind of myth.
But, in company with R.A. Forsyth (1963: 325–34) who makes a

similar point, I do not mean to imply by this that the poetry is pure fantasy. Hardy testified to Barnes's avoidance of 'dreams and speculations' and to his 'exceptional knowledge of rustic life' (Hardy 1879: 469). I suggest it is the sort of myth that Roland Barthes deals with in *Mythologies* (1957), myth which we referred to in Chapter One as a partial truth. That is, the dialect's usual arbitrary signifiers, in this case of day-to-day rural living, may be removed from their narrow and conventional connotations and become instead potential signifiers of a second – mythical – order. They can be read not simply as references to the landscape and people, their homes and their church, their crops and their animals, but as signs of certain selected underlying values and concepts – in this case those 'rich but frequently overlooked sources of nature' which Barnes wanted to concentrate upon and preserve, whatever the outward changes in local culture.

Max Keith Sutton believes Barnes's concentration upon a particular part of rural living is not evasive to the point of fantasy but is, in its special concentration, a *clarifying* myth. For his original enormously appreciative audience, who responded to the resonances of his myth, it was 'a way of dealing with reality, not of avoiding it' (Hardin: 1979: 34, 39–40). Whilst Barnes did not choose a political 'drift' that was overt, through an aggressive tone or strident calls for reform, he did staunchly profess a belief in the dignity and importance of his people which, as we saw above, they undoubtedly welcomed.

And yet, Barnes's belief in localness, though certainly well-intentioned and expressed in poetry of subtle skill and beauty, is not in the end a complete triumph for the rural community. For Barnes's affirmation of the local – a special circle of language, custom, work and domesticity – is ultimately constrained. He speaks out for Blackmore literally, in its dialect. He shows strength and wisdom in the community effort, trusts in God, and preserves in his myth the beauty and energy of the natural world. But this local strength may not, in the end, survive. Barnes's localness, though it is not so parochial and innocent as to be ignorant of the outside world, does not fully manifest its strength in the growth that stems from adaptability. Instead it remains controlled and constrained. It has a sense of its own dignity and beauty – a small thing, well done – but not of its full potential, of growth and adaptability in a changing world: it does not attempt to go forward.

Indeed, Barnes himself evidently doubted that his beloved local culture could survive. But, rather than challenge, or adapt to the full implications of change, which he had to recognize both in Darwinian theory and industrial revolution – the former destructive to his faith in God, the latter an attack upon much that he defined as 'loveworthy' in man and nature – he chose to retire from his school into the secure boundaries of his vicarage, and into the formal harmony of his poetry. Yet here he wrote less and less in the dialect, and more in standard English. The voice of these later poems is still largely that of a countryman, frequently a labourer. In a way it is as though Barnes is making use of the facility that many rural people, like Hardy's Tess, possessed, the ability to switch from dialect into the national English now taught at school. But dialect was becoming an anachronism: to use it for his poetry was no longer to genuinely speak out on behalf of the community. Besides, though these standard poems may be largely restricted to the kinds of registers appropriate to a rural worker, they display clearer signs of the teacher, vicar, and man of wider horizons that Barnes had become, than those identifiable in the dialect work. There is more metaphor, more questioning, more speculation – even more recognition of loss. Though the sun rises afresh in a standard English poem entitled 'Dawn' (Jones 1962: 933), Barnes regrets that it 'comes not to shine/On any early friends of mine'. And it seems unutterably sad that he ended the poem, and perhaps his own life, begging, as the new dawn spreads over the land, to go on dreaming of his dearly loved past not in the special language which truly signified that old life – but in what he had always called *common English*, now the standard language of the changed world.

> Come orchard out from shade to light,
> 　Come apple trees, and hives of bees;
> Rise Hambledon in thy blue height;
> Come mead, and cows of red and white,
> Though night dreams flee as here I roam,
> Still let me dream myself at home.

Notes

1. Andrew Lang is quoted in an unsigned article, 'A Wessex Virgil', in *Times Literary Supplement*, 1 July 1944, condemning Barnes as 'a weariful writer of misspelled English'.
2. Page references, given at the end of each quotation, are to Barnes's 1879 collection, *Poems of Rural Life in the Dorset Dialect*. Bernard Jones's 1962 collection brings together all the poetry, the dialect and the standard English.
3. Trevor Hearl (1966) gives an excellent account of Barnes's career as a schoolmaster.
4. The orthography of Robert Hill's poetry ('Rabin Young' 1811–1908), also born in Sturminster, suggests a rather different sound.
5. Uttered speech can be described as a set of tone units. Each of these has a nucleus where tone movement takes place. The point between each

unit – marked by a sense of pause, sometimes long, sometimes barely perceptible – is called a boundary.

6.   Two hundred and fifty copies were printed by George Barclay, London, under the auspices of H.R.H. Prince Lucien Bonaparte, 1859. He visited Barnes in Dorchester on two occasions in 1859. His was not the only French interest: Barnes was visited in 1860 by le Chevalier de Chatelaine who had translated some of the poems into French.

7.   Interestingly, Snell (1985) argues that Hardy was not representing reality in his images of Tess and other women in the fields. A variety of factors perhaps, including the kinds of feelings Barnes articulates here, may have contributed to their exclusion from field labour.

CHAPTER FOUR

Women and Language:
Power and Possibility

Differences between male and female language have long been misunderstood. They continue to be so, in ways which diminish woman's linguistic potential. Moreover, although women have undoubtedly suffered through the language of men, sufficient has been said and written about their verbal reduction. What follows – particularly by distinguishing language as regenerative System from language as standardizing, reductive Myth – looks towards women's linguistic power and to the possibility of its development. It is a sexism of hearing, rather than a sexism of word and grammar, which stands most in our way.

Idle Chatter

For centuries English men have apparently cherished the English language as their own. They have firmly believed (their) women abuse and misuse it and insisted that female silence is definitely golden. For these patriarchs, male language is standard, Correct Language, the norm and the goal – though a goal unattainable by woman.

In the eighteenth century (as Jennifer Coates points out, in her excellent analysis of recent research into language and gender [1986: 16–29]), such men scorned a woman's ill-considered 'pomp of utterance'. In male opinion, these noisy women even had the affrontery to make up new words that adulterated the 'fixed and permanent standard of language'. Worse, female speakers evidently led the young male child linguistically astray, for the sixteenth century found wanton nannies teaching 'noblemen and gentilmennes chyldren' a pronunciation that was 'corrupte and foul'.

Coates (1968: 24–32) finds that such complaint did not lessen with the onset of linguistic science. According to Otto Jespersen, writing in 1922, women were woolly minded since – 'much more often then men' – they 'break off without finishing their sentences, because they start talking without having thought out what they are going to say' (1922: 250). The ladies of his day were evidently simple-minded too. For Jespersen firmly believed that men excelled in a kind of Chinese Box arrangement of complex syntax, and so could set clauses, subordinate, relative, and conditional, intricately one within the other. Women, on the other hand, could do no more than string a few simple sentences together with the occasional 'and' (1922: 250). Nor could they read very efficiently. True, women were observed to read faster than men, and even to remember more of what they read. But Jespersen insisted that 'this rapidity was no proof of intellectual power . . . some of the slowest readers were highly distinguished men' (1922: 252). And Havelock Ellis comfortingly removed all stigma from their slowness, reassuring such men that a slow response to written language is actually a sign of profound capacity to reason, since quick reading is possible only if 'every statement (is) admitted immediately and without inspection to fill the vacant chambers of the mind' (Jespersen 1922: 252).

Still, could it be – just possibly – that these early linguists may have been too hasty in their patriarchal eagerness to command the language? Might their evidence have been a little suspect? Early researchers were primarily nineteenth-century dialectologists, mainly interested to preserve fast-disappearing local dialects before the onslaught of a more uniform standard English taught in National Schools. At least, they were concerned to preserve the *male* dialect. Their research questionnaires abound with probes to establish local words for plough, rake, barn, ale and tobacco. They do not seem to have been over-keen to collect words from the female domain. Naturally: these researchers were themselves mostly men. And Coates (1986: 45) finds that more recently Griera, responsible for the Linguistic Atlas of Catalonia in 1928, gave the following reason for his own concentration upon male subjects.

> The reasons for my doing so are: the impossibility of . . . [women] maintaining attention during a long questionnaire lasting several days; the fact that their knowledge of objects is, in general, more limited than men's, and, above all, their lack of firm concepts which is reflected in imprecise naming of objects.

This lack of 'firm' conceptualization might of course, seen from a different and pro-female vantage point, be interpreted as an admirable flexibility, a sign of an open and questioning mind. But women are not always, any more than men, inclined to interpret linguistic evidence in favour of female strength. Very recently, I was asked to take part in a psychology student's research. My speech patterns in mixed conversation were, unknown to me, being monitored for – so-called – male and female characteristics. These included, it was eventually explained, *sound male logic* and *female wiles* like the paralinguistic signals of fluttering eyelashes and arm waving. Evidently those sexist stereotypes which trivialize the female persist. Most disconcertingly, the student working within this distorting male bias was a woman.

I am not suggesting that difference between male and female language does not exist. It would be surprising if it did not. For as we have seen, language is, virtually by definition, full of variety. English is composed of a large number of dialects – of which standard, prestige English is really but one – and, besides, each dialect varies again in terms of *register*, as a user selects from its repertoire an accent, syntax, lexicon, and also metaphor appropriate to the situation. We do not, that is, produce the same language in the pub, the board-room and the bedroom. And it is more than reasonable to suppose that gender, as well as region and situation, should play a part in this selecting and organizing of language.

However, even those acknowledgements of difference, related to gender, which are essentially sympathetic to women's use of language and therefore of most interest to us here, are not necessarily more accurate than the blatant misrepresentations we have just considered. Deborah Cameron, in her challenging discussion, *Feminism and Linguistic Theory* (1985), is undoubtedly right to point out that linguistic 'evidence' has sometimes been used erroneously in order to prove that language is a patriarchal weapon to female oppression. She is not for a moment denying the existence of an oppressive patriarchy, nor saying that language plays no part in it. But, for the sake of its effective curtailment, she is arguing that the destructive relationship between male power and language must be more precisely evaluated. To prevent misleading and counterproductive arguments, linguistic methodology and theory require careful application.

That care is especially important if we are intent not only on discovering sources of disadvantage but are looking, about all, to affirm the powerful resources that women – as well as men – have available to them through the existing language system.

Plainer Speaking

It is the over-simplification of complex feminist arguments about language, particularly in their popularization, that does women's language as great a disservice as its male ridicule. The common assertion that all women are expressive, kind and gentle conversationalists – whenever boorish and tough-talking men do not violate their body-speaking language with interruption and cold logic – has the emptiness of all sweeping generalizations. In its determination to preserve a male/female opposition it is as erroneous as the anti-female convictions we have just considered. The true picture on each side of the gender divide is much more complex and varied. For young women speak differently from old women; black women speak differently from white women; working-class, middle-class, professional, non-professional women – and men – all speak differently. And the contrasts multiply when we compare spoken language with written language.

Besides, when 'evidence' of male and female language difference is 'discovered' it is frequently spurious. Take, for example, the linguistic red herring of the French feminine *e*. It has been supposed that its muting is a perfect example of woman's suppression. And it is true that if the 'feminine' morpheme *e* is taken as a metaphor for the female, then French might provide some sort of symbol of female silencing. But, on closer inspection, it is not a very effective symbol because, although the letter itself remains mute, an *e* at the end of an adjective, necessary when the adjective modifies a female noun, causes its immediately preceding consonant, normally silent when attached to a masculine noun, to be pronounced. *Le petit mur* contrasts with *la petite chaise* and the latter's voiced adjectival *t*. Thus the 'feminine', far from being powerless, actually forces a linguistic change. And of course, in writing, it has always had the power of visibility.

Yet this kind of linguistic hair-splitting is no more proof of actual, or even symbolic, female supremacy than it is of female marginalization. In the French language, masculine and female gender do not, as a rule, bear direct correlation with biology. It is difficult to find a suspicion of masculinity in *le mur* or femininity in *la chaise*.[1]

I am not saying that syntactic gender is irrelevant to the issue of women's marginalization, including that of female English speakers. I am pointing out, rather, that certain charges of syntactic sexism, apparently but mistakenly proven by linguistic methods, can draw attention away from the real sources of difficulty: that is, those *opinions* and *myths* about men and women which lie behind the language, are disseminated through it, and which affect women at least as much as the system itself.

For instance, Ann Bodine (1975) explains that however intrinsically unrelated gender may be to biological sex, our grammar books have, for centuries, insisted that the generic masculine has virtues of 'naturalness' and 'propriety'. She notes that John Kirkby wrote (1746: 117): 'The Masculine Person answers to the general Name, which comprehends both Male and Female: as *Any Person, who knows what he says.*' We shall return to this issue in more detail presently. But, for the moment, suffice it to say that presumably neither my tinkerings with the French *e*, however logical, nor its enforced voicing, nor a determined English use of, say, *s/he* or *his/her* will, of themselves, easily alter such bigoted conviction. It is not what you hear, but the way that you hear it . . .

Yet feminist myths can also, unintentionally, be as damaging to women's language as the opinions of misogynists. Women, distracted by patriarchal power, do not necessarily hear any more clearly than those men who are obsessed with their own mastery. Such women may assume this mastery is inevitable – and that in it language plays an unchallengeably determining role.

For instance, a version of determinism appears to be at the root of misconceptions about the syntactic system. For behind the trivial matter of the aforementioned muted *e* lurks a much more important premiss: the conviction that women, all women and not just the French, are at the mercy of a cold, controlling – determining – male grammar and therefore need uniquely female language. But such a belief ignores the fact that language's potentially unlimited creativity – for both sexes – depends, as we saw in Chapter One, partly upon the workings of the (presently existing) syntactic system. Moreover, concepts of determinism are also involved in other language and gender arguments.

The title of Dale Spender's highly influential *Man Made Language* (1980) is not helpful in this respect. It focuses on male dominance and might suggest at a casual glance that the book proves absolute masculine control through linguistic determinism. The book does bear its title out to an extent – but only to an extent. Spender, intensifying the ideas of Whorf and Sapir with regard to linguistic relativity, writes:

> Language is *not* neutral. It is not merely a vehicle which carries ideas. It is itself a shaper of ideas . . . In this context it is nothing short of ludicrous to conceive of human beings as capable of grasping things as they really are, of being impartial recorders of their world . . . Human beings cannot impartially describe the universe because in order to describe it they must first have a classification system. But, paradoxically, once they have that classification system, once they have a language, *they can see only certain arbitrary things*. (Spender 1980: 139)

But, whilst Spender certainly claims that it is largely men who have created the world and its shaping language, and done so to their own advantage – 'The names which men have supplied have been biased . . . There is a "loud silence" when one searches for the meanings of women in the language' (Spender 1980: 54) – she does not, whatever the implications of her title, insist that women cannot and do not either see around these male meanings or create their own. She does not insist that women are helpless. She does accept that we can create meanings and that we are not always silenced. But still, some of Spender's arguments may be misleading.

As an example of 'the names which men have supplied' she looks at 'motherhood'. She appears to claim that men are responsible for creating a limited understanding of the word, a meaning of 'something beautiful, that leaves women consumed and replete with joy' (Spender 1980: 54) – and, crucially, can leave women who do not experience such joy feeling guilty failures. But Spender also describes women objecting to images of motherhood that isolate, as if they were the only reality, its most fulfilling aspects. In this way she accepts that women can see, and do point out, that childbirth may be painful, that rearing children can be a difficult, dirty, and disheartening experience. She explains that it is possible, though difficult, for women to see around the 'normal' accepted meaning, even if society is reluctant to allow them to explode its comforting myth.

Still, why should Spender, or anyone else, automatically assume that men alone have created the 'normal', narrow, misleading meaning? Presumably because, where accepted, it can be inaccurate in a way that is distressing to women, and because a basic premiss of extreme feminist thinking is that men are at the root of all evil.

But it is not *always* inaccurate. Motherhood (as Spender freely acknowledges) can be fulfilling in the most positive and loving of ways. Surely women who knew this played some part in creating and confirming the conventional meaning of the word? Surely they did not all wait for men to tell them this was 'motherhood' and so they could enjoy it?

Besides, an over-estimation of male control of language, and an overly simple concept of relationships between language control and behaviour, may blind us to more complex issues. Dr Estela Welldon, a psychotherapist and a clinical tutor at the Portman Clinic, acknowledges that idyllic images of motherhood can intolerably pressurize a mother who is struggling with a very different reality. But still we should not forget that mothers have power: 'The power of the womb distinguishes women from men and leads to the power of motherhood – truly as potent as, and usually more far-reaching and more pervasive than, the power of money or law or social position' (Welldon 1988: 40–1). Moreover, the power of the womb is, tragically, not always beneficent. 'Odd though it may sound, motherhood provides an excellent vehicle for some women to exercise perverse and perverting attitudes towards their offspring, and to retaliate against their own mothers' (1988: 63). True, this kind of perversion may be related to men through the power of patriarchy. 'Perhaps if women had a longer tradition of belonging to the power structure their attitudes to men and children would not be governed, as they are now, by a weakness which they strive to turn into possessiveness and control' (1988: 105). But it is clear that we cannot make simple oppositions between dominating men and dominated women, and between male makers of language and disadvantaged female accepters of 'their' symbolic law. The final sentence of Welldon's book notes: 'it is worth stressing that the clinical evidence supports the maxim: "Never underestimate the power of a mother"' (1988: 158).

The temptation to follow concepts of linguistic determinism and destruction to their bitterest and simplest end is therefore to attribute to language – and particularly to men – an exclusive power which neither has. It is to turn attention away from the complexity of power structures outside of language. It is to ignore human – male and female – choice and agency. It is to forget that language is a capacity shared by both sexes and all peoples which women, as well as men, can to some extent manipulate. It is thus to perpetuate a myth of female inadequacy and to contribute unwittingly to female silencing.

In what follows, therefore, we shall be turning the spotlight off male mastery. We shall be looking instead toward the potency and potential of the regenerative system of language as it may be used, controlled, by women as well by men. Language is deterministic to a degree. But it can be challenged and changed. In its potential for creativity it is not determinate.

CREATIVE POSSIBILITY

Syntax

I believe we have, in our existing language, all the resources necessary for both sexes. But some feminists feel that women need a wholly new language, if they are to speak and write effectively from a female standpoint.

Their arguments begin at the beginning with the acquisition of language in childhood. We have seen (Chapter One) that acquiring language appears to be partly the result of innate predispositions and partly the result of socialization. What then, if anything, has being born male or female got to do with the beginnings of speech? Or what – if anything – has acquiring language to do with the social formation of gender identity, with becoming a 'proper' boy or girl? More or less everything, it would seem, in the opinion of the French psychoanalyst, Jacques Lacan. For the phallus, to Lacan, rules acquisition of the symbolic order which is language.

Lacanian thinking argues that the need to name, to use the labels of language, can only begin with a dawning awareness of difference and with a sense of the possession or loss of something to label. So, as the child becomes aware of separation from and loss of the mother's body – in Freudian terms, at the Oedipal phase of development – s/he at the same time encounters language, the symbolic order. Moreover, our culture – transmitted partly through language – recognizes the phallus as *the* symbol of power. So, taking advantage of the order's traditional male mastery, men become men: women know their lack and become women in the shadow of the symbolic order's patriarchal preference. (Some of Lacan's views can be found in translation in Sheridan 1977, and an extremely helpful explanation of those relating to feminism is contained in Cameron 1985.)

But Luce Irigaray, herself a French psychoanalyst and a feminist, is not surprisingly critical of the emphasis placed by Lacanian theory upon female *lack*. She prefers to speak of female difference, and argues that this includes the existence of a special female language, quite apart from the standard 'male' symbolic order. We have already said that difference of gender is quite as likely as any other distinction to result in a difference of language. But Irigaray believes that our different, special language is not, in its most distinctive form, openly manifested by women. Instead, as our culture's patriarchy reproduces and confirms itself, generation by generation, our alternative language is suppressed. If heard, Iragaray believes this female language would have 'nothing to do with the syntax we have used for centuries, namely . . . subject, predicate, subject, verb, object . . . [for] female sexuality is not unifiable' (1977: 64). Furthermore,its words would have a rich flexibility of meaning beyond the unique meanings of male discourse.

We shall return to words later. But Iragaray's call for a non-unifying syntax cannot be taken too literally in support of a new female language. She herself is not specific about its description, and relates it as much to body signals as to language.

> . . . what a feminine syntax might be is not simple nor easy to state, because in that "syntax" there would no longer be either subject or object, "oneness" would no longer be privileged, there would no longer

be proper meanings, proper names, "proper" attributes . . . Instead, that
"syntax" would involve nearness, proximity, . . . I think the place where
it could best be deciphered is in the gestural code of women's bodies. . . .
In suffering, but also in women's laughter. And again: in what they
"dare" – do or say – when they are among themselves. (Irigaray 1985:
134)

But as we saw in Chapter One, without the combination of our
present syntax with the lexicon, the one unifying – to use Irigary's
verb – the other, our ability to communicate, in mixed groups or
woman to woman, would be drastically impoverished. For this
unification is a form of energizing, a releasing – not a repressing –
of the power of sounds, words, rhythms. The linguistic double-
articulation and structural system that we possess as humans, male
and female, is a characteristic which contributes greatly to our
differentiation from other creatures with their less creative communication. Deny yourself this grammar and try talking about anything –
linguistics, gender, politics, even the weather. Other than roughly
labelling, with animal simplicity, feelings of pleasure, fear, surprise
and the like, the experiment seems doomed to failure. And –
however vital the expression of feeling – logic and lucidity, helped by
syntax, are surely not male monsters that should be strangled at birth.
Syntax is not a linguistic strait-jacket from which women (and men)
would quite rightly wish to escape, and nor, therefore, can it be used
as an appropriate metaphor for repressive patriarchal power. We
'depend' upon structure, certainly, but as a means to infinite creativity.
Besides, given the arguments for innate language capacity, syntax
would seem to have, at some basic level, an element of universality
which is likely to resist change and which in any case belongs to both
male and female.

The creation of a new and different female language, syntactically at
least, would appear then to be ineffective and unnecessary as a means
of assertive expression. But there are different ways of developing
Lacanian theory, including the approach of Julia Kristeva.

The Semiotic

It is frequently asserted that women, when they are not silenced by
patriarchy, are more emotional and sensitive communicators than
men. And Julia Kristeva's thinking (she is Professor of Linguistics at
Paris University VII) might be taken as supporting evidence, for she
describes a repressed 'feminine' quality in language that is closely
linked to the body. But her arguments are not directly relevant in
praise of women's difference, or in evidence of women's repression.

For, although she relates language difference to 'femininity' and 'masculinity', gender is not for her directly equatable with biological sex.

Kristeva suggests that in the child there exists a *semiotic* state. Her use of the term 'semiotic' is more specific than its general use in communication studies. It is, she explains, a

> . . . pre-verbal functional state that governs the connections between the body (in the process of constituting itself as a body proper), objects and the protagonists of family structure. But we shall distinguish this functioning from symbolic operations that depend on language as a sign system – whether the language [*langue*] is vocalized or gestural (as with deaf-mutes). The kinetic functional stage of the *semiotic* precedes the establishment of the sign . . . (Moi 1986: 92)

The semiotic modality of signification begins therefore, in Kristeva's view, at a time before the child is a fully knowing, fully developed subject. It is linked, in Freudian terms, to pre-Oedipal oral and anal drives. It is not totally lost, however, when the child matures and acquires symbolic language. It remains recognizable for Kristeva in the rhythms, intonational flow and textual disruptions of mature speech. Indeed, she believes that the symbolic and the semiotic are 'inseparable . . . and the dialectic between them determines the type of discourse (narrative, metalanguage, theory, poetry, etc.) involved . . . (Moi 1986: 92).

Kristeva notes that Mallarmé (1945: 382–7) had recognized the semiotic aspect of language – in writing – and she explains his concept thus:

> Indifferent to language, enigmatic and *feminine*, this space underlying the written is rhythmic, unfettered, irreducible to its intelligible verbal translation; it is musical, anterior to judgement, but restrained by a single guarantee: syntax. (Moi 1986: 97; italics mine)

We have seen how the semiotic is anterior to judgement. But in what sense is the semiotic, for Kristeva, feminine? And is syntax – which she describes as its 'restraint' – in consequence somehow male?

First, and most importantly, Kristeva is not saying that the semiotic is a marker of female sex, even given her premiss that it arises in the pre-Oedipal stage which is linked to the mother, for Kristeva sees the pre-Oedipal mother encompassing both the masculine and the feminine. She is saying, however, that the semiotic element of communication shares the kind of marginalization – repression – that is forced upon women. Yet Kristeva continually resists definition of 'female' and 'feminine' except as a state of marginalization by the patriarchal order. And some men, as well as women, may be so placed. It is in this non-biological sense that she describes the semiotic as 'feminine'.

It follows, then, that symbolic language, with its 'restraint' of syntax, should not be understood in Kristeva's theorizing as the province of the biologically male. However, it might be termed 'masculine' because, with its logical, cultural, intellectual semantics and shaping syntax, symbolic language can be opposed to the 'feminine' marginalization of the semiotic: and for Kristeva it comes after the semiotic, combines with and can dominate its remains. But as we have already noted, she finds the semiotic and the symbolic ultimately inseparable and she is not of course rejecting wholesale the energy of syntax as destructively restrictive: with reference to Mallarmé she spoke of syntax's 'restraint' – but defined restraint as a necessary 'guarantee', and Mallarmé called it a 'pivot' for intelligibility (1945: 383).

Nevertheless, Kristeva does see the semiotic, in its relationship to the unconscious, as having a particular value. For her it is a value which can pressurize the symbolic and sometimes emerge from marginality. In *Psychoanalysis and the Polis* (1982) she refers to the French (male) writer, Louis Ferdinand Céline, in whom she finds an effective balance of all signifying modalities.

> It is as if Céline's stylistic adventure were an aspect of the eternal return to a place which escapes naming and which can be named only if one plays on the whole register of language (syntax, but also message, intonation, etc.). (Moi 1986: 317)

She finds Céline making this full play in the following way and to the following effect.

> Laconism (nominal sentences), exclamations and the predominance of intonation over syntax . . . because of the influx of non-meaning, arouse the non-semanticized emotion of the reader . . . [and] give an infra-syntactical, intonational inscription of that same emotion which transverses syntax but integrates the message. (Moi 1986: 316–17)

But are Céline's adventures so remarkable? Is the semiotic, and its emotional implication, ever truly marginalized (and thus in this respect 'feminine')? Kristeva finds 'desyntacticization' in Céline's 'ejection' of *la vache* ('the bitch') – 'I had just discovered war in its entirety . . . Have to be almost in front of it, like I was then, to really see it, the bitch, face on and in profile' (Moi 1986: 315).[2] Presumably Kristeva values the sentence's arrangement because it is to some extent emotional, manifesting the semiotic in its disrupted and intonation/stress-injecting effect. Yet it is hardly an adventure, since it is not really desyntactization but the use of a syntactically regular appositional phrase – a phrase, that is, which merely repeats, but in a different term, the subject or the object. It is a manouevre fairly common in speech and writing.

Besides, Kristeva herself notes that a particular intonational contour, marked in one of Céline's stylistic 'adventures', is found in 'the emotive or relaxed speech of popular or everyday discourse' (Moi 1986: 315), and she does not specify the gender of speakers. She finds this a partial 'proof that it is a *deeper* organizer of the utterance than syntactic structures'. Probably so. (See, on this point, papers by David Crystal, 'Prosodic Development', and Patrick Griffiths 'Speech Acts and Early Sentences' (1979) which describe the early use of prosody in children and its later development, in co-operative conjunction with syntax, into adulthood.) But it is also proof that such intonation is far from marginalized, at least in speech.

Of course: prosodic features, like rhythm, stress, intonation, are an integral part of talking. But even writing is 'heard' by the reader with his/her own imposition of prosodic pressures. For prosodic features are needed just as much as syntax in order to express judgement as well as emotion. Try saying out loud – or, as you read, hearing in your head – the grammatically unremarkable *The cat sat on the mat* without any rhythm or tonal flow! Its meaning is then minimal, certainly without judgement. But choose to stress *cat*, or *sat*, or *mat*, or even *the* or *on*, and the utterance/utterer is beginning to mean, and to express feeling, Such meaningful/judgemental signalling is not eliminated by writing. It may be more encouraged in some writings than in others (we have seen that Kristeva emphasizes this) via, for example, the shaping patterns of poetry. But it is always there, to some extent, even in the most regular of grammatical structures, as the writer, male and female, conceives the sentence, and as a subsequent reader reimposes his/her own prosodic significance.

Céline is not then precisely right to claim a totally destructive, domineering quality in symbolic language when he writes ' "In the beginning was the Word." No! In the beginning was emotion. The Word came afterwards to replace emotion as the trot replaced the gallop' (Céline: 1966–9: vol. II, 933). 'Feminine' emotion, in the form of the semiotic, is not, of itself, easily repressed. And Kristeva herself implies that it is within the capacity of both men and women.

Neither the semiotic then, nor syntax, seems intrinsically biased towards men or to women. Neither aspect of language appears to be at the root of female linguistic disadvantage. But what about words? They have been condemned as cultural determinants, guilty of degrading and destroying women. Yet it is not a fat and pompous

Dictionary, falling readily and obscenely open at certain offensive words – slag, bitch, whore and the like – that should figure in the dock. In a poem by Robin Hamilton, the guilty parties look altogether more human: male, certainly, but maybe female too . . .

Signification

Robin Hamilton's cartoon parable has a bitter-sad wit. He writes (1985: 163):

Semantic Fairytale

When Hanzel and Grettel came to the witch's house
(The crumbs of comfort they'd scattered all eaten up)
They could almost taste the tales she'd spun to make
Her walls, the language of the bricks fresh as new bread.

So Hanzel peeped through a lively image set just
Child-head high, and saw the tables well laid out
With magnificent words – Love, Fame, Honour; even
Happiness was there like a bright cake at the centre.

In they went without even a murmur of regret left
In their pockets, while the witch snapped them up
With her dexterous tongue – popped Hanzel into the oven
Fired by Duty, clapped Grettel in a cage of Motherhood.

Instead of escaping they came to love the words that lapped them:
Hanzel wore his Duty like a fine cloak, and never had to think
What he'd tell the children: Grettel in her cage chirruped
Like a songbird, and only wished to become a parrot.

Vocabulary, the poem's major theme, is for many commentators on gender and language (including for example Dale Spender, Mary Daly, and Monique Wittig) a prime element in sexism. It seems to them man-made and man-orientated. But is it *the* crucial element in language and sexual inequality? To what extent are words themselves intrinsically and individually powerful? Alternatively, how far are they merely tokens, of changeable value, and in this case, who controls them?

That we can lie, tell jokes, be ironic – skewing slightly the relationship of the signifier with its signifieds, the relationship of language to experience – is some evidence that language is a system, yes, but one of manageable tokens. Words hardly mean, independent of their human utterance. Still, at the same time, at the moment of utterance, they become part of speaker/writer-hearer/reader experience, with a force beyond the token.

Hamilton finds *both* men and women subject to this force and in the thrall of language. 'Love, Fame, Honour', and also 'Happiness', are set temptingly before Hanzel as well as before Grettel, and there seems no reason to confirm stereotypes of foolish feminine hysteria by arguing that we are more susceptible than men to the temptation of words. But nor does Hamilton confirm that the English language offers men a better lexical deal than women: being baked in an oven is probably not a great improvement on imprisonment behind bars. There are surely snags in dutifully observed male roles as well as in motherhood. And yet, whatever snares language holds for men, in reality women are plainly in some way disadvantaged by words which, at the same time, perpetuate patriarchal control. How much of this is avoidable?

One of the biggest linguistic difficulties for English-using women is the pronoun system. In English we do not of course have a catch-all, female-plus-male-plus-neuter term in the singular, only a choice of *he* or *she* or *it*. As a result, women find themselves lumped together with, and lost behind, the masculine priority of sweeping generalizations like, 'Mankind progressed beyond the apes. He walked upright from the forest and acquired language.'

But this imbalance has not always been encouraged by all languages. Mary Ritchie Key points out (1975: 20) that Aztec was quite different. Its third person singular is *yejua*, a pronoun untranslatable into English for it can refer to our *he*, *she* or *it*, and, most importantly, to a combination of these. English could produce, on paper, a similar composite term: something like *s/he*, or *s/he/it*. Some such alternative is being made in a great deal of writing, particularly academic, and certainly prevents the image triggered by the words being one of perpetual masculinity. I found it salutary to be asked to write *s/he* in a text designed as an introduction to art. A stock mental image of man-with-novel-play-painting-sculpture-music, etc., had evidently lurked unconsciously behind my sense of 'the artist' and, surprisingly and embarrassingly, it was an effort to think otherwise. But such a deliberate change is only effective in writing. It has no clear phonemic distinctions: *s/he* sounds very like *she*. A totally new-sounding word would thus be necessary. *His/hers*, *she/he* could be said of course, but these dual terms are cumbersome and would need single composite replacements to preserve the flow of speech.

More crucially, to make such a replacement would require a major rethinking, not so much about language itself, but more about gender and social place. It would involve the fundamental acceptance that *both* sexes are present *and* correct! A simple proposition – yet the physical presence of women, however vital, does not of course guarantee our acknowledgment and certainly not our welcome.

Janet Morley (1984) discusses the Christian Church's determination to speak and write of 'men of God', 'brothers in Christ'. She is puzzled by the furore caused when women object to this linguistic exclusion: it is, say their patronizing critics, such a trivial point – don't women know they are automatically included in *mankind*? But why, Morley wonders – if the issue really is so trivial – do its detractors seem to believe its raising 'is positively satanic' (1984: 60).

The reason, she suggests, is that women have been eternally scapegoated, blamed everlastingly for 'mankind's' sins (and here, for mankind, we may assuredly read 'women') and therefore they have been rejected. Yet to reject is in a sense to banish part of the rejector's own self, that despised part which belongs to all 'mankind' but which only women have been chosen to epitomize. And here Morley quotes Susan Griffin (1983: 101):

> The projection of a denied self onto an enemy never works. And, in fact, not only does it not work, but the enemy is perceived as someone who gets stronger and stronger and stronger, because with every effort to imaginatively diminish and reduce this enemy, the enemy still returns.

This, says Morley,is why the feminine continues to be denied in the Church's language. Or if not denied, we might add as Nelly Furman (Greene and Kahn: 1985: 64) notes, the feminine is firmly bounded, the female role precisely labelled when the marriage ceremony pronounces a pair 'man and wife', defining and differentiating the woman only with reference to the man. And this denial or limitation makes easier a resistance to woman's full contribution in the life of the Church – and elsewhere.

It is true that a revised Bible has recently been published (the *Revised English Bible*, September 1989). This translation limits language that might be considered sexist in the *New English Bible* (New Testament published 1961; Old Testament and New Testament together, 1970) from which it has been developed, but only in regard to words which did not carry a specific gender in the original, ancient texts. The new Bible would seem to continue therefore to reflect the culture of its time of writing, but to make no radical concessions to today's different attitudes.

Presumably God therefore remains male. Accord to *The Times* (15 December 1988: 3) a report prepared in readiness for the General Synod is certainly adamant that male pronouns will be maintained for God in a revised Alternative Service Book. And this will please many people, if not feminists. Morley quotes *The Times* leader (8 October

1983): 'The available alternatives to "He" are "She" and "It". The traditional language makes the best of those three choices: one would prefer not to have the Holy Spirit called "It".' Well, yes. A depersonalization of God, to 'It', may be a reduction of God, losing essential implications of the Trinitarian formula. And to reject maleness would be to deny masculine value. But why is 'He' *better* than 'She' . . . ?

Had English the resources of Aztec, *The Times* would not be forced to make a sexist choice: three pronouns and the gender-limited nouns related to them would not be the only available alternatives. The Aztecs' supreme being was a dual god, with male and female countenance and the regenerating ability of both. It (but the Aztecs had the more expressive pronoun *yejua* which, as we have seen, means something like *he-she-it*) was called 'Ometeotl': *ome* = 'two', *teotl* = 'god'. Yet, despite *yejua's* duality, the Aztec's (even though they had a plural form available) spoke of Ometeotl in singular grammatical form.

But of course this concept of plurality was the choice of Aztec culture: it was not a concept necessarily pre-determined by their language – although their linguistic system could easily communicate and confirm their image. We – if we so wished, if our culture believed God had similar duality – could create a suitably expressive pronominal aspect in our syntactic system. Some members of the Church do find evidence of femininity in the Christian God. Other do not, but the Bishop of Durham, the Rt. Revd David Jenkins, regards their arguments as old-fashioned: 'This is not worth taking too seriously except as a psychological thing, a neurotic thing, and a bothersome thing' (*Guardian*, 19 September 1988: 4). However, it will remain a profoundly bothersome thing to those in agreement with Bishop Jenkins until the 'psychology' and the 'neurosis' alter and – in consequence – language expressive of God alters.

Which brings us back to Hamilton's image of Hanzel and Grettel and to a secular as well as to a religious lexicon. For Hanzel *chooses* to see duty as fine, Grettel is *happy* to sing a song of motherhood. She apparently does not notice, unlike Dale Spender, the confining bars of her cage: singing contentedly, she aspires simply to parrot-hood.

But she is not forced to sing the same old tune. Words are neither unchallengeably deterministic nor unquestionably man-orientated. They are always subject to interpretation, and to rejection or acceptance, according to context and inclination. Except for cases of onomatopoeia, they are mostly conglomerations of sounds, arbitrarily assigned to signification. Of themselves they are insert, vapid, empty carcasses. Their power derives from the power of those who use them and in the process shape their signification. It is the process of assignment – not the word itself – which is potent. It is the user of language – more than the system itself – that is deterministic. And we do ourselves a disservice if we somehow suggest that women do not have the thinking-power to resist linguistic inertia and, at the same time, imply that only men have the wit and linguistic capacity to seize its vital potency. The very fact that Mary Daly can see a multiplicity of possible meanings in a signifier, can identify a 'male' element and can replace it, as she does in *Gyn/Ecology* (1978), with a 'female' significance (*crone-logical*, *the-rapist*), attests to the vulnerability of the signifier itself.

Language is a system, yes. But it is, as we saw earlier, particularly in our discussion of Chomskyan and Hallidayan models of language (Chapter One), a system which is, by definition, creative. And, in its creativity, it is available to both sexes. Women's problems, despite Betty Friedan's fears (1963), need not be without a name.

Naming the Problem

Women can, and of course do, write and speak of their own lives, expressing themselves as they wish. They have done so for a long time and certainly, with the rise of the Women's Movement, have begun to speak louder and louder of their objection to patriarchy.

Besides, speaking up for ourselves, as women, is not simply a matter of changing individual words in response to our untraditional perceptions. We have, and always have had, expressive resources – available to both sexes – without which words are very little. As we have seen, earlier in this book and in our discussion of Kristeva's theory of the semiotic, the power of language derives from a combination of the lexicon with syntax, rhythm, intonation, gesture and the like. All of these are present, to some degree, in both the spoken and the written language. Their interpretation lies in their relationship with context. 'What a man!', exclaimed rapidly with rising intonation and smiling face, has one meaning. The sentence is capable of quite another, said with falling tone, sluggish rhythm and dismal look. Vocabulary is at the mercy of these extra-lexical resources: The Dictionary is vulnerable to irony and wit.

And so, combining all of language's signifying forces, Anna Wickham has been able in the poem below (which was first privately printed in 1911) to use the old words while yet implying – to anyone who will listen – the special, unconventional meanings they held for her, in her own personal context.

Divorce
A voice from the dark is calling me.
In the close house I nurse a fire.
Out in the dark, cold winds rush free
To the rock heights of my desire.
I smother in the house in the valley below,
Let me out to the night, let me go, let me go!

Spirits that ride the sweeping blast,
Frozen in rigid tenderness,
Wait! For I leave the fire at last,
My little-love's warm loneliness.
I smother in the house in the valley below,
Let me out to the night, let me go, let me go!

High on the hills are beating drums.
Clear from a line of marching men
To the rock's edge the hero comes.
He calls me, and he calls again.
On the hill there is fighting, victory, or quick death.
In the house is the fire, which I fan with sick breath.
(Smith 1984: 166)

Wickham invests the word 'house', and also 'fire' 'nurse' and 'warm', with significances which challenge their conventional power, a power which is usually linked to a traditional concept of gender: the Myth of Wifehood. She does so by linking house with the stifling implications of 'close', the rhythm of the line drawing attention to its (in this context) odd adjective. She nurses the fire, yes, but, fanning it with a breath that is sick, the poem's speaker is in consequence self-destructive, and the verb 'smother' demands a painful, pathetic emphasis, which Wickham achieves by its placing in the poem's metrical scheme. So it is that 'loneliness' can become insidiously 'warm', emotion achieve no grand passion but wither to a 'little-love', the alliterated 'l' in the word's insistent repetition defying the reader to ignore the miserable paucity of a situation in which the woman colludes.

I am using the term 'myth' – the myth of wifehood – with the implications discussed in Chapter One, defining myth more as partial truth than as fantastic falsehood. This particular myth has concentrated upon woman keeping the home fires burning. And of course these fires have, in reality, been welcoming, sustaining sources of vitality for both sexes. Moreover, woman's image as soothing, healing nurse has more often than not been an accurate representation of actuality. But the myth is, by definition, incomplete and Wickham turns its word-coins over, revealing meanings they can hold on their other sides. The 'house', traditionally and mythically understood as a source of protection and family unity, may now be seen, in the context of this poem's surrounding language, as a potentially stultifying, diseased goal.

But Wickham is, of course, a product of her own particular context and her own time. Through her poem she forms a fresh and personal myth, yet inevitably it cannot be for everyone and for all time. And, some years on from the writing of this poem (Wickham died in 1947), and no doubt for many women in its own time as well, the poem's clear equation of desire and achievement with the attainment of a hero who, even if he is merely symbolic of freedom, is a patriarchal male if ever there were one, tramping along with his warring comrades and summoning a woman to the presence, is not specially appealing. Well, perhaps there is a banality about these particular lines which hints at mockery. On the other hand, there seems no irony in Wickham's suggestion of personal complicity and guilt in the building, nursing, of her sad home. Her acceptance is, perhaps, a legacy of the Victorian myth, the concept of the Angel in the House, that keeper of goodness and the status quo – and the scapegoat for male iniquity: John Ruskin's woman who may be granted place and power (in the home and to man's specification) but who, in return, 'must be enduringly, incorruptibly good . . . infallibly wise – wise, not for self-development, but for self-renunciation' (Ruskin 1865/ 1907 edition: 60).

The Angel is a persistent myth, reaching out (as we shall be arguing in more detail later) to the end of this century. But there is no *essentially linguistic reason* to fear that it, or Wickham's particular version, should have the last word. The myth of the male hero, galloping in to take and revive the poor, defeated, ineffectual and only half-alive female – the scenario that Wickham chose as her alternative goal – is neatly demolished in a much more recent fairy-tale, written by Zoe Ellis, when, aged seventeen, she found the language, inventing a word here, updating another there, to express her alternative vision (*Sunday Telegraph*, 15 September 1985 and *Mini Sagas*, 1985: 218).

What the Sleeping Beauty would have given her right arm for.

This princess was different. She was a brunette beauty with a genius of a brain. Refusing marriage, she inherited all by primogenesis. The country's economy prospered under her rule. When the handsome prince came by on his white charger, she bought it from him and started her own racehorse business.

Certainly this princess is different. No symbolically simpering blonde, from her brown hair onwards she is intelligent, powerful, capable, successful. And she is a heroine without need of a hero. She is also clearly a Thatcherite. But then, the myth can always be re-written . . .

A Deaf Ear

Yes, but who will listen? Women have at their disposal all the creative possibilities of language: syntax, the semiotic, and signifiers. Women can name their problem, can tell new tales. But merely changing the terms of myths cannot guarantee instant altered perception all round. Different stories may be told, but they could fall so easily on deaf or stubborn ears. There is a sexism of hearing.

Even if women recognized a linguistic disadvantage *en masse*, and spoke up, as some feminists would like, in a new female style and syntax, they would not necessarily be heard. The assumption by women of their own language style, need not, *of itself*, secure equality in difference. Tamar Katriel's discussion (1986: 105–8) of Elinor Keenan's study (1974) of Malagasay speech norms makes the point. In Malagasay it happens to be indirectness – not the powerful directness that is a marker of western 'male' communicative prowess – that is considered an ideal speech style and is therefore assumed by men.

> Women, like children, are considered to lack subtlety and sensitivity, and have leeway to engage in direct, confrontational discourse. They are acknowledged norm breakers; their directness, though disvalued, is not only tolerated by men but is actually utilized by them in strategic ways to express criticism and censure, which they are prevented from doing . . . [Thus] the cost of indirection, which implies a weakening of the community's ability to exert social control, is partly offset by the interactional counternorm applicable to women. By socially circumscribing direct, confrontational talk and associating it with a less prestigious social position, one can use it to perform social functions without disrupting the expressive order. (Katriel 1986: 107)

Katriel notes that, in consequence of their different language, women 'play a dominant role in conveying social information, as in disputes' (1987: 107). But of course it is a perverse, male-ordered, dominance. And female English speakers would need to be certain of good listeners before they could be confident that a different language would be a better means of self-assertion: in a world dominated by a particular discourse, its proponents deaf to alternatives, theirs could be condemned as a meaningless babble.

When Luce Irigaray wrote *Speculum de l'autre femme* (1974) she did not go so far as to write in the new grammar she advocates. Instead she appears to have chosen a half-way house by 'miming' male discourse. For example, the book began as a doctoral thesis and it retains something of this academic form, a form which, emanating from a power structure dominated by men, might be called 'male'. All female language is in a sense miming if it is assumed that male expression is (in line with Lacanian thinking) its standard model and its master but when, as Toril Moi suggests is the case here, the mimicry is a conscious acting out, 'it doubles [the mimicry] back on itself', thus, 'raising the parasitism to the second power' (1985: 140). But some of Irigaray's hearers were not sympathetic to her individual viewpoint and language. They refused to hear her, for her response to Lacan's work led, after the publication of her book, to her expulsion from his *École freudienne* at Vincennes.

But then, Thorne and Henley believe that women's language use is generally misheard and undervalued: 'no matter what women do [in language], their behavior may be taken to symbolize inferiority' (1975: 153). It is certainly true that women's attempts to use language forcibly have sometimes been deliberately ridiculed – their intentions misheard – and used in evidence against feminist politics. Cheris Kramarae (1981: 113) quotes the following trivializing over-extension of lexical development: 'It was interesting to see how a group with obviously persongled egos were able to personipulate an organization the size of ours into looking like a pack of fools. "Chairperson" indeed!' (Shimberg, 1971: 2).

And if response to the carefully considered assertive language of women is disappointing, the situation is unlikely to be better in reaction to spontaneous everyday speech. Here, when women's language is truly powerful, it can be deliberately misheard through downgrading. Gossip, for example, can be essential to the social well-being of both sexes since, as Nicholas Emler argues, it is a vital and exceedingly complex means of processing the kind of information we need to have in order to function well socially. Discovering who is on good/bad terms with whom, who is about to leave a job, a spouse, a house, what changes in work or community the grapevine predicts, helps us to plot our own course. Besides, we use the same language channel to release our own emotion, to express anger or affection that cannot be shown to the person concerned. But gossip is derided as scandelmongering tittle-tattle. Its power is thus neatly trivialized. And tradition links it with women. Yet gossip is not the prerogative of the female sex. Men 'gossip' together as much as women – only they call it politics![3]

Gossip or 'politics' may be single-sex occupations. But what about mixed conversation? Who, when men and women talk together, is really listened to? Who gets the last word? Jennifer Coates (1986) gathers together recent research into masculine and feminine communicative competence and I am indebted to her for the background to the following argument.

By definition, conversation involves taking turns. But turns can be affected by *overlapping* and by *interrupting*. We overlap when we cut in around the final word, beginning our turn a fraction early. Interruption involves a much earlier invasion. Now, data collected by Zimmerman and West (1975) finds men overlapping and interrupting women's talk far more than each other's speech. In one study, men were observed to interrupt their women co-conversationalists a staggering forty-six times compared with two interruptions of men by a woman. Although women were seen to overlap each other sometimes (but not, be it noted, interrupt), they did not take the same liberty with men. And language disruption *is* a liberty taken. Both overlaps and interruptions, most particularly the latter, seize a turn out of turn. They are a violation of one of the defining conventions of conversation, preventing the current speaker having her/his total say. And men, in these studies at least, certainly seem much more prepared to infringe a woman's rights to speak than vice versa.

Yet it is not that women cannot speak up for themselves. Even the feminist method of allowing silences in women's meetings, deliberately waiting for reticent speakers to have their say, and supposedly a method indicative of 'natural' feminine co-operation, is some indication that such groups are familiar with competitive women, women who are perfectly able to dominate conversation – at least amongst their own sex. But there is a sense in which women collude in their silencing by men. There is evidence that we may be concerned not to inhibit male talk. Women listeners appear prone to interjecting minimal responses like *mhm*, *right*, *yes* which suggest interest, a desire to hear more. On the other hand, Zimmerman and West found male speakers frequently denying minimal responses to their female partners in talk. In such cases a wall of silence can be as powerful as speech and a demoralizing experience for the recipient who may feel ignored, trivialized, mocked.[4]

It is true that, discouraged but not quite defeated, a speaker may try to compensate for a lack of encouraging minimal responses by using a particular kind of question, a *tag* question, to trigger reaction. A tight-lipped partner may be prodded into sound if an *isn't it?* *wouldn't it?*, *won't it?* or *can't it?* is tagged on to the end of a bit of speech: 'Well, it is my holiday as well as yours, isn't it? . . . And it would be nice for me to have a break too, wouldn't it?' So tags may be a fairly powerful, demanding linguistic tool. But they are, in this kind of context, a kind of rear-guard action, the product of an insecurity that is compounded by deaf ears. And Holmes (1984) found rather more women than men using them. Indeed, women can be eager – far more so than men – to persuade others to speak.

Cueing in

Fishman (1980) found women inviting response by asking two and a half times as many information-seeking questions (of the kind requiring yes/no answers) as men. And Brouwer (Brouwer et al. 1979) heard women asking more questions of men than of other women! But whilst these women might hope not only to confirm or deny information but also, like those using tag questions, to encourage the beginnings of a dialogue in which they can participate, in fact their questions could well trigger male monologues. For if a man accepts an invitation to talk he may respond with vigour. Swacker (1975) observed that, when asked to describe some pictures, female subjects responded with an average contribution of a brisk 3.17 minutes. The men averaged a dazzling 13.00 minute solo performance!

Still, there is another kind of tag question. Holmes (1984) draws attention to their use as *facilitators*. That is, they can be tagged on to a statement in a manner which, like the 'weaker' version, is intended to draw out an addressee, but does so in a way that stems from the user's sense of control, not his/her inferiority. A questioner can thus tempt a hesitant child, student, interviewee, guest at a party, into a response. Being asked simply, 'You are from Edinburgh, aren't you?', allows the addressee to join in the conversation comfortably, without fear of making a mistake. (This more confident use of the tag is of course distinguishable from the other not through syntax or vocabulary but through differences of tone and probably body language. Firmness replaces the quaverings – or obvious belligerence – of anxious insecurity.)

Now, Holmes heard more women than men using the 'stronger', facilitating tag. But although this might seem evidence of women's ability to command and control their hearers, this kind of facilitating language can also lead us into difficulties. If its users are not careful it can be another kind of collusion in their silencing. The oral elements of the General Certificate of Secondary Education examination, in its English tests taken by sixteen-year-olds in the United Kingdom, provides an example of the problem.

A student at Loughborough University observed preparation for this examination in a local school and questioned pupils and staff about their conception of effective oral work. She notes:

> The boys believed that their teacher was looking for: someone who 'talked a lot', had interesting views, could dominate the conversation, and accept others' views to some extent. The girls believed a good oral candidate was a good listener, had interesting views, [but also] accepted others' views and did not argue for the sake of argument . . .[5]

The teacher in this case personally rated the role of facilitator and listener in a conversation highly. However, he said it was hard work to mark 'within the exam criteria'. Naturally. A silent examinee who has handed the stage over to someone else provides little to grade. Although the exam board (The Midlands Examination Board for English Oral Communication Assessment, 1988: 26) did specify the need to listen carefully, it judged this primarily on the basis of further talk: that is, it welcomed 'evaluating what is heard, seen and read', by 'showing sensitivity to the audience and situation in the use of the appropriate speech style, and in the manner of presentation'. The helpful girl may show sensitivity to audience and situation, but if this is done in the form of facilitating language she earns no personal credit whilst helping another speaker to success. In this school the girls were seen to 'become supporters, and give the floor to the boys, thereby disadvantaging themselves'. And their helpful facilitating allowed the boys to do exactly what they rightly thought was required of them. Whilst the girls remained obligingly silent, the boys 'talked a lot' and thus satisfied exam criteria which included the ability to convey information, opinions and attitudes, 'clearly', 'accurately', and in 'an interesting and authoritative way'.

There is a sense then in which women may unwittingly invite their silencing by men. They may have been practising for it since childhood. For there is sociolinguistic evidence, as well as the theories of psychoanalysis we mentioned earlier, that the acquisition of language in childhood is closely linked to difference and to learning gender roles, to discovering what it is, in a particular culture, to be a 'real' girl or boy – and to learning female weaknesses. There is evidence (Liebermann: 1967) that babies alter the pitch of their voices according to the sex of their addressee: that is, they tend to choose a lower pitch when 'addressing' their fathers, a higher one when addressing their mothers. They are, from the very start, hearing and imitating possible gender role-models – including males who traditionally possess power and females who lack strength and control. And if linguistic politeness and unassertiveness are observed more in adult females than it is in males, then it is probable that girl children will follow suit. Engle (1980) found mothers, much more than fathers, consulting rather than directing their children's wishes:

'Do you want to do such and such?' rather than 'Do this, that or the other' . On the other hand, both mothers as well as fathers (Greif: 1980) appear to interrupt girls more than boys.

It would not be surprising if such experiences degraded a girl's sense of difference with the demoralizing realization that what she might want to say, and the way she might want to say it, is of little value – unless it is deferential. Boys, on the other hand, are confirming their possession of power through learning to direct and demand.

So, is the situation utterly bleak? Are women, despite their language capacities, doomed never to be heard? Hardly. The studies we have mentioned are certainly an indication that manipulative talk – talk and tactics that refuse to hear another voice – exists. But common sense indicates that the small talk they describe is not representative of every English-speaking woman. It is not difficult to cite, amongst public and personal acquaintance, counter-examples of women who are successful speakers in a variety of mixed as well as single-sex groups.

Moreover, it is not always women who are the losers in conversational games. Men may also be silenced. One explanation for this puts the situation into a perspective that is optimistic for women's language.

Powerful and Powerless Language

During the 1988 Lambeth Conference, I listened to six bishops discussing on television (*Lambeth Walk* BBC 1, 31 July) a few of the topics which they were currently debating with their colleagues (six hundred of them, all of course, in 1988, male) during their three-week visit to England from their communities across the Anglican world. A bishop from an African community was invited to begin the programme with reference to the question of polygamy. He said, quietly, briefly, and succinctly that he had regretted the ironic absence of women in this particular debate. Immediately, as if he had not spoken, precisely the same point – no different – was made again, by a bishop from England. This time, however, it was stated in a more assertive tone, with more complex syntax (of the Chinese Box variety admired by Jesperson) and was accompanied by much emphatic gesticulation. Before the end of the programme a similar maneouvre was repeated, again as if the African had never spoken.

This television debate is of course only one small anecdotal example. But I mention it because during the programme the African bishop himself raised the issue of language and disadvantage. He wondered if the western bishops appearing on the programme with him had happened to notice that he and many of his friends from the African world had been very silent during the conference. The trouble was, he said, certainly a matter of language. But it was as much a difficulty of the language these African delegates were listening to, as of the language they themselves used. A great deal of what was being said 'passed over their heads', not because English itself was a problem to foreign visitors, but apparently because Lambeth's chosen discourse was mystifying. This seemed to be largely because many issues of the debate were irrelevant to emerging churches. In consequence, complex ideas – about, say, the ordination of women as bishops – were unfamiliar. Thus, the language of their expression, by now habitual and readily on tap for those accustomed to debate the matter, was understandably hard for bishops who had other priorities in mind to grasp and to produce quickly in discussion.

No doubt the tables would have been turned if African issues had dominated the debate: Western bishops would have been less at ease with the relevant discourse. Leet-Pellegrini's work on conversational dominance (1980) demonstrates, hardly surprisingly, that a well-informed speaker is more likely to control a conversation than someone with less knowledge. But who, in the first place, decides what is relevant to the agenda? Whoever is in control of its drawing-up. And it is the possession or lack of control – more than their biological gender – which contributes to women's *and* men's choice of language and, also, to the way in which that language is heard. Indeed, O'Barr and Atkins (1980) prefer to speak not of women's language and men's language but of *powerful* and *powerless* language, power which is derived in the first place from the speaker's situation.

For, whilst analysing the speech of witnesses in an American trial courtroom, they found linguistic signals of power and of weakness in both sexes. They heard both men and women exhibiting the kinds of features which resemble Robin Lakoff's description of what she has called (1975) 'women's language', the kind of language which is so often (as test responses in O'Barr and Atkins's study confirmed) interpreted as indicative of a lack of power. Such features include hedges ('it was, *you know, sort of*, difficult . . . '), super-polite forms, marked intonational emphasis, empty adjectives, and hypercorrect grammar and pronounciation. But these were not used by those witnesses – men *and* women – who had unusually high status in terms of job, education, or expertise particularly related to the case. They were used instead by housewives and by men who were either unemployed or who had lower-status jobs: by those, that is, whose situation was itself without power.

O'Barr and Atkins argue, however, that since women tend to be the powerless in society they, more frequently than men, manifest speech signs that are heard as weakness, signs which allow and perpetuate their lack of strength. This is hardly surprising and those women who, we noted above, have made themselves heard must have done so not simply through their powerful style of language – since this could so easily go unheard – but through their achievement of powerful position, the result not only of their own abilities, of course, but in part the consequence of whatever co-operation they have found in a patriarchal culture. A powerful position not only helps to shape a subtle, controlling command of the linguistic system but, equally importantly, ensures a deferential ear. Mere lessons in a theoretically more effective use of language, rehearsing Eliza Doolittle fashion adventurous intonation curves, subtle syntax and conversational power games, will not, on their own, give easy access to self-assertion. Parrots are not especially powerful. Unless they sit on the top perch. On the other hand, given a change of situation that increases confidence and control in other respects, then language may follow more or less unconscious suit.

And fortunately things are, if slowly, changing for women and in consequence for our language. Work by J. and L. Milroy (Milroy & Milroy 1978: Milroy 1980), in a district of Belfast, demonstrates the point. The changes in this case have to do with standard English, particularly in terms of accent. Standard English is of course prestigious – but, paradoxically, non-standard English has in some circumstances a prestige all of its own. Coates explains (1986: 76), that whilst standard speakers may be

> . . . rated highly in terms of competence, regionally accented speakers are rated highly in terms of personal attractiveness: they are perceived to be serious, talkative, good-natured, and as having a sense of humour. This suggests that there are also rewards, though of a different kind, for those speakers who choose non-standard forms.

Now, in many speech communities women tend, more than men, to vere towards a prestige standard, particularly in formal situations. On the other hand, there is a tendency for men to opt for the non-standard. These choices have some relationship with class. It is well documented that working-class groups appear to signal their solidarity and difference from other classes by uniting linguistically and diverging from the standard (Coates 1986: 76). Yet Coates finds evidence (Trudgill 1974) that gender also plays a part in choosing language alignment. She suggests (1986: 77) that 'By using non-standard forms, male speakers signal their solidarity with each other . . . linguistic differences between women and men can be seen as functioning to maintain their separate identities'.

This is not such a simple and immutable male/female division as might be supposed. Coates argues that integration into a community plays a part in gendered language difference. She discusses social network theory, first mentioned in sociolinguistic analysis by Blom and Gumperz (1972) and becoming well-known through the Milroys' Belfast study. A person whose contacts – friends, workmates, relations – all tend to know each other, may be described as belonging to a *closed* social network. Someone whose personal contacts are not so closely linked may be said to belong to an *open* network. The latter situation is more prevalent in socially mobile, highly industrialized societies, whilst rural and traditional working-class communities manifest denser social networks. But network strength may also differ between men and women – not surprisingly, given their traditional divisions of occupation. The Milroys' work in the Balymacarrett district of Belfast found men, in traditional ship-yard employment, manifesting signs of tight-knit networks: the local women, remaining at home and not able to increase their relationships through work, belonged to less 'multiplex' groups. These differences in network strength were found to correlate with linguistic difference. The men shared a non-standard speech: the women, at home in less tight-knit groups, did not. In Belfast's Clonard district, however, the situation appeared to be reversed. Here unemployment leads to men finding work outside the area or remaining at home: their networks are therefore less dense. The young women, on the other hand, do find work, local work, and thus it is they who belong to the multiplex networks. And it is they, rather than the men of the Clonard district, who display signs of a socially unifying non-standard language.[6] I am not of course relishing the men's disadvantage here, but pointing out that language change, in response to social change, is possible.

NEW MYTHS FOR OLD

Evidently then, given situational changes, language too will alter: the system is not inflexible and it will bend to match and emphasize change. But, naturally, change relates not only to economic pressures, like those in Belfast. And the linguistic alterations that follow suit are not limited to phonemic variation. Other factors, especially the Women's Movement, have obviously inspired alteration in the position and strength of women, and in the signification of the language surrounding them., Feminism has challenged the man-biased Myths of Womanhood.

Feminism's own language, and its own scrutiny of language, have played an enormous part in the Movement's influence. Despite Mr Auberon Waugh's conviction that linguistics is a 'job-creation scheme for idle academics with nothing better to do' (*Sunday Telegraph*, 23 October 1988), feminists working within the field of communication and gender have certainly highlighted language that can be prejudicial to women and also language styles to which women respond. Increased awareness, fostered by their work, is making insensitive sexist use of the lexicon and the English pronoun system more difficult. Persistant use of *Ms*, *chairperson* and the like, have begun to silence the ridicule that greeted these innovations in their early days. In addition, educationalists are taking account of the likelihood that girls and boys may come to school conditioned towards a different communicative competence. Whilst, as we have seen, this recognition may not yet have been taken into account in the GCSE oral examination requirements, it has been considered in recent work on science teaching. Jan Craig, with the assistance of David Ayres, reported her findings from a small study of two parallel classes of ten- to eleven-year-olds learning science (Craig 1988: 25). In Class A the girls were most interested in the subject: in Class B the boys were more enthusiastic. There were a number of significant differences between the classes but, most importantly from our point of view, they were marked by different language strategies. The teacher of Class A (the one the girls most enjoyed) generally used a 'high proportion of open-ended questions in which pupils are encouraged to describe their work and listen to each other': Class B's teacher used a 'high proportion of questions asking for answers and facts'. As we might have expected, the girls seem to have appreciated being encouraged to listen and being given the chance to speak at some length. Jan Craig notes that all the 'girl-friendly' strategies she observed have been 'put forward by Barbara Smail for girl-friendly secondary science teaching' (Smail 1984).

Moreover, I have been stressing the expressive possibilities already open to women, already available through the power of language we now have – so long as we can find the opportunity to use them and so long as they are listened to. And feminists, despite some anxieties about the strictures of a 'man-made' language, have had little difficulty in producing, from the existing system, the language they need, at least for their polemic purposes. But most importantly, given a sexism of hearing, they have been able to make themselves increasingly heard as they have begun to speak from positions of greater authority, gaining some ground in education, publishing, media, politics.

So, from increasing strength in academic life, the Feminist Movement has taken its chance and drawn attention to the already existing language of women, to voices from the past which, although they have spoken, have simply been ignored. For instance, Dale Spender's *Mothers of the Novel* (1986) argues against the traditional (male-inspired) understanding of the growth of the novel: she insists that 'it was women and not men who made the greater contribution to [its] development' in the eighteenth century. Jane Spencer's *The Rise of the Woman Novelist* (1986) looks closely at some of these early female contributors to the genre.[7] She points out, however, that 'women's writing is not the same as women's rights' (Spencer 1986: xi). If writing is permitted, allowed, believed to be an acceptable feminine occupation, then of course women will put pen to paper. And Spencer argues that in the eighteenth century 'feminization of literature defined literature as a special category supposedly outside the political arena, with an influence on the world as indirect as women's was supposed to be' (Spencer 1986: xi). Eighteenth-century women might have been encouraged then, in their day, to write. But it follows from Spencer's argument that their contribution in the context of influential literary development would have been, for male critics at least, readily forgettable. Now, however, feminist critics have replaced these and other women writers back on the agenda – and this time for serious consideration. Indeed, male critics have been encouraged to follow their lead: for example Roger Lonsdale, in his pioneering anthology of eighteenth-century women's poetry (1989).

Feminist literary criticism has given female voices a special, new hearing, one that does not automatically tune out, for male preference, sounds of a feminine political tenor. It has also demanded, in addition, that male voices be listened to more carefully and more critically. It has re-examined readings, interpretations, which fit what Maggie Humm calls a 'form of theology . . . [in which] only males can be ordained as priests' (1986: 5). And so, women reading as women – not merely echoing patriarchal voices and decoding the text in masculine favour – have deciphered, and drawn critical attention to, the influence of Myths which are prejudicial to women. No reader, once aware of their insights, can confront the old texts in the same old way. The Shrew seems not so much Tamed as crushed; Lady Chatterly is not so much released as confined in her sexual roles; and Hester Prynne, with her Scarlet Letter, refuses to be relegated to supporting actress in Reverend Dimmesdale's drama of expiation.

But what of language apart from that of high culture? The message encouraged by the Movement has of course passed beyond the academic, so it is hardly surprising that we saw Zoe Ellis's Princess, catching its drift, taking charge of her own emancipation, and declining to be wakened from innocence by an obliging Prince's kiss.

Still, as yet Prince Charming need not feel too threatened. Alternative consorts are still available to him. For willing princesses live on in the Myths of Language, deaf to feminist insight. The mythical Angel in the House, who so troubled Anna Wickham and who appears to be, in her docile perfection, a first cousin of Cinderella, Sleeping Beauty, and Snow White, is still around. And she exerts an influence beyond the realms of fantasy. She is present – pure and delightful beside modern-day versions of the old Scarlet Woman, Scold, Whore, Hysteric and Dumb Blonde, who are all alive and well despite feminist protest – in fiction's perfect Little Woman: she who is mother, housewife, nurse, and sexual companion. The story of this ideal woman, raised to perfection by man, happy at his right hand and two steps behind, sells women's magazines and lines the paperback shelves.

And, given such enthusiastic welcome, she extends her influence beyond the fictional and into the language and lives of any women and men who accept and perpetuate her attitudes.

Emulating her in reality is, however, a tricky and frustrating business. True, the Angel has sometimes been updated – into Superwoman, Daughter of the Twentieth Century. Yet Superwoman is still, like the Angel, super mostly on male terms, by male definition. And she is beyond the reach of most normal women. For the blurb on the back of her blockbuster cover (an example is easy to find – her look-alikes are everywhere) praises her meteoric rise from rags to riches, achieving perfect male-adored beauty and, in moments between Board Meetings, giving birth to marvellous offspring who are their father's pride and joy. On the way she has usually been given a leg up by a lot of luck, modern technology, high finance, a clutch of nannies and, naturally and most importantly, Prince Charming in modern dress. And there is still not a speck of dust on her mantelpiece. For real women, coping with demanding children, dirty houses, and the drearier kind of husband, frustration, envy – and guilt – cannot but follow in the wake of reading about this twentieth-century paragon.

And popular fiction tends to increase that guilt still further. For angelic superwomen are accompanied by other, less lovely, storybook creatures. Perhaps we should not be too hard on Robin Hamilton for imagining that wicked tongue, the one that snared Hanzel and Grettel in his poem, in the mouth of a Witch! No doubt he intended his witch to stand only for the deterministic forces, *both* male and female, of education and cultural. (Besides, his own feminist credentials are excellent. Indeed, because of the dual possibility of his Christian name – Robin – he has been mistakenly included in an anthology of feminist women writers!) However, Hamilton did not himself resist the temptation of language tradition. He merely took over an old tale, with its conventional casting of female in the role of wickedness, and thus played a part, however accidental and however small, in continuing the sexist myth that women are generally to blame when they do not make it to angelhood.

I have chosen a woman's magazine, and a story from it, at random (Moggach 1988). In one way the tale has moved with the times. Its vocabulary is extended to include a 'homosexual', a 'woman computer expert', and a 'one-parent family'. But its heroine is still victim – and perpetrator – of the old myths.

She knowingly, and to her eventual shame (for the object of her attentions turns out to be gay, and so her 'sins' cannot be purified in marriage), plays the Scarlet Woman, fake-tanning her legs and borrowing her daughter's make-up in an attempt to seduce a lithe and very professional tennis coach. But of course she herself is inadequate, shades of the old Dumb Blonde, her game hopeless on and off court. Or so she says, for she tells her own self-mocking story, neatly whittling herself down to Little Woman proportions. Besides, the Wicked Witch has popped up again. Only this time she looks suspiciously like a nasty caricature of Superwoman. For here she is in the guise of the lady computer expert – the one who 'ran off' with our heroine's husband. And there she is again as a failed wife, a 'loud, muscular woman', who recently departed for Canada on 'some self-seeking mission'. These two are responsible for our heroine's divorce (she herself is, naturally, pure and blameless), and for that of a further man in the tale (which, as we shall see, turns out to be very convenient). Our poor heroine, however – who incidentally has a variety of part-time jobs that either 'make ends meet' or else are 'fun', nothing so selfishly successful as computering – bears traces of the Hysteric: 'Since being alone, I hadn't worked out what sort of woman I was'. But then, just in the nick of time, she does remember, from the old days, what it is she wants to be: 'a sane, whole mother'. Fine, but apparently this can only be achieved by Getting Her (second) Man. Still, despite this rather baffling logic, at least the gentleman in question is as pure as our heroine, since, conveniently, he was the one left by the Witch's over-loud understudy. Man the second is, in addition, extremely and traditionally patronizing. It was, he points out politely and without so far as I could see a shred of evidence, not the gay tennis pro but 'me you wanted all the time'. Then, gently kissing her, he wakes our heroine, Sleeping Beauty, to the realization that she is, miraculously, whole again: as mother, friend, bed-fellow, housewife, nurse, and, since this is the twentieth-century, part-time secretary.

No: it is not the system of language that militates against women, but the myths that language is called upon to carry and which, in consequence, limit its development and the developing, changing perceptions of its users. Looking for 'male' language, 'female' language, even 'androgynous' language, is a red herring if we are searching for aspects of the system that can be pinned down as intrinsically sexist or non-sexist. Syntax and prosody are there for the taking, for meaning, by men and women. Far from being a restrictive and standardizing strait-jacket, syntax is an energizer, an essential springboard to the creativity of words. Nor, in practice, do we confine ourselves to the neatly perfect noun-phrase-verb-phrase patterns beloved by linguistic theoreticians. We, men and women, and not only certain artists, habitually and to meaningful effect, disturb, interrupt, embroider and complicate this basic pattern without losing its directive energy. Rhythm and intonation convey subtle messages above and beyond the words that carry them.

Language is subject to the pressures of emotion, creativity and change, and its control is only iron amongst unthinking users (like Hanzel and Grettel) going through the motions of unaltered experience – and refusing to hear and repeat anything but unchanging myth. It can play into the hands of the deterministic, but it need not be determinate. It has power and also possibility: both are possessed by men and by women. So it is counterproductive to confuse the symptom of female language disadvantage with the root cause of the malaise.

It is essential to distinguish language the facility, the capability, from the myths people – men and women – make and, through it, maintain. We might focus our attention less upon the system and more upon its uses and users, more upon the myths we choose to hear. For it is these myths which continue to reduce women. It is these which, limiting women's aspirations and pandering to men's dominance, continue to keep women from spheres of influence and strength: spheres from which new myths may be loudly proclaimed and unavoidably heard.

Notes

1. Frank Palmer points out (1981: 120) 'the feminine la sentinelle . . . may refer to a strapping young male'. He explains that, in French, most occupational names such as *sentinelle* are feminine: historical facts have overruled the obvious semantic probability that male creatures will be referred to by masculine nouns and female creatures by feminine ones.
2. 'Je venais de découvrir la guerre toute entière . . . Faut être à peu près devant elle comme je l'étais à ce moment-là pour vien la voir, *la vache*, en face et de profil'.

3. Emler discusses the issue of gossip in a forthcoming publication, 'A Social Psychology of Reputation' in *European Review of Social Psychology*, vol. 1, eds. W. Stroebe and M. Henstone, Chichester, John Wiley.
4. Not that we can automatically equate deafness with arrogance. Clare Campbell notes (*Marie Claire*, October 1988: 51–6) that Zela West-Meades of Relate (the new name for the National Marriage Guidance Council) believes a man's silence can be the consequence of early experiences which he has interpreted as female betrayal. And Margaret Ramage, a marital therapist, warns in the same article that forcing a man to talk can put him under counter-productive emotional pressure.
5. Undergraduate dissertation, Sex Differences in Language and the GCSE Oral Examination, written in 1988 at Loughborough University (Department of English and Drama) by Emma Dowson.
6. Significant phonemic change was noted. In particular, the young Clonard women used more backed variants of /a/ in words like *hat*, *man*, and *back*.
7. Spencer does not 'claim that in any respect, thematic or stylistic, women's writing is *essentially* different from men's' (Spencer 1986: ix) but argues that their position in a patriarchal society has contributed to the shaping of their work, leading them to either internalize and reflect – or, alternatively, oppose – that society's notions of femininity.

CHAPTER FIVE

Healing Narratives

Could mortal lip divine
The undeveloped freight
Of a delivered syllable
'Twould crumble with the weight.
(1970: 602)

I want to begin with this warning poem, written by the nineteenth century American poet, Emily Dickinson. For although language and perception, and language and personality, are first cousins, limits may be imposed upon the power of words and syntax.

Dickinson seems to be implying, albeit through a different metaphor, that an utterance can be only the tip of an iceberg. And it is true that the implications of language are multiple and extensive. For the hearer to respond to every nuance is a huge task of interpretation. It involves intelligent and intuitive assessment of word, syntax, sound, tone and rhythm. It needs recognition of speech 'acts', acts that may be intended apart from the overt meaning of uttered words: after all, saying that you smell smoke is as likely to be an act of warning as a statement of simple fact (Austin: 1982: Searle: 1969). But these depths of language, like the lurking depths of an iceberg, may be difficult for a hearer to judge accurately. Linguistic clues can be limited or ambiguous. This may be due to impaired communicative competence, or it may be intentional. Intonational signals, for example, can lack clarity. But Labov and Fanshel believe this need not be a deficiency of speech. They argue (1977: 46):

Speakers need a form of communication which is *deniable*. It is advantageous for them to express hostility, challenge the competence of others, or express friendliness and affection in a way that can be denied if they are explicitly held to account for it. If there were not such a deniable channel of communication, and intonational contours became so well recognized and explicit that people were accountable for their intonations, then some other mode of deniable communication would undoubtedly develop.

But of course, apart from deliberately masking what we believe to be true, we can also be reluctant or unable to understand totally what we hear – or say. For the full implications of the 'undeveloped freight' in an utterance, to return to Dickinson's poem, could be too awesome, challenging or painful, for even their speaker to bear if it were completely explicit, totally acknowledged. We may listen to people's stories then – the subject of much of this chapter – but their total meaning can elude us and even the teller of the tale may not be fully aware of the shadowy forms beneath its outward display.

Still, a cautionary reminder is just that: a warning, and not a total ban. If we did not make some attempt to assess and take account of an iceberg's hidden limits, a disastrous collision might well follow. Much the same is true of the personal narratives that permeate our lives so extensively that Roland Barthes has said (1977: 79) story-telling 'is simply there, like life itself'. Tale-telling does not only concern itself with imaginary events and it is not only discoverable between the covers of books and magazines, on the radio and television. All of us, whether or not we are professional artists or performers, relate – mostly in conversation – narratives of our personal lives. The practice of personal narration is a constant habit, so much so that we may not be aware of its crucial importance. Yet the psychologist Theodore Sarbin believes that 'Survival in a world of meanings is problematic without the talent to make up and to interpret stories about interweaving lives' (1986: 11). He has claimed 'universality' for the story 'as a guide to living and as a vehicle for understanding the conduct of others' (Sarbin 1986: x).

We saw evidence of fictional story telling as a (dubious) guide to living in the final paragraphs of the previous chapter, where real-life perceptions and attitudes appeared subject to moulding or confirm-ation through the story-myths of popular art. But the personal, everyday telling of tales can also lay claim to being an art form, and a powerful life-shaping one at that.[1] For, like fictional narrative, it requires not only the organization of events into some sort of chronological order. It involves in addition the shaping and interpret-ation of these events. As we tell our personal tale we stand back from it (like the author of fiction, shaping characters and scenarios, indicating causality and consequence) and bear interpretive witness to our actions. 'One thing leads to another', remarks the story giver of the here and now, as s/he recalls the past: 'Looking back, I can see why'. The personal tale is a reconstruction of experience then, subject to the influential direction of its teller, selecting, highlighting, and connecting some events and their consequences, choosing to ignore others. The process of the tale's creation is in this sense a heuristic device. As such the anecdote might take a respected place alongside the rationality of definition and logical argument. Moreover, the telling of the tale is not only a recalling and restructuring of experience – it is itself an experience. It has the power to crystallize or shape perception, affecting the teller and hearer. Seen this way, personal narratives bandied across the dinner-table or recounted over the garden fence must become much more than entertaining trivia.

So the personal story is a relevant subject for discussion in a book which deals with the powerful creativity of language, particularly the power of language outside of, or unconventional in, art. Besides, it is this element of creativity, this element of the 'non-standard' – the term being understood not as an opposition to standard prestige English but more generally, implying change and development from an earlier norm – that can make narrative a healing art. Robinson and Hawpe's concept of 'narrative repair' is relevant here. They write:

> Narrative repair is potentially an unending process. Retrospection, or reminiscing, can be viewed as a process of testing the continued validity of life experience stories. Sometimes new information relevant to an incident is discovered which creates discrepancies in the accepted story, but more often interpretive perspectives change prompting reevaluation of the casual model which organized the original account. (Sarbin 1986: 123)

The ability to loosen the elements of an existing personal story then, rather like shaking up the pieces of an kaleidoscope, can allow a fresh look at a standard perception. The process has the creativity of the artist. And it can be a healing creativity. I am not suggesting that physical or psychological suffering is in any way illusory, or that it be denied in the telling of a fantasy tale: I am saying that its slotting into the framework of a life story may be done in different ways, some less painful than others.

An adaptation of W.V. Quine's metaphor of a sphere (Quine: 1963, 1969) makes the point. It is a metaphor illustrating his concept of the linguistic system, a concept which maintains that there are different types of sentences of different epistemological status.[2] Those sentences standing on the edge of the sphere refer to day-to-day, verifiable knowledge: Quine calls these *occasion sentences*. Those sentences in the centre of the sphere represent our most deeply rooted knowledge, the memories and ideas we carry with us and hold to be true: Quine calls these *standing sentences*. If standing sentences are challenged by occasion sentences – day-to-day happenings – which do not appear to match the previously held sense of self and the world, then either the standing or the occasion sentences will need to be adapted if the individual is to be able to cope with the discrepancy. Mancuso and Adams-Webber (1982) propose that resolving discrepancies between memory and fresh data is a basic motivation of psychological functioning: it would seem that the telling of the tale, the personal narrative, is one way of bringing the two sorts of sentences into some sort of comfortable liaison.

The attempt to do so may be made privately as we talk to ourselves, going over in our heads – silently or out loud – something that has disturbed us. It made be made in conversation with a friend. Or the tale may be told to a therapist. These contexts of tale-telling, and the part played in them by a story's recipient, are significant. They can all facilitate a marriage of standing and occasion sentences but some may do so in ways which achieve a more authentic and healing compromise than others. So we shall be looking at the patterns of conversation that surround personal narratives. And we return here to our theme of the non-standard. For the discourse patterns that seem to encourage the most useful narratives are unusual.

We shall be looking at the contexts of story telling in due course. But first, the story itself. How exactly is a story structured; what are its essential formal elements? Wherein lies its flexibility and, consequently, its potential for healing?

LIFE STORIES

Narrative Structure

Labov's description of the probable structure of personal narrative, told in conversation of some kind, is the best place for us to begin (Labov and Waletsky 1967: Labov 1972: Labov and Fanshel 1977). For Labov and Waletsky, the basic unit of a narrative is a clause which refers to an event and which is placed in a chronological order: 'The basic narrative units that we wish to isolate are defined by the fact that they recapitulate experience in the same order as the original events' (1967: 20–21). The majority of these units will be found in the part of the story that Labov calls *complication*. Their order cannot be changed without to some extent changing the story – as sentence (2) below, tampering with the framework of the English nursery rhyme, demonstrates.

(1) Jack and Jill went up the hill. Jack fell down. He broke his crown.
(2) Jack and Jill went up the hill. Jack broke his crown. Jack fell down.

A rational chronology may also be lost.

(1) Jack and Jill went up the hill. Jack fell down.
(2) Jack fell down (the hill). Jack and Jill went up the hill.

Labov concentrates on clauses of physical action. But Emerson pointed out that words are also deeds: in this sense, speaking and thinking too would qualify as events.

There will also be other components to the narrative. it may begin with an *abstract* which quickly sums up the crux of what is to come: *I'll tell you about when Jack and Jill went hill-climbing*. It signals that conversational dialogue should be suspended for the moment because its speaker is about to start telling a tale.

Then, between the abstract and the complication there is likely to be some sort of orientation, the who, when, what, and where of the tale: *Jack and Jill were on water-collecting duty*.

One or two elements may come right at the end of the tale telling. There is likely to be a *result*, what finally happened: *Then Jill came tumbling after*. And finally there may be a *coda*, which is a sort of signing-off and a return from the past time of the story to the present moment of its telling: *Well, that was the end of that. Would you like another cup of tea?*

But there is one more vital element in fully-fledged narrative: *evaluation*. The story we have been piecing together so far – without evaluation – is as follows.

> I'll tell you about when Jack and Jill were on water collecting duty. Jack and Jill went up the hill. Jack fell down. He broke his crown. Then Jill came tumbling after. Well, that was that. Would you like another cup of tea?

Any listener would be entitled to wonder, 'So what? What did she tell me all that for?'. The account is dramatic, it is true. But it does not explain just why the drama is worth retelling. The story has no *evaluation*. But all would be clear if sentences something like the following were inserted before the coda: *It was bound to happen. Children really shouldn't be asked to carry heavy pails.*

This sort of evaluation is part of the present, of the moment of tale-telling. The narrator is looking back on events, stepping outside them and assessing them from the here and now. But evaluation could have taken place at the time of the action and another sentence, recalling it, would then have been inserted in the narrative: *Jill kept saying the bucket was too heavy for them*. Here the story's narrator is recalling an assessment made at the time of the escapade.

We shall look at this practice of evaluation in some detail. It is – particularly because of its adaptability – a core element in the healing nature of narrative.

Labovian Evaluation

Jack and Jill's story was assessed quite openly and directly. The narrator believes it just goes to show that children should not carry heavy buckets: indeed, Jill herself said so at the time. However, neither kind of clear evaluation – either in the present or recalled from the past – is made in the following 'tale'.

The Spaceman and the Dinosaur

There was a spaceman and he met a dinosaur and they went to the dinosaur's house and played on the swings and then they brushed their teeth. They went to the pub and played on the swings and then they went home and brushed their teeth and went to bed.

The above is the work of Alexander Osmond-Brims, aged four and three-quarters, published in the *Telegraph Sunday Magazine* (15 September 1985: 31) and *Mini Sagas* (1985: 46). A dinosaur home-owner presumably takes the tale out of the realm of personal narrative! Moreover, this story/fantasy was not told as part of a conversation, the kind of personal tale-telling context we shall be discussing: Alexander tape-recorded his words, his father wrote them down, and the end result was second under-eighteen place in a *Telegraph* story-writing competition. But – quite apart from its charm – the tale will still be useful in our discussion since it helps, by contrast, to emphasize the essential qualities of adult narration.

Alexander's narrative is very like what Rothery and Martin (1980) call a 'recount', simply a number of events temporally sequenced. However, his narrative competence will develop. At present Alexander is still 'leap frogging' from event to event. When, for instance, did the visit to the pub take place? Were there two swing episodes or is Alexander referring, twice, to the same post-pub happening?. But this haphazard tendency of young story-tellers normally progresses (see Peterson and McCabe 1983) to chronological recounting which eventually, at about five years old, stops abruptly at some apparently high point. Even at this stage, however, the story does not usually offer a result on the adult model. But causal linking between events develops and progresses with age, until eventually tales emerge resembling the Labovian model, having evident purpose and point-of-view. There is probably no need to assume some innate storying capacity in order to explain this narrative acquisition. It becomes feasible when the linguistic facility of displacement (discussed in Chapter One) is mastered and when a concept of time is understood. Narrative content will become available as social experience grows –

and an increasing human need to make sense of experience must foster the practice of evaluation and interpretation.[3]

This is a practice followed not only by the teller of the tale but also by its recipient looking for a point. Though Alexander may not have pointedly evaluated his tale, adult audiences are tempted to speculate. Michotte (1963/1946) demonstrated a human readiness to project cause-and-effect stories on to the simplest of stimulus materials. So we wonder what Alexander's recount is *really* all about and cast around for possible casual links to turn it into a complex narrative. I am inclined to suggest that tooth-brush training is at the root of it all!

Yet adult evaluation – making sense of the data as it were – does not always take the clear-cut form of overt commentary outside of and upon the narrative clauses describing the complication of the story. (Jill came tumbling after. *She always said the bucket was too heavy for them.*) It can also be part and parcel of the narrative clauses themselves.

Evaluation of this kind is present in Zoe Ellis's tale. This is another literary narrative but, like Alexander's recount, her example is still useful in our discussion of personal stories. For whilst Alexander's recount was helpful by contrast, Zoe's writing contains elements similar to those frequently present in personal narrative. And it gives rise to discussion of others. Zoe just overtook Alexander to win the *Telegraph Sunday Magazine* competition. She wrote:

What the Sleeping Beauty would have given her right arm for

This princess was different. She was a brunette beauty with a genius of a brain. Refusing marriage, she inherited all by primogenesis. The country's economy prospered under her rule. When the handsome prince came by on his white charger, she bought it from him and started her own racehorse business. (*Mini Sagas* 1985: 218)

We have already heard Zoe's story (in Chapter Four). We could not at the time fail to miss its triumphant feminist point. To this end its narrative clauses are plainly evaluated outside of themselves. That is, Zoe stands right outside the events of the tale and declares, from her vantage point in the present, that her heroine is 'different' and a 'genius': this is the point of the story, and the precise cause of its events.[4] In addition, had she wished, she could have allowed the princess to evaluate her own actions as they were happening. She might have added (had there not been a fifty-word limit for the competition) something like, '*So now,*' *said the princess to herself,* '*I shall live happily ever after*'. But, quite apart from external comment-ary, Zoe also suggests evaluations which are part and parcel of the tale, embedded in its narrative clauses.

For a fuller discussion of internal evaluative possibilities, see Labov 1967, 1972. Briefly, we can note here that one way for the oral narrator to indicate his/her perspective, or evaluation, of a narrative clause, is through *intensifiers*. These are often gestural or phonological. For example, vowels may be lengthened: *She was a ge-e-e-nius of a brain*. (There is potential here for mixed or confused evaluation. The words uttered seem to state one thing. But their accompanying gestures, or intonation patterns, can offer a contradictory message. 'She was a *genius*', said with emphasis upon 'genius', but with eyes raised to the heavens, can turn compliment to ridicule.) Or there can be *explicatives* which, prefaced by *although, while, because* and so on, attach an explanatory subordinate clause to the main clause: *Because he had sold his horse, the handsome prince went by bus*. Or there are *correlates* that link events or attributes together through complex syntax: *Refusing marriage, she inherited all by primogenesis*. There may also be what Labov terms *comparators*, embedded into the narrative clauses themselves. These draw attention to the point of the tale by relating an event to something different and thus illustrating its own comparative importance. Zoe paves the way for a subtle example of this as soon as she remarks (the remark itself is an example of external evaluation), *This princess was different*. How was she different? We soon discover that, for one thing, the princess was brunette and a genius. But the significance of these – comparative – facts depends of course on our knowledge of the phrase 'dumb blonde' and the current feminist climate.

Naturally. Narratives must depend for their evaluation upon both personal and cultural attitudes. When Laura Bohannan took the story of Hamlet to the African bush she encountered (as she recalled in a paper entitled 'Miching Mallecho' [Morris 1956: 186]) a bewildering difference of evaluation – right from the moment when the village elders congratulated Claudius for doing the honourable (African) thing and swiftly marrying his brother's widow. 'But it is clear', said one of the old men to Bohannan, 'that the elders of your country have never told you what the story really means'.

However, not only Labovian evaluation, external and embedded, but also the chosen narrative clauses of a tale may be personal variations on a cultural theme. And being the result of choice – frequently syntactic choice – their form too can be a kind of evaluation, a way of personally perceiving.

Seeing Through Syntax

1) Verb phrases

Polanyi (1978: 1981) and also Tannen (1979) find cultural values influencing the telling of individual stories, guiding their selection of events and the perception of these essential elements. Sutton-Smith (Sarbin 1986: 83–88) analyses the fictional stories of groups of western children. He finds that their plots tend to develop through four stages, each representing a gradually increasing sense of ability to overcome difficulties. But he suggests that 'from the cross-cultural evidence presented by the Marandas (1970), it is also clear that there are many societies where no such belief in one's ability to overcome the fates exists'. In these cultures stories apparently do not go beyond the first or second of the western levels. Now, although these are fictional tales, and we are most interested in personal narrative, these observations seem relevant to our purpose since the confronting of difficulty is at the heart of therapeutic tale-telling.

The first of the four 'western' levels describes a conflict. For example, a frightening monster appears. But at this earliest plot stage no response to the conflict is recorded. (Alexander Osmond-Brimm's dinosaur and spaceman tale does not imply either conflict or strain, but we suggested that this comes from an even earlier stage in narrative development.) At the next stage of plotting the conflict may be evaded – the protagonists escaping or being rescued from the monster – but the danger is not nullified: the monster lives on. At the third level the monster will be rendered powerless in some way. The final stage, which Sutton-Smith labels 'transformation', sees the danger completely removed without any possibility of its further return. Sutton-Smith suggests that the older the child, the nearer his/her plots 'approximate to the hero myths of the Western world within which heroes and heroines brought under duress, undertake task which resolve their problems' (Sarbin 1986: 89). On the other hand he also notes – relating fiction to fact – 'we find that some of our younger children, even five-year-olds, occasionally tell the fourth level stories, and so we wonder whether or not this particular series of steps might not be functionally related to need achievement, or to an inner locus of control' (Sarbin 1986: 87).

This account of children's fictions is most useful in our discussion of evaluation by structural choice when it is linked with Greimas's narrative model of six *actants* (1966). In a sense, Sutton-Smith describes the *verb phrases* of narrative clauses: the protagonists *conflict, evade, restrain,* or *transform*. Greimas, on the other hand, deals with the *nouns* of narrative clauses – and these may vary according to a narrator's perception of events.

2) Noun Phrases

Greimas proposed that six roles, or *actants*, underlie all narratives. They make up three interrelated pairs:

> superhelper-giver/receiver-beneficiary
> subject/object
> helper/opponent

Folk-tales, especially their prettified modern versions, are particularly suitable for analysis into these categories. For instance, our pantomime versions show poor downtrodden Cinderella (Greimas's *subject* and potential *receiver-beneficiary*) dreaming of a happier life and, eventually, her handsome prince (*object*). Buttons is a faithful supporter (*helper*). But the Ugly Sisters do their best to interfere (*opponents*, and thus a source of Sutton-Smith's conflict element). Therefore Prince Charming and Cinderella are only able to meet because of the Fairy Godmother (*superhelper-giver*), who transforms the girl's appearance and whisks her to the palace, in this way overcoming her opponents and nullifying the conflict.

However, a modern romantic tendency to dwell upon magic in the tales and to create a superhelper with fantastic powers, is not present in these stories in their earlier forms. A superhelper did exist in them, but s/he was not a magician in the supernatural sense and Iona and Peter Opie point out (1974) that Cinderella's story was never one of miraculous transformation from rags to riches. It is not therefore the model for the paperback blockbusters we mentioned in the previous chapter, where a once downtrodden woman's accumulating power is the prize, and the original personality with its original conflicts and struggles is utterly transformed with the minimum of real-life likelihood. On the contrary, Cinderella is a tale of 'reality made evident' (Opie 1974: 11). The fairy godmother/superhelper merely creates an opportunity for that reality to be brought to the surface and recognized. In the story told by Charles Perrault (whose *Histoires ou Contes du temps passé. Avec des Moralitez* was published in Paris in 1697, and whose Cinderella is at the root of our modern English versions) the girl was – really – of 'unparalleled goodness' and of high birth. The tale demands that these values be acknowledged as inherent and not as superficial additions. So it is important that Prince Charming confirms Cinderella's intrinsic value by proposing to her not in her elegant trappings at the ball, but in her rags. The fairy-godmother never allows the silks and satins to remain after midnight. She does not do so in our modern versions either, but we may now choose to underplay the point that her 'magic' is merely to help

Cinderella reach out for her rightful prince, and her prince to find and cherish the girl that existed, unrecognized, undervalued, all along. The Opies (1974: 12) write of this and other tales: 'Enchantment, in practice, is the opposite of the golden dream. The wonderful happens, the lover is recognized, the spell of misfortune is broken, when the situation that already exists is utterly accepted . . .

John Ruskin was surely correct then when he introduced (1868) *German Popular Stores* as follows:

> Let [the child] know his fairy tale accurately, and have perfect joy or awe in the conception of it as if it were real; thus he will always be exercising his power of grasping realities: but a confused, careless, and discrediting tenure of the fiction will lead to as confused and careless reading of fact . . . therefore it is a grave error, either to multiply unnecessarily, or to illustrate with extravagant richness, the incidents presented to the imagination.

His comment, in relating fiction and fact, makes helpful bridges for us between the two kinds of stories, fictional and personal. Both kinds can be described with the help of Greimas's model: both require the same close attention to their most authentic evaluations possible. A therapist – who may be any competent story-hearer, amateur or professional – listening not to fictional tales but to personal narrative, can be regarded in a similar light to Greimas's superhelper. S/he is not precisely present in the story as it is being told, but in listening s/he plays a closely related and extremely powerful role. It may be that a story-teller will come to a listener hoping for the kind of magical problem-solving transformation that never took place in folk myth. If so, s/he is likely to be disappointed. On the other hand, the skilled listener (whom we shall consider below in a discussion of therapeutic contexts) can encourage in the teller the kind of evaluatory 'magic' that makes evident a particular version of the narrator's reality: in this way the spell of misfortune could be broken.

I have said that all of Greimas's actants, not merely the superhelper, can be recognized in personal narrative as well as in folk-tales. Giver/receiver, subject/object, and helper/opponent all have their counterparts in real life. So it is not surprising that all appear in the noun phrases of the following personal narrative. Its content, too, is reminiscent of Sutton-Smith's analysis of children's stories. Like the first level of these, the verb phrases of the narrative focus on conflict. In looking forward to a solution, the story anticipates later levels. Most importantly, its verb and noun phrases are united in *transitivity* structures, so it will be helpful to extend our syntactic approach to narratives by examining these. We referred in Chapter One to

Halliday's systemic grammar and its concept of options. Some of the language options we can choose relate to the system of transitivity. We select first the option *transitive* or the option *intransitive*. If we choose transitive then we are concerned, roughly speaking, with processes which pass from one person or thing to another. *The child played in the living-room* is intransitive. But *The child played the piano in the living-room* is transitive. Taking the transitive option means making certain choices. We shall be opting for a process – usually expressed by a verb (played) – and then for certain (in Hallidayan terminology) *roles* expressing *participant functions*. For example *actor* (the child) and something like *goal* or *patient* or *beneficiary* (piano): these are represented by and large by nouns. There may also be *circumstantial* roles (in the living-room). This is a most superficial account of Halliday's description of transitivity. For one thing, some processes are 'mental', and in this case we cannot talk easily of actor and goal: *processor* and *phenomenon* may be better (as in, for instance, *I liked your wallpaper*). The reader will find a full discussion in Halliday 1973. However, this brief reference is sufficient for our purpose in examining the following story.

This tale has a similar form to the one described by Labov, beginning with an abstract, followed by an orientation, then a complicating action, followed by a result and ending with a coda which brings us back into the present. Labovian evaluation is here both external and internal.

3) Transitivity

I want to tell you about when Peter went. We had been married about four years. I had the twins in the first year. And then Ruth was born. I shouldn't have had them so close together, should I? Well, I couldn't get the twins to sleep in the day from the start. And then I couldn't seem to get Ruth settled on to cereals and that, so she was always being sick. Peter's mother said I should have fed Ruth myself – and the boys: then they'd all have been a lot happier and healthier. So it was bound to get Peter down, wasn't it? I was so tired. And I looked such a mess. It's really no wonder he went, is it? He came home at lunch-time one day. I hadn't even cleared the breakfast things. And I hadn't got the boys out of their pyjamas. I hadn't got Ruth's lunch either, and she was yelling. Well he just lost his temper. And I can see why. I suppose it wasn't surprising. He just said, 'That's it. You're useless, aren't you? I'm going!' And that was that. It's been a year now. Tell me what to do! I just want him back.

The subject, in Greimas's sense, is in this case also the teller of the tale: we'll call her Mary. The object is the missing Peter. If he will only return,the Mary will be receiver. His mother might rate as a dubious helper. But Mary hopes her hearer will turn out to be super-helper, giving the tale the chance of a new ending. As for an opponent, Mary seems to have cast herself in a number of roles including this one: she is subject, potential receiver – and her own worst enemy. If only she had not had the children so close together, if only she had breast-fed them, then they would have been wonderful and she would have been energetic and beautiful. Peter would have got his just deserts.

On the other hand, listening to her story one might wonder if she was really her own opponent, the agent of all her own misery. Possibly Mary wonders too. After all, she does tag 'should I?' on to her own evaluation of the close births, and also asks her listener to confirm – or deny – her assessment that it was all 'bound' to get poor Peter down and force him to escape. But the professional listener/superhelper cannot answer Mary's questions for her, only urge her to consider her narrative clauses again and again, checking to see if any other evaluation of them is possible and helpful.

It is significant in this evaluative respect that virtually all the clauses in Mary's story have her, in terms of *transitivity*, as agent of her conflict. A choice within the transitivity system is a choice of an evaluative kind. Mary's chosen syntax reflects her sense of herself as 'doer': she sees herself as being agent of most of the narrative clauses she relates. They imply, syntactically, that she has caused all the trouble: *she* had the twins close to the next child, couldn't get them to sleep, couldn't feed Ruth properly, and so on. We can imagine this particular tale's sequel, Peter endorsing its implications and narrating to friends in the pub the consequences of what he too sees as his wife's provocative actions: 'I was forced into it. I was driven to go, you know. I couldn't help it. She let the situation get completely out of hand.' Mary remains the agent in Peter's tale-telling. He is subject (except in 'I couldn't help it') only in *passive* syntax which implies an agent over-ruling his own will: 'I was forced into it (*by Mary*)'; 'I was driven to go, you know, (*by Mary*).'

Peter could be right. Possibly Mary was an inadequate wife and mother. Possibly he was the victim of her deficiencies, their children suffering through her incompetence.

Or is it possible that Peter too played some role in – was partly agent of – their distress? Maybe he gave little support. He could, surely, at least be held responsible for his own reactions. There is also the possibility that there may have been joint, or even several, responsibility for the couple's difficult situation. One would think that each, husband and wife, played some part in the rapid conception of the children. And it is not improbable that the twins and Ruth are by nature, and diet notwithstanding, a difficult trio.

If any of these possibilities occurs to Mary, then she might choose different transitivity roles, filling Greimas's *actant* 'slots' in different ways, finding in a revised tale-telling different sources of the kind of conflict that is central to Sutton-Smith's narrative model. A new story might choose to share responsibility. Mary could even resist, in her personal story, the influence of the larger cultural myth of female inadequacy and guilt.

> We had the twins in the first year. And then Ruth was born. We shouldn't have had them so close together. The twins wouldn't sleep in the day from the start. And Ruth didn't take to cereals. It's not surprising Peter felt so fed up. And it's really no wonder I was so tired.

The choice of transitivity roles, the syntax of the narrative clauses, is thus a kind of evaluation. Moreover, it provokes reselection from the lexicon. Mary may now be seen as 'enduring' rather than 'failing': it is no longer she who, in the terms of Sutton-Smith's model, is provoking conflict.

The new language is not inventing a fantasy. Rather, it is bringing to consciousness, for consideration, a reality that could always have been present yet not previously recognized: 'sensed' but not 'experienced', to use these words in Crites's particular understanding of the terms. He explains (Sarbin 1986: 160):

> Many such things register in my consciousness, are perceived but not experienced, heard but not listened to. Here I must acknowledge a terminological quibble. I think it is useful to reserve the word 'experience' for what is incorporated into one's story, and thus owned, owned up to, appropriated. It will follow from this usage that many things are experienced retroactively. The close air, my labored breath, my co-worker's agitation had to be sensed at the time or they could not have dawned on me later, and of course it is common to use the word 'experience' for all such sensations . . . I prefer to say that most of the things that are sensed are never experienced, and that only those that are attended to are experienced, some things only slowly clarifying themselves as I become aware of their significance for my story. From this point of view 'experience' is a single, vast story-like construct, . . .

Change the story line then, and in this respect a person's experience – which the language crystallizes – is adjusted. For language is a kind of filter through which what we sense must pass.

Not only transitivity roles, and their related verbs, may change in the re-evaluation of a tale. There are other syntactic possibilities. These require not so much a change towards completely new role perceptions as the revelation of already existing language representations.

4) Deep Structure

Bandler and Grinder rightly claim that 'Magic is hidden in the language we speak . . . webs that you can tie and untie are at your command if only you pay attention to what you already have (language) . . .' (1975: 19). We need, that is, to recognize the *deep structures* lying behind the surface structures of the language that we actually utter. For all that lies in the deep structure may not reveal itself in the spoken/written word.

We are developing this argument out of the Chomskyan deep/ surface structure model of language, discussed in Chapter One. This model describes our *knowledge* of language. It is unlikely, as a general rule, to be a description of the way in which we normally produce and comprehend language (Aitchison 1989: 152–200; but, for a rather different view see also Kress and Hodge 1979: 15–37). However, it seems to be knowledge that we can draw upon when we wish – and its conscious retrieval may be psychologically revealing and powerful.

It will be recalled that expansions, and also transformations (involving the deletion, permutation, or addition of new language elements), are Chomskyan concepts that can describe the 'deep structures' that we know lie behind the sentences that we choose to utter 'on the surface'. For instance, a deep structure that is assumed to consist at one point of Noun Phrase – Verb Phrase (NP – VP) may expand to NP – VP – NP. We know that this would describe the structure of a sentence heard as *Peter left me*. However, we may choose to say simply *Peter left*. In this case we know that the option to expand the Verb Phrase to include a second Noun Phrase in the structure does not figure.

The perceptual concomitants of such choices could be psychologically important. For instance (though naturally we would need the context of the utterance to be certain), the chosen lack of *me*, the second NP, could be an evasion of pain, a decision – conscious or unconscious – to avoid acknowledging the totality of an experience by focusing on the person and his leaving but sliding away from the self, the person left. On the other hand, acknowledging the choice, recognizing our knowledge of its deep structures, may be self-revealing.

Similar choices, with scope for similar self-deception and self-revelation, are exemplified by the following sentences. Both, though different on the surface, share a similar deep structure: the structure of the second, however, can be described as having also gone through an optional passive transformation.

(1) Mary forced me.
(2) I was forced by Mary.

The choice of sentence (2) opens the way to a further option, which we have already heard taken by the imaginary Peter: the deletion of reference to agency in the phrase *by Mary*. Taking these options allows the speaker to evade specifying responsibility for the forcing. But, if called upon to recognize this structural/semantic evasion, and to supply the missing agent, the speaker will be encouraged to think more deliberately about agency and responsibility. Did Mary really 'force' him? What does *forcing* mean? Did Mary physically push him out? If not, did she do certain other things which led him to go? And could being *lead* to go really be described as being *forced*? Isn't being *lead* to do something closely related to *choosing*? If so, Peter – not Mary – was, at least in part, the agent of his own departure.

Sometimes, however, perceptual distortions described by transformations from deep to surface structure are more difficult to identify. There is a confusing ambiguity in the following sentence as a result of *nominalization*: 'Loving people can be a tremendous strain.' What is meant? Is it the *process* of loving people that is a strain for the lover? In this case the deep structure of the utterance would involve two separate clauses, something like:

(a) (Someone) loves people.
(b) . . . can be a tremendous strain.

Sentence (a) has a structure that we can describe as transformed from a clause with its own NP – VP – NP structure into a single noun phrase which has become the first NP of the ambiguous utterance.

On the other hand, the sentence could mean that the *people* who love are themselves a strain, a pressure upon the beloved. In this case it would have the following clauses in its deep structure and have gone through a series of transformations, involving relativization, to produce an apparently identical nominalization but one that has a very different implication.

(c) People love.
(d) People can be a tremendous strain.

Whoever utters the sentence, and whoever hears it, will need to be very clear about precisely which meaning, which deep structure, is involved, in order for its sense to be totally experienced. Asked to describe his marriage, Peter might have said, 'It can be a tremendous strain'. 'It' is a further step in evasive nominalization. If challenged he could choose to replace the pronoun with 'loving people'. But does he mean he finds it hard to actively care for Mary – or that he finds Mary's loving a strain upon himself?

The reductive potential of nominalization is an essential theme of Roy Schafer's *A New Language for Psychoanalysis* (1976). The 'new' language of the title is termed by Schafer 'action language', a language that shuns nominalization.

5) Living Language

Schafer explains that a concept of the person as agent has always been central to psychoanalytic understanding. Events are created, not merely encountered. Therefore he reinforces the argument that a person's account of events – their story – is open to interpretation, to re-evaluation. But he suggests that two languages have traditionally been involved in psychoanalysis (one of the healing contexts to which we shall return). There is *action language*, which can narrate these events. But action language has been, in Schafer's view, merely the 'necessary but personally unacknowledged servant' of Freudian *metapsychology* (Schafer 1976: 362), that second language which translates the first into the quasi-physiochemical and quasi-biological language of force, energy, mechanism, sublimation, function, structure, drive and so on. The language of metapsychology is reasonably complete and definite, if open to challenge. Action language, on the other hand, has not been developed into a clearly codified, formalized, rule-based system. It is a deficiency which Schafer sets out to remedy. We cannot here do justice to Schafer's complete formulation of action language, nor detail his reasons for departing from the language of Freudian metapsychology. But reference to a number of his central arguments helps to develop our current theme.

For example, Schafer begins his description of action language with the following rule (Schafer 1976: 363).

(1) One shall regard every psychological process, event, experience, response, or other item of behaviour as an action, and one shall designate it by an active verb and, when appropriate and useful, by an adverb or an adverbial locution that states the mode of this action.

These actions, which should be taken to include thoughts and unconscious as well as conscious activity, are not then to be spoken of syntactically as properties – nouns – that people possess. People do not, that is, *have* feelings, or habits: on the contrary, they *feel* in such and such a way, or they *behave* habitually in such and such a way. *He was behaving very hostilely* could be voiced as *His hostility was marked*, with an accompanying loss of focus on personal agency.

In consequence, entities such as drives or regulatory structures will not be invoked by action language: for preparation for an activity is yet another, earlier, action. 'Whereas *to wish* is to perform an action of a certain sort and thus is a notion that is compatible with action language, a *wish*, in the sense of an autonomous dynamic agency, is now an inadmissible conception' (Schafer 1976: 354). Actions cannot be said to have causes,

> for within the action system these causes must always be mediated by the person's interpretations, constructions, or understanding of them; consequently, an infinite regress would be entailed by any effort to state the cause of a personal interpretation . . . (Schafer 1976: 370–371)

Schafer goes on to say that there can be no once and for all correct statement of an action. An action can be referred to in a number of ways: it is a manifold of possibilities. It can be designated on different levels of generality or abstractness, or from different points of view which can even be maintained in one and the same person. Our fictitious Mary saw herself agenting all her difficulties. She might *also* come to see some of the distressing activity agented from outside of herself, and then recognize her own (personally agented) activities in response to these. 'Whenever one designates an action in a new way – one does so often in the course of psychoanalytic work – one creates a new action without cancelling out the old' (Schafer 1976: 365).

It is significant also that actions should be seen as performances – not as achievements. In consequence words of inability are inappropriate. One performs or does not perform an activity. *Cannot do* refers to *not doing*. Refusal to perform an action is itself a kind of action. ' "Won't" refers to an action of refusal that, logically, is distinct from the action one refuses to perform' (Schafer 1975: 371). When the imaginary Peter claimed *I could not help it* he may, by the rules of action language, be heard to say *I did not help it*: he chose not to. (If Peter had needed muscular strength to resist Mary's 'forcing' this would have been a different matter in action language, because wrestling, like cooking or musicianship is, for action language, a skill rather than an ability.)

So Schafer appears to understand 'experiencing' in a similar manner to Crites, as a person giving meaning to that which previously has only been 'sensed': experience is not unmediated phenomena. We have been concentrating on sense mediated largely through syntax: seeing through our chosen syntax. But I want to look now at another fundamental power of language: the choice of *metaphor*. For the metaphorical language we select is not mere embellishment – Alexander Pope's stylish 'dress' of thought – but is also a way of experiencing.

Metaphor

The work of Lakoff and Johnson, which we referred to in Chapter One, will be illuminating here. *Metaphors We Live By* (Lakoff and Johnson: 1980) argues that our conceptual system is fundamentally metaphorical. But many of the book's examples might suggest that our use of metaphor can limit perception, and thus experience, by militating against action language. For we have a tendency to nominalize that which we sense, metaphorically, into entities and substances. For instance, we often talk of the mind as a machine: *My head just won't work today. It won't get into top gear.* And machines have particular properties. So we may see this one as very sensitive and fragile: *Her mind simply snapped.* Nominalization in metaphor is psychologically problematic, then, in that it can create allies and enemies, entities and substances with lives of their own, outside of our 'selves': thus, *her mind went to pieces*, or *life cheated them*, or *her emotions ran away with her*. In these cases responsibility is shifted from human agency to imagined and elusive entities. We can find ourselves destroyed by phantoms.

Nevertheless, we can use a kind of action language in company with the nominal core of these metaphors, placing ourselves as agents of the related verbs: *I made my mind work overtime.* Besides, the notion of making the mind work is not necessarily untrue, even though the mind is not 'really' a machine. Lakoff and Johnson counter the diametrically opposing concepts of subjectivity and objectivity with their own preferred middle ground of *experiential understanding*. They demonstrate that the metaphors we 'live by' are neither wholly imaginary and subjective, nor wholly 'actual' and objective. They are instead grounded in, imagined out of, that which we have sensed. And it is the awareness of our own physicality that encourages us to imagine other sensed phenomena as if they had shape and form. Understanding them in this way can make it easier for us to reason about and react to them. If such reasoning and reaction 'works', in that it does not challenge any other parts of our conceptual system, then our metaphorical understanding has been acceptable: in this way it is 'true'. The possibility of 'making the mind work' might be a helpful and accurate concept, developing a sense of control, energy, potential.

But metaphor can still permit self-deception. For we experience through metaphors which, whilst highlighting some aspect of that experiencing, at the same time hide the recognition of others. Thus we can talk of arguing, for instance, as if we were warring: *I won that round*; *She will have to defend her position better next time*. In the process we can lose sight of the potentially co-operative, agreement-reaching aspects of argument.

We can speculate upon the kind of metaphors that could be structuring – hiding and highlighting – the fictitious Mary and Peter's concept of their situation. We talk of love, and love relationships, in various metaphorical ways. We may associate them with health, or madness, or journeying, for example. Lakoff and Johnson include as metaphors of health *it's a sick relationship/ their love is dying/ their marriage is reviving*. All of these involve nominalization and, most importantly, imply a passivity on the part of those involved in the relationship. As for madness, take the metaphorical images of insanity implied in *I'm crazy about her*, or *She's driving me wild*. Lack of control is emphasized here and the imaginary Peter could well have thought in these terms, at least before the pressures of home life and children, since he appears to see his emotions as forced upon him, quite outside of his agency. If, on the other hand, Mary and Peter had been inclined to experience their marriage as journeying, then they might have thought in terms of difficult roads, lost ways. Entities are envisaged here, it is true, but the couple could have understood themselves relating to these as active agents, co-drivers and map-readers along a route which, chosen and negotiated together, might well take a turn for the better – or else reach a mutually agreed stopping point.

So metaphor – or perhaps we should say *metaphoring* – is not always culpable. It can play its part in healing narratives, for it is a use of language which gives us much of our flexibility of perception, allowing us to re-evaluate the story line, to find new language and thus new meanings – and new experience. Mary and Peter might discover, over a period of telling their story, the relevance of the familiar journeying metaphor. Or they might even create something completely fresh. Lakoff and Johnson explore the meaning potential in viewing loving as collaborative artistic creativity. This would involve recognizing the work element of loving, its need for co-operation, its uniqueness in each experience, its shared aesthetic – and even its need for funding! Once envisaged, the metaphor can crystallize sense into experience, a perception that will play its part in the languaging of future experience.

Languaging and Listening

We have been looking at a variety of ways of languaging, particularly those involving choices from syntax and metaphor and the incorporation of these into narrative form. But are some of us more able than others to use language in a creative and healing way? Can we be taught to do it better? Do some circumstances, more than others, encourage us to review our language and thus our lives? Can we, for instance, re-evaluate in talking to ourselves? We certainly do, sometimes, adjust our tale-telling without the immediate influence of a partner in talk. To see this we have only to contrast the private diaries that were written in the trenches of the First World War with the letters – brutal details softened, perhaps impossible to share – that these diarists wrote home; and then compare their letters with the poetry they produced later – emotion recollected in some sort of tranquility – away from the front.[5] However, the presence of other people, especially in conversation of some kind, is particularly likely to inspire re-evaluation. Their questions and reactions can provoke re-appraisal. But listening to stories takes a variety of forms, and our discussion so far raises a number of questions about their comparative efficacy.

Listening friends, for instance, can discourage exploration, endorsing the story we first tell because they are anxious to assure us of their understanding and approval. Besides, Grice (1975) has drawn our attention to the *maxims* which we unconsciously follow in conversation: speaking relevantly, reasonably accurately, unambiguously, and giving neither more nor less information than our hearers require. So, to close associates we may not spell out – and thus consciously consider – every detail of our story.

Other friends however, with other motives, may choose to challenge our tale, persuading us towards a different telling. But (we recall the standard and occasion sentences of Quine's sphere) any new story has to take its place in the teller's current scheme of things, or else disrupt the scheme itself: non-professional listeners do not always have the skill, or the wish, to assist this compromise. Moreover, friends may impose upon the tales they are told evaluations which have more to do with their own particular life stories: we remember 'Miching Mallecho'!

Trained listeners, then, are likely to be more helpful. In the first place, not knowing the tale-teller's background in detail, they encourage him or her to reveal and at the same time consider more information than s/he might relate to a friend. But how, precisely, will they listen? How and when will they encourage new evaluations? How will they know when a more useful understanding has been reached? How do they prevent their own stories shaping what they hear? These are the kind of questions we shall now address, turning from stories and their tellers to the contexts in which they are told.

The three professional contexts we shall consider do not use the 'standard', conventional language of everyday conversation: they are all, in some sense, linguistically unusual. All three encourage, through various kinds of language and to varying degrees, the autonomy of the story teller. Change is a deliberate goal of the second and third (neuro-linguistic programming and psychodynamic therapy). But although change may be the end result of talk to Samaritan volunteers – the context with we shall begin – it is not precisely the motivation which inspires this organization.

LISTENING WITH CARE

The Samaritans

Most personal story-telling takes place orally, within a conversational context. The part of the tale that Labov calls the abstract – *I'll tell you about Jack and Jill's disaster* – signals that a narrative is about to start; other participants in the conversation generally become quiet and attentive. Nevertheless, in ways we have just suggested, the usual conversational context can inhibit a therapeutic telling of tales. It would appear, however, that members of the Samaritan organization – volunteers answering the telephone to people calling for their help – disregard many of these norms and thus encourage a rich story-telling.

I am concentrating in the following observations on telephone calls to Samaritans, not on face-to-face visits to their centres. Samaritan calls are totally confidential, so I have been able to listen only to the training of volunteers and to their role-playing callers. But the members of an urban branch of the organization, their regional training officer and also their national training adviser, confirm the following assumptions – made on the basis of these training sessions – about the language they use during authentic calls.[6]

Everyday conversation involves, above all else, turn-taking: like tennis, knocking the talk-ball back and forth across the net. When the caller is ringing primarily with the problem of loneliness, than the Samaritan may well chat reciprocally. But, when the caller has a different or more specific cause of distress, then the Samaritan is unlikely to take a full conversational turn. Instead, the volunteer will relinquish the stage to the caller. I use the word 'stage' deliberately. The caller, in a sense, acts out a drama, with the listening Samaritan taking the place of an audience. I am not, as I shall explain, choosing the metaphor lightly: the use of the word 'drama' is not intended to hint at the imaginary or at over-reaction. (And interestingly, Sutton-Smith argues (Sarbin 1986: 69–73) that story-telling grows out of the kind of play-acting children perform, beginning in their earliest months with face games played with parents or peers.)

Like a politely attentive theatre audience, the Samaritan audience does not interrupt callers. Yet in everyday conversation interruptions do take place. We looked at these, and the feminist argument that men interrupt women more than vice versa, in the previous chapter. The effect of interruption upon the silenced speaker – male or female – and the less invasive practice of overlapping the end of someone's remarks, can be painfully destructive. For if language is a demonstration of self, then its constant interruption is not only a violation of a speaker's right to language, but also a negation of that silenced speaker's own person. It is an experience that could well bring a caller to the acceptance and encouragement of a Samaritan's unusually passive, patient listening. But silencing is done not only by a more powerful partner. It can also occur when the story-telling is too painful to be heard – except by the patiently listening Samaritan.

Samaritan listening is, however, of a particular kind. Total silence can be disconcerting, leaving the speaker uncertain of his/her reception: is s/he being ignored, rejected, ridiculed? Silence can be another weapon then, like the practice of interruption. It too, inflicted by a partner at home or work, may bring a caller to the Samaritans for the comfort of their *active* listening.[7] *Stabilizers*, like *um*, *yes*, *go on*, are part of normal conversational practice, reassuring noises that encourage a speaker to continue with the story. The Samaritan uses a great many of these, confirming the caller's right to speak and the listener's interest and acceptance. To return to theatre imagery, it is like an audience clapping hands in appreciation and anticipation of more to come.

But a caller may actually ask for applause, wanting not only the reassurance of these stabilizers but also a confirmation that is even more explicit. In consequence *tag questions* are a prevalent feature of calls to the Samaritans. Tags can be marks of uncertainty. We make a statement. 'I was right.' And then we undercut ourselves, show ourselves to be less sure, by asking for confirmation, 'I was right – wasn't I?'[8] Yet Samaritans are unlikely to give an answer. Definitive statements are not part of their language. In fact, their syntax is, overall, highly selective.

A potent image, used in their training, clarifies the reasons why. Callers, people in distress, are imagined as down in a dark pit. Volunteers answering the phone are looking over the edge of the pit.

They can react in one of two ways to the person in darkness. They can put a metaphorical ladder down into the pit, and shout out instructions for getting on to it. Or they can climb down the ladder themselves and, as far as is possible, share the darkness. But instructions, *commands*, are not really viable: because from the safe edge of the pit no outsider knows precisely the condition down in its depths. There may not even be an escape route, a fundamental point in Samaritan thinking to which we shall return. Ignorant of conditions down in the pit, the listener cannot comment – make *statements* – about it. S/he cannot even extend stabilizing murmurs of understanding support to the point that these become assertions like 'I know'. A volunteer put it succinctly: 'If you claim to know, you take half the other person's feelings away from them.' But listeners can be willing to get to know, willing to comfort by sharing the darkness as far as possible. They must avoid commands and statements then, but they will ask *questions*.

Even here there are limitations. Samaritans will generally choose *open*, not *closed* questions. They are unlikely to say 'Was that bad?', because, put this closed way, the caller need only say 'Yes' or 'No'. But, if the question is opened up, phrased something like, 'How did that make you feel?' and asked in a gentle and sympathetic tone, then 'yes' and 'no' are not options. On the other hand, the caller has a chance, if he or she wants to take it, of telling his/her story.

The Samaritan generally makes sure this chance to tell is there for as long as the caller wants it. So, again unlike normal conversation, the volunteer rarely uses conventional conversation closures, polite phatic endings like 'I must go now, someone is on the other line', or 'I'm wanted in the other office'. We return here to the imagery of theatre and audience. In the theatre an audience, like the Samaritan, waits for the actor on the stage to say when the curtain is going to drop on this particular act of the drama.

Moreover, theatre audiences change for each performance: Samaritans are likely to do the same. Counsellors and therapists, on the other hand, may offer future appointments. As for listening friends, the normal closures of normal conversations tend to consolidate the relationship between parties in conversation and refer to some future meeting: 'See you tomorrow night – you can tell me more then.' But Samaritans will avoid these conventional closures and future plans because they are not forming an ongoing relationship with their caller. They will not say when they will be available to receive another call – a repeat performance – and a different volunteer may well answer the phone.

But saying they are not in a relationship with a caller is not of course the same thing as saying Samaritans do not care. On the contrary. They remain the caring, appreciative, patient audience – an audience which may change tomorrow night. The playwright Harold Pinter told the National Student Drama Festival in 1962 (Pinter 1983: 14–150):

> One way of looking at speech is to say that it is a constant strategem to cover nakedness . . . what takes place is a continual evasion, desperate rearguard attempts to keep ourselves to ourselves. Communication is too alarming . . . To disclose to others the poverty within us is too fearsome . . .

But communication may be less alarming if it is shared with an unknown, with someone who does not have to be faced again, with a person who offers care without the pressures and responsibilities of relationship. Samaritans can do just this. Their unusual telephone language permits revelation. Face-to-face conversations in their centres may be different. Because these include facial and body gestures and can involve touching, they may be nearer to a conventional language exchange than the phone conversation, and volunteers think that, except in cases of a very recent trauma, visitors do not tell their stories as revealingly as they do over the phone. Their telephone callers, on the other hand, take the stage and tell their life stories without inhibition.

This revelation, shared with a sympathetic hearer, is likely then to be a relief and a profound comfort. Loving acceptance is the Samaritan's prime aim and their great achievement. They do not deliberately set out to change. As we have said, they start from the premiss there may be no escape route for their callers, no ladders out from the pit. In this case the Samaritans can do no more – and will do no less – than give their unqualified and loving acceptance. Nevertheless, their caring acceptance gives callers the time and the encouragement to tell and re-tell their stories in an unpressured situation not readily available in everyday conversation. In the process – almost as a by-product – it is possible that change of heart and attitude may occur.

However, in our second context of story telling, the neuro-linguistic programming of Bandler and Grinder, change is the essential goal. But stories are not so much told and rejigged here, as their future versions prepared for. That is, the possibility of different reactions to future events – reactions that have yet to figure in narrative clauses and/or their evaluations – is considered and prepared for. Bandler and Grinder do not claim that their method is effective in every instance but they believe it can be helpful in the case of phobias, habits, some physical problems, learning difficulties and also group interactions.

Neuro-Linguistic Reprogramming

Given their emphasis upon change, it is appropriate that Bandler and Grinder should have titled one of their books, *frogs into PRINCES* (1979). But in this case neither a fairy godmother nor a kiss from a beautiful princess is needed to inspire transformation in the client seeking personal change. Moreover, the neuro-linguistic therapist need not even know precisely what a client feels his/her problem to be: the therapist, unlike the Samaritan, will not ask exploratory questions. The 'superhelper' of Greimas's model is indisputably the client's own self, privately choosing new patterns of thought and behaviour in response, in the first instance, to the instructions of the therapist: later, neuro-linguistic techniques become the client's own. As Bandler and Grinder explain (1979: 146):

> This particular process differs significantly from normal therapeutic and hypnotic techniques. We simply serve as consultants for the person's conscious mind. He does all the work himself. He is his own therapist; he is his own hypnotist at the moment. We're not doing any of those things. We communicate directly only with his consciousness and instruct it how to proceed. It's his responsibility to establish and maintain effective communication with the unconscious portions of him that he needs to access in order to change. Of course, once he learns to do that – using this as an example – he can do it without us. That's another advantage. This process has autonomy for the client built into it.

What the client is instructed to do, essentially, is talk to his/her unconscious. S/he is required to 'go inside', to ask what intention the unacceptable behaviour s/he has come to treat seeks to fulfil. When s/he knows his/her own answer, then s/he is required to imagine alternative, equally effective but less distressing behaviours. Finally s/he is to make an 'ecological' check which considers whether or not these new behaviours are acceptable to his/her whole person. In order to know the answer to this personal, interior check the client is to be 'sensitive to any response . . . feelings, pictures, or sounds. . . .' s/he experiences' (Bandler and Grinder 1979: 147). A chosen new behaviour may then be linked up, through suggestion, to some future relevant event. Given this *bridging*, the newly chosen and acceptable behaviour should take place at appropriate times in the future.

It is impossible, in the space available, to do justice to the various forms this second context of therapy takes (Bandler and Grinder 1975, 1979, 1982). But I believe its practitioners would not object to the suggestion, reinforced by the shortness and simplicity of my explanation,that their methods can be easily and rapidly effective. Steve Andreas writes (Bandler and Grinder 1975: i):

When I was first introduced to Neuro Linguistic Programming I was both fascinated and *very* skeptical. I had been heavily conditioned to believe that change is slow, and usually difficult and painful. I still have some difficulty realizing that I can usually cure a phobia or other similar long-term problem painlessly in less than an hour – even though I have done it repeatedly and seen that the results last.

Sometimes, in the third and last story-telling context we shall consider, a problem may be solved equally quickly. But here change is worked for through an intense examination of the past, present, and possible futures. So it is more likely that tales will be told over a long period, and that particularly profound changes will come about gradually. Here the listener plays a role different from that of either the neuro linguistic programmer or the Samaritan. Yet the client's autonomy remains of paramount importance.

This final context, of psychotherapy, is examined through a reconstructed interview with Dr Bernard Ratigan, formerly Senior Student Counsellor at Loughborough University of Technology and now Principal Adult Psychotherapist for the Nottingham Psychotherapy Unit at St Ann's Hospital, Mapperley. The interview form is particularly suitable to the interdisciplinary nature of our theme, which relates linguistic concepts and methods to the 'art' of language in a variety of fields, literary, sociological and psychological. I am grateful to Dr Ratigan for his comments which in my view clarify and extend the major tenets of this chapter. We begin by discussing the kind of language frames within which Dr Ratigan's patients tell their stories, and go on to story-telling and the story-teller.

Psychodynamic Therapy

1) The language context

Dr Ratigan, when people first come into your room to talk to you, you seem to me not to use *phatic* openers, the kind of remarks that we conventionally make to each other in order to break the ice, get things going: polite enquiries about health, say, or a run down on the day's weather. *I never do.*
I get the impression that you also discourage your clients from using phatic beginnings.
That's not how I see it. When someone comes in talking about the weather I'm thinking, 'What does this mean?'. Is it a social thing because they aren't used to the clinical setting – which I can quite understand – or is there another message here? I am wondering what it is they are finding hard to say.

So you are encouraging the client to start work with you immediately?
That's right.
There don't appear to be phatic remarks made at the end of sessions with you, either. When you first meet them, you show new clients a clock on the table between you and explain that after fifty minutes the session will have to end, whatever point it has reached. You initially control that ending by saying, when the time comes, something quite brief like, 'It's ten to three now'. But after a few sessions the client learns to draw things to a close for him/herself. Why do you work this way?
I'm trying to encourage autonomy. The fifty-minute session, starting and finishing on time, has a function of getting an autonomous part of the patient moving. It gets them to pace themselves and to use the time to get the story, or the episode of the story, all in. It draws them to take responsibility for their story.
Is that responsibility to do with sorting the story out, for one's self?
Yes. It's a sorting out at a deep level though, not just on the surface of the tale. I'm trying to encourage an internal sorting out. Often people come to see someone like me because they are in an internal chaos and when they face themselves and get their story into that fifty minutes they also seem to be putting a boundary round the internal chaos.
Now can we look at – listen to! – the kind of language you use inside the fifty minutes? You don't make conversation in the usual sense at all, do you? You say very little. And if we consider the language you use in terms of its grammar, it seems to me that, rather like the Samaritans, you make very few *statements* about the client, and virtually none about yourself. Nor do you use *commands*. Mostly, then, you ask *questions*. But even these are kept to a minimum – just sufficient to get the client talking, and to keep him/her talking. Clients do feel they have to keep talking, don't they?
Yes. There definitely is a pressure in the clinical situation, to put the focus on the patient. The word patient is interesting. 'Client' is not right because the person coming to therapy suffers in the session. I don't mean this in a cruel way. But what happens in the fifty minutes is serious business: work.
So your patients work hard, doing most of the talking in a session. But you reward their remarks with a lot of what I'd call *stabilizers* – like *um, yes, go on*. They let people know you are listening. They imply you are interested and understanding. You use a lot of facial gestures too, most of them encouraging. So I think patients feel you approve of, and care for them. And as a result they 'dare' to keep on talking?
I think that's fair comment, yes.

Sometimes, though, you deliberately interrupt a patient's talk and invite them to change what they have just said. You often ask them to modify statements they have made. You might encourage them to change the verb. You might hear a patient say 'I couldn't do that' but you ask them to repeat the sentence as 'I didn't do that', or even 'I wouldn't do that'. Or else you might ask a patient to change a pronoun. If they say 'You feel rotten when that happens', or 'One feels rotten when that happens', you often want them to rephrase to something like 'I feel rotten'. Why do you encourage these alterations?

I'm offering ownership, ownership of actions and feelings.

Well, we looked earlier in the chapter at the potential for syntactic and lexical change. But how deep into a person do you think these language alterations go? In what sense might a person change their view of themselves, particularly their sense of ownership, in consequence of changing their language?

I hope the change of language is an irritant. The people using it are encouraged to see themselves not as victims but as actors. They can choose to recognize themselves as responsible. And they are then at liberty to try to expand that responsibility.

Your patients are always being encouraged to see themselves as individuals, responsible individuals, aren't they? And it is their personal session. They do not get the impression, during it, that you are prepared to share yourself with them, do they? I think this is partly because you appear to discourage questions, either about yourself or about your opinion of the patient. In fact, if patients ask something like 'Was that right? Do you think I did the right thing?', you will draw them to try to answer the question for themselves. You will decline to comment and encourage them to express support for themselves verbally.

That's how it is. Generally I'm extremely passive. Openness from the therapist is a very powerful tool to be used with great care and not promiscuously. Otherwise it can so easily become seduction.

Does your passive approach fit a particular school of therapy?

I think it is very much derived from psychodynamic, psychoanalytic ideas where the therapist is relatively neutral and creates a context box by time. You give the person as much attention as you can, then let the person get on with it and you watch the interaction with them. The image I had the other day was that it's like a kind of stream where I am some sort of reed or plant but my feet – my roots – are firmly in the ground. I'll be moving all over the place through the force of the patient, the pressure of the session. But I'm still rooted. Beginning therapists tend not to be rooted – they are all over the place – or else they are too rigid.

You may be passive then – but still there is combined activity in a session: it is a dynamic discourse?
There is an energy interchange – in which I am relatively passive. The patient puts his or her feelings – out of their interior chaos – on to, in to me. I receive them and s/he can feel the chaos contained.
But isn't this transfer of feeling to you quite different from the personal control of chaos, the achievement of coherence, through the narrative process and its evaluative potential?
They are linked. One leads on to the other. For instance – people who have been sexually abused as children: that abuse really is totally out of consciousness. I have to help them through the return of the repressed, and the transfer of feeling, on to some sort of meaningful coherence for now.
So people really do tell you stories, within the context of your sessions?
The sessions are absolutely awash with stories. If they are not present this may be a signal of continuing inner chaos. Disintegration of language can signal disintegration of the internal world. Disintegration can be at the level of syntax. But it can also disrupt the narrative form.
I'd like to ask you now about that narrative form.

2) Narrative in the session

Just to draw things together – why, in your view, do you think we tell you our stories?
I believe story-telling is a basic human need. Narration makes sense of the world. And there have always been socially sanctioned people – priests, shamans, witch doctors – who listened to the story-telling. But it seems to me that we live in a kind of centrifugal sort of society which is collapsing around us and the natural ways, the traditional community opportunities for telling stories, are disintegrating. Social change limits them, particularly as people move out of their closer-knit communities. But there is still a tremendous hunger to tell our stories. It's like the child hurrying home from school to tell mummy what s/he has been doing.
So in a sense you replace the missing opportunity? You replace this missing role. But is it simply being heard by you that matters or – I keep coming back to the story – the re-organization and re-evaluation of chaos through the tale?
It's both. It works at different levels. Patients are bringing me stories which are codes. And it is our job to decode these together: people and their stories need to be validated by the hearer.
Talking of validation, Labov mentions (1967: 34) that 'self-aggrandizement' seemed to be a motivation of the particular personal

tales he was examining. These were not being given in the clinical context though. However, do people coming to you also twist their story to their own advantage – to get the validation you mention, perhaps?

If people do skew their stories and I don't at once sense it, it comes out later, over a number of sessions. But I'm not there as a member of the secret police to suss out people's fictions. I'm there to let people see their own fictions for themselves and to know what they are for. I'm interested in the notion of the con. We all have cons and the setting I'm offering helps people to see what their personal cons are – and what they are for – and then move on.

Much of Labov's work on personal narrative (1967, 1972) was done with men –

Well, men are a problem of course. Men are an enormous problem. Heterosexual men with a male therapist are often wanting to assert themselves through their stories. Women at first don't seem to be doing a similar thing, describing themselves in the same way.

People describe themselves, you say. But would it be true to say that in therapy language is *experience*, as much as description?

I believe patients think it is describing. But it is more than that. 'Look at my world', they ask when we start work together, and I will, but I'm waiting for them to focus on them and me in the here and now and on their inner world. I'm waiting till I get the code to their inner world. Till I can say 'it sounds to me as if you are saying something about . . .'.

So the stories change, little by little?

Yes. It's as if the patients are nudging on a ratchet towards something which is disclosing about themselves, working the code out, and I offer preliminary and tentative understandings, decodings, to check I'm hearing right. We get a fresh start each week.

Are you looking for one authentic story, for one ultimately perfect decoding?

No. I'm not of the Sherlock Holmes school of psychotherapy. I'm looking for resonances across the web. When I've been working with someone for years I seem to remember the stories. Often these narratives come as readings of dreams and in these readings there will be resonances of other dreams the patient has told me about. At first the patient remembers the currently acceptable reading of the dream, but over a period of work – perhaps a long period – the dream may make a different sense, have a different reading.

You are saying that the narrative clauses of the dream remain very similar, but that their evaluation changes?

Yes. And evaluation is always a provisional understanding. But it gets more valuable, not more valid precisely. It is a question of readiness:

later readings might have been too difficult to face earlier.
Perhaps we don't really want to get to the end of the story? It may
not be liveable with?
Well, I don't think there is an end story. Just a series of approximations.
My therapeutic task is to offer patients their story in a tolerable way. If
it is too powerful at the time it can destroy the world they have got
going for them. Or if they aren't ready it will bounce off them. The
patient is really doing the work and until they are ready to tell the new
story they won't.
What you are saying now seems to me to relate to comments we made
earlier in the chapter about Quine's sphere, and its model of standing
and occasion sentences. Is there an explanation here of a patient's
tendency to go over and over the same story, with the same, standard
evaluation, again and again? Are we waiting, hoping for the two sets
of sentences to shake down together comfortably?
Perhaps. A patient will go over the same story repeatedly until the new
story has arrived; that is, when the perspective on the old story has
changed. That's at a conscious level. Maybe, at an unconscious level,
punishment is involved in the constant retelling.
What happens when the patient leaves your room, when you aren't
there to encourage re-evaluation of the story, and the kind of
'responsible' language you endorse? Does the drive towards new
language fade as you are removed from its context?
I often know that therapy is taking off when someone tells me what
they told me in their head during the week! Sometimes they even pick
up on a story they have obviously been telling me inside their heads –
and have forgotten I wasn't actually there to hear it! I mentioned
earlier the child needing to come home to its mother to tell its story of
the day. The need decreases as the child becomes more secure and
independent. The child can leave the mother because mother is in a
sense inside him/her now. S/he doesn't need to keep coming back to
tell the story. There is something of the child/mother relationship here
in therapy. Therapy is a weakened version of this.
Can we learn to tell our stories better – in some therapeutic sense
more helpfully – as we grow, in life and in therapy? Do you think
there are different kinds of story-tellers, some more competent, as it
were, than others?
Yes, I do. Different personalities make different story-tellers.
So can we turn now from concentrating mainly on the form of the
tale to its teller?

3) Story-Tellers

If organization of the tale and its evaluation are so important, are people whose work is *self-consciously* centred upon language the best tale-tellers? Are they best able to heal themselves?
Far from it. Academics for instance, precisely because they use language so fluently, often have a real handicap! An academic understanding – a metaperspective of cause and effect – may cut a patient off from feelings. Academics have a structure which can mean they don't have to experience their cut-offness from their feelings. Scientists and engineers in particular tend to tell me what they thought about something in their lives, not what they felt. Their hurts are covered beneath a massive superstructure of education and learning. We need to undo that towards a much closer relationship that doesn't evade through pseudo-understanding. People from arts and social services are generally speaking more comfortable saying what they feel.
What if we go to the other extreme from academics, to people with learning difficulties: what kind of story-tellers are they? How effective, psychologically, are their stories?
In the past, therapy tended to be seen as the preserve of intelligent, verbal, successful people. But I think we have evidence to show that it can be effective even with people who have been described as mentally handicapped, suffering from major learning difficulties, even with autistic people. If you can get the language medium right you can communicate. You can use the language of, maybe, painting, music, or play – and play is important with adults too. These languages all tell stories. In fact, these stories may be easier to decode than the ones from people apparently more gifted with words. Their narrators can be easier to reach.
How does your own, personal story affect reaching people, and affect interpreting their tales?
Being in therapy oneself is a central part of training, so you learn your own story and your own blind spots. The people who are very like me, I have most blind spots with, though. But I am on the look-out for these. Being in therapy yourself also teaches you humility and respect – you realize the courage that patients have to come to you!
A therapist's theoretical background – say Freudian or Jungian – is, like your own personal tale, a narrative framework within which you may work. How does this affect your decoding? Can it encourage pushing on the ratchet (you mentioned this earlier) towards a story evaluation that the patient might not have chosen?
Possibly. Sometimes. But therapy is only about a hundred years old and we have to accept this for the time being. There are more gains

than losses from having these frames. My particular Kleinian approach is seen by some as a very non-giving technique. But it helps me work at depth with very disturbed people. And besides, it's a bit like learning music. You have to learn a technique – someone else's story, you might want to say – before you can go on to compose your own music.
Can you describe something of your own guiding analytic story?
I start off from the position that the infant is born mad and becomes sane, more or less. But there are always crazy bits left inside us. You've only got to be expecting someone to turn up at a certain time and they don't and you think they never will! It's to do with the dread in all of us, from infancy, of impending chaos. And in every adult – the most wise and sophisticated of us – there is an infant: if s/he is put down will s/he be picked up again, will the feed come, will the breast come back, will the mother/father come back?
So how do we come to expect to cope with chaos, to control the craziness?
Most times the world is actually predictable, and if we are moderately well looked after we mostly learn to cope with the rage. But it is still just one step away. And if the experience in childhood is more traumatic, then a person can't make basic trust with another human being.
What connection can we make here with language in therapy?
There is a link with sounds – pre-verbal language. When mother talks to baby she uses sounds and baby recognizes them and her. Then there is echoing, mother to baby. There can be regression in therapy to remember these earlier, long forgotten bits. Patients may actually act and sound, here in this room, like a baby and this is part of the therapeutic process. They are remembering things to do with their relationships with their mothers. I am made to feel this by projective identification. And in response I find myself making the kind of pre-verbal sounds of the mother.
Are these sounds linked with the stabilizers you use to keep patients talking?
They may be linked, but they are much more – they are me trying to reach what you might call the mother register.
You don't – unlike, say, the neuro-linguistic reprogrammers – tell the patient what you are trying to do, do you? Doesn't this make the relationship unequal?
For my approach, to tell them is an imposition. They don't need to know. The theory is my speculation, and it may only give ammunition to the sick part of the patient and then they become a spectator rather than a participator.
So – to draw things together – your context of words seems to encourage, through language, a patient's participation and his/her

autonomy. Moreover, it may involve a kind of language behaviour that recalls a pre-verbal state. But I want to concentrate again, finally, on the telling of stories, and the changes their narration may shape. You endorse *responsible* language from the patient. And you seem to have confirmed that re-evaluation is vital, leading, in your kind of therapy, towards both insight and to change. But aren't narrative clauses themselves inviolate? Nothing can change them? 'I broke my leg', or 'I got divorced' – these narrative clauses are absolutely fixed. So isn't there a limit to the kinds of shifts of perception that we can have? After all, I did start this chapter with a short poem that reminded us of the limits – as well as the powers – of language.

Well, let's think about terminal illness. A patient says, 'I have cancer', or 'I have Aids'. Those are inviolate narrative clauses, surely. But coming to terms with limited longevity . . .

Coming to terms – you mean shifting perception, evaluation of the clause? A person says, 'I have got Aids – I am dying, the end is coming but . . .'

'I am living' You are helping that patient to live, to say 'I have got Aids, I am living . . .'

So the core clauses may remain, but perception of them, even those of limited longevity, can profoundly alter?

When faced with life-threatening illness there seems to be an increased need to tell stories, to make sense of lives past, present and future. People with a restricted life expectancy can often be helped to do all kinds of things, to settle things.

I don't mean to trivialize, but is it like getting the story told inside the hour with you? You know precisely how your time, your life, is limited: you have got to fit things in?

Yes. You could say that every end of every hour is a little death. And other breaks with the therapist over a period – for holidays, illness – have to be prepared for, worked towards and within. So has the final termination of therapy. We have to find meanings in the break itself, in an ending of a story.

Dr Ratigan's comments apparently confirm the vital therapeutic function of narrative. It would seem that Barthes was right to claim that stories are 'simply there, like life itself' (1977: 79). But more than this: they are givers of life. We end then as we began, with Emily Dickinson. We may not always (lacking skill, or strength, or desire) recognize the 'undeveloped freight of a delivered syllable'. But still the potential power of words is awesome. And all of us, choosing carefully from the language systems and structures at our disposal

may – encouraged by good listeners – be creative, regenerative
tellers of tales.

> A Man may make a Remark –
> In itself – a quiet thing
> That may furnish the Fuse unto a Spark
> In dormant nature – lain –
>
> Let us deport – with skill –
> Let us discourse – with care –
> Powder exists in Charcoal –
> Before it exists in Fire.

Notes

1.   M.L. Pratt (1977: 67, 69), notes the similarity of the two forms of story, literary and naturally occurring, and writes: 'What is important about the fact that literary narratives can be analyzed in the same way as the short anecdotes scattered throughout our conversation? To begin with, it casts grave doubt on the Formalist and structuralist claims that the language of literature is formally and functionally distinctive . . . the formal similarities between natural narrative and literary narrative derive from the fact that at one level of analysis they are utterances of the same type.'

2.   I am indebted to Valerie Webb for drawing my attention to this metaphor. She discusses its implication for narrative in her unpublished MA dissertation (Birmingham 1979), *Personal Narrative as Experiential Organization: A Linguistic study with Philosophical Implications*.

3.   Ong (Tannen 1982: 12–24) suggests that a preoccupation with chronology and the analytic interpretative practice has been encouraged and developed by our chirographic, typographic, electronic culture. Oral narratives of the ancients were 'not much concerned with exact sequential parallelism, which becomes an objective of the mind possessed by literacy' (Tannen 1982: 19): the oral epic was instead episodic, without climactic linear plot development. Ong appears to be referring primarily to the effect of chirography and technology on modern written narrative, but perhaps oral personal narration might also be affected by our literate sense of controlled plot line.

4.   The story's title – in this case, virtually its abstract too – extends external evaluation of the tale, standing before it to tell us that the behaviour we are about to witness is to be admired.

5.   A discussion of the language of war diaries, by R.K. Chan, will appear in *Parlance*, vol. 2, 1: August 1990: 'Narrative clauses in the diaries of World War I: history, experience, or fiction'?

6.   I am grateful for the supportive assistance of the Peterborough Branch of the Samaritans, particularly their Regional Director Denis

Lake, and the National Director of Samaritan Training, Norman Whiting.

7. However a member of the Peterborough Branch explained to me his feeling that, during a long call, sufficient rapport may be achieved for the caller to take, and benefit from, the 'right' to silence.

8. Samaritans themselves us tag questions, but these are of the facilitating kind discussed in Chapter Four.

In Other Words . . .

In January 1989 a Leicester theatre staged a linguistically unusual play, with an unusual audience. A consideration of its implications draws together the threads of all we have been saying about the power and creativity of varieties of language.

As we waited in the bar before the performance we were surrounded by Leicester people. The vast majority were, as you would expect, native English speakers. But there were also a few Asian men and women, representative of the very large Asian community in the city. The Asian contingent were in the minority, standing in a group together. But the situation changed as the start of the performance was announced.

The Haymarket Theatre has a main auditorium and a studio theatre. The Asian people moved towards the studio; virtually all the English took their seats for the comedy playing in the main theatre. But we went into the studio too – and looking around found ourselves in the minority, an English trio surrounded by local Asians and very few other Europeans. Yet the minority/majority issue became irrelevant as the lights went down. The play's language saw to that. For *Kirti, Sona and Ba* is written and performed in a mixture of Gujarati and English. And the story it has to tell – written by an Asian woman, Jyoti Patel, and an English man, Jezz Simons – might apply equally to any family in the city of Leicester, whatever its racial and cultural background.

Despite the use of Gujarati, we English speakers had no difficulty in following the play. As Jyoti Patel says, for the English in the audience it was rather like listening to someone in the same room speaking on the telephone: the other part of their conversation, on the other end of the line, is not directly accessible – but you can guess at its contents from the bit you do hear, and from the facial expression and body language of the speaker when s/he is silent. The play's English utterances are not translations of previous Gujarati comments. But the playwrights have skilfully blended the two in a way that leaves the gist of the dialogue comprehensible to all. As for the Asian audience, its members were hearing nothing strange. Outside the theatre they will normally use something of each language, switching from their original language to the language of their adopted country, depending upon context and content.

The contexts and content of this play were also recognizable to everyone in the audience. Its first couple of minutes, and its closing seconds, are about racial tension. There is no doubt that the three women in its story live in a city that is not entirely welcoming. And from our different parts of the city, in our different ways, we both, Asians and English people in the audience, recognize a reality that exists outside the theatre doors. But within this outer frame of racial difference, Simons and Patel have written, in the small, separate and relatively private circle of the family garden, a drama of family life. That drama is the stuff of everyday occurrence for all, Asian or European, who are sitting around the stage watching it unfold. Seen through the women in the family, it includes sibling rivalry, care of the aged, feminism, teenage revolt, death of partner and parent and, above all, loneliness – the difficulty of making contact with another human being.

The play focuses upon an elderly widowed mother, trying to live without her husband and to carry on bringing up her daughters. The fact that she has to do this in a country not her place of birth must inevitably sharpen Ba's anxiety and loneliness. She has brought plants with her from home, a reminder of Kenyan life. Tending them in English soil, in a small brick-enclosed bed in the yard, she tries with difficulty to help them flourish. It is a symbolic act. For in the same way she is trying, despite her own confusion, to help her daughters mature in a new place, maintaining their traditional culture but assimilating something of the new which now surrounds them.

This part of the play touches specifically – can perhaps only be truly understood by – those in the audience who have left their countries of origin. But all of us watching know, whatever our race, about daughters like Kirti who stay at home to help their parents. And we all know of other daughters, like Sona, who go away to the big city, trying to leave family problems behind in order to 'find themselves' as individuals; girls, like Sona, who are drawn back to visit and find their roots remain where they always were – but now they have introduced new perspectives, new tensions, that threaten to fracture the old family group. Kirti and Sona are representative of a generation, not a particular race.

After their mother's tragic death – an accident occurring when she is trying to support Sona – the two girls decide, whatever their personal differences, to stand together against the old guard in the family and against the racial tension outside: in the last moments of the play, wearing their traditional dress, they preserve their cultural background but are set to be individuals of the next generation. This finding of identity and sense of place is not the prerogative of any one culture, or unfamiliar to those who remain within one geographical area all their lives. And Ba's loneliness and bewilderment are known to every widow who, without her husband, is no longer sure of her self and her place.

In every culture too there must be girls who find it difficult to talk to their mothers. Kirti and Sona are no exception, though Kirti – the stay-at-home daughter – uses mostly Gujarati with her mother and manages fairly well. Sona sees the gap between herself and her mother widening; she has more difficulty in communicating than Kirti because she needs to make Ba comprehend yet another life, beyond their home in Leicester. Sona has been to the capital, reads *Cosmopolitan*, and is an actress with a walk-on part in *Eastenders*. So she brings a gift of an English plant for Ba and tries to talk to her in English. But it is an evasive, uncomfortable, aggressive English, full of taboo words, usually with a Leicester accent, but sometimes with a mimicked RP. No wonder. Sona is confused, hurt by lack of success in London, and by old wounds from within the family. The hostile layer of language conceals and protects. She finds it difficult to talk to her sister, too. Mostly the girls share English and Kirti asks Sona, with irony, if she has forgotten the ritual words for a Hindu religious ceremony. Sona's memory is certainly rusty – but still, needing to compromise, to live with both cultures (she loves the fairy-lights which remind her of both Asian festivals and of Christmas) she tries to remember and repeat the comforting, traditional phrases.

With our discussion of male/female language in mind, we may agree that these three women, being women, have special experiences to communicate. But we can all, male or female, English or Asian, recognize the *struggle* to communicate, to achieve autonomy whilst yet keeping contact with the security of the family group, to reveal – and to conceal – ourselves. Something, however, *is* lost on the native English speaker, unfamiliar with different circles of Asian language. For the chosen Asian language is Gujarati and we may not be aware that there is something 'non-standard' about this choice. Hindi or Punjabi would normally be used. For Hindi is understood by most Asians, and in any case Jyoti Patel thinks these languages 'sound more attractive' than the rather guttural Gujarati she has chosen. (The point is reminiscent of Tennyson's concentration upon the harsh and Barnes's choice of the mellow.) An unusual language is being given a hearing, then.

But there is nothing stereotypical about this play, from its language onwards. Its very form can seem unusual to an Asian audience. It lacks the opulence and melodrama familiar from traditional Asian stage and screen: it seems more authentic. And this is true as much of content as of form. For the play's characters do not match the conventional studies of harsh parents, arranged marriages and hostility to European influence, mediated by English directors and widely disseminated by television. Jezz Simons told me how particularly delighted the elderly women in the audience were to find themselves portrayed accurately and sympathetically in Ba.

Their pleasure is reminiscent of that enthusiastic reaction to William Barnes, reading poetry to local people in their own language about their own lives: the narrative is healing. But Jyoti Patel noticed that 'the white men in the audience also saw their own mothers in Ba'. Therefore, in a way, the play reaches further than the dialect poetry of Tennyson or Barnes. These poems were written by one kind of person, apparently about another, and read – if read at all by those who do not figure directly in them – in separate arenas. Tennyson's upper-class readers could not see and laugh at themselves in his Lincolnshire characters. Barnes's London enthusiasts saw the beauty in the rural life he described but, observing from a distance, did not notice the shadows on his landscape. Besides, these two artists, wishing to preserve the power of dying languages, were not concerned – unlike Thomas Hardy, and unlike Simons and Patel – with the diachronic movement of language. *Kirti, Sona and Ba*, on the other hand, is written in the changing language of the present and the future, a combination, made necessary by a new kind of multi-racial country. Circles of language express difference between groups – but these, English and Gujarati fitting together, comprehensible to all, are symbolic both of distinction and of similarity. Moreover, they represent compromise. Tom Leonard's Glasgow poetry asserts with fierce courage the independence of a city and a kind of people. The language of this play speaks out for people trying to preserve their own identities and, also, to step into another circle. Listening English-speakers are invited to join them.

By the same process whereby [man] spins language out of his own being, he ensnares himself in it; and each language draws a magic circle round the people to which it belongs, a circle from which there is no escape save by stepping out of it into another.[1]

Note

1. This translation from Wilhelm von Humboldt, first referred to in the Preface, is quoted in Ernst Cassirer's *Language and Myth*, 1946, translated by Susanne Langer, New York, Dover Publications (p. 9).

Bibliography

Preface

Cassirer, E. (1946), *Language and Myth*, translated by Susanne Langer, New York, Dover Publications.

Honey, J. (1989), *Does Accent Matter? The Pygmalion Factor*, London, Faber and Faber.

Kingman, Sir J. (1988). *Report of the Committee of Inquiry into the Teaching of English Language*, London, Her Majesty's Stationery Office.

Proposals of the Secretary of State for Education and Science and the Secretary of State for Wales, June 1989, Department of Education and Science and the Welsh Office.

Thomas, E. (1964), *Selected Poems of Edward Thomas*, ed. R.S. Thomas, London, Faber and Faber.

Times Literary Supplement, July 1 1944, p. 321.

Chapter One

Aitchison, J. (1989), third edition, *The Articulate Mammal*, London, Unwin Hyman.

Aitchison, J. (1987), third edition, *Teach Yourself Linguistics*, Sevenoaks, Hodder and Stoughton.

Barthes, R. (1973), *Mythologies*, translated by Annette Lavers, London, Granada.

Bernstein, B. (1971, 1972, 1973, 1975), *Class, Codes and Control*, London, Routledge and Kegan Paul.

Black, M. (1979), 'More About Metaphor', in Ortony, A. (1979).

Brown, R. (1958), *Words and Things*, New York, The Free Press.

Brown, R. (1970), *Psycholinguistics, Selected Papers*, New York, The Free Press.

Cameron, D. (1985), *Feminism and Linguistic Theory*, London, Macmillan.
Cazden, C. (1972), *Child Language and Education*, New York, Holt, Rinehart and Winston.
Chomsky, C. (1969), *The Acquisition of Syntax in Children from 5 to 10*, Cambridge, Mass., M.I.T. Press.
Chomsky, N. (1957), *Syntactic Structures*, The Hague, Mouton.
Chomsky, N. (1959), Review of Skinner's *Verbal Behavior, Language*,35, 26–58.
Chomsky, N. (1965), *Aspects of the Theory of Syntax*, Cambridge, Mass., M.I.T. Press.
Chomsky, N. (1985), *Knowledge of language: its nature, origin and use*, New York, Praeger.
Cluysenaar, A. (1976), *Introduction to Literary Stylistics*, London, Batsford.
Cole, P. and Morgan, J. (1975), eds. *Syntax and Semantics, III: Speech Acts*, New York, Academic Press.
Crystal, D. (1976), *Child language, learning and linguistics*, London, Edward Arnold.
Fromkin, V. and Rodman, R. (1988), fourth edition, *An Introduction to Language*, New York, Holt, Rinehart and Winston Inc.
Gardner, R.A. and B.T. (1969), 'Teaching sign language to a chimpanzee', *Science*, 165, 664–72.
Greenberg, J.H. (1963), *Universals of Language*, ed., Cambridge, Mass., M.I.T. Press.
Grice, H.P. (1975), 'Logic and conversation', in Cole, P. and Morgan, J. eds. (1975)
Halliday, M.A.K. (1973), *Explorations in the Functions of Language*, London, Edward Arnold.
Halliday, M.A.K. (1985), *An Introduction to Functional Grammar*, London, Edward Arnold.
Hockett, C. (1963), 'The problem of universals in language', in Greenberg (1963).
Hymes, D. (1971), *On Communicative Competence*, Philadelphia, University of Pennsylvania Press.
Labov, W. (1969), 'The logic of nonstandard English', *Georgetown Monographs on Language and Linguistics*, vol. 22, 1–31.
Lacan, J. (1966), *Écrits*, Editions du Seuil (a selection translated by Sheridan 1977).
Lakoff, G. and Johnson, M. (1980), *Metaphors We Live By*, Chicago and London, University of Chicago Press.
Larkin, P. (1964), *The Whitsun Weddings*, London, Faber and Faber.
Leech, G.N. and Short, M.H. (1981), *Style in Fiction. A Linguistic Introduction to English Fictional Prose*, London and New York, Longman.
Lenneberg, E.H. (1967), *Biological Foundations of Language*, New York, John Wiley.
Lewis, C. Day (1954), *Collected Poems*, Jonathan Cape/Hogarth Press, London.
Lyons, J. (1977), *Semantics*, 2 vols., Cambridge, New York and Melbourne, Cambridge University Press.

Lyons, J. (1985), *Chomsky*, Glasgow, Fontana.

Ortony, A. (1979), ed. *Metaphor and Thought*, Cambridge, Cambridge University Press.

Palmer, F. (1971), *Grammar*, (second revised edition, 1984) Harmondsworth, Penguin.

Sapir, E. (1921), *Language*, London, Harcourt, Brace and World.

Sebeok, T.A. (1968), *Animal Communication*, Bloomington, Indiana University Press.

Sheridan, A. (1977), *Jacques Lacan: Écrits. A selection translated from the French*, London, Tavistock Publications.

Skinner, B.F. (1957), *Verbal Behavior*, New York, Appleton-Century-Croft.

Sontag, S. (1983), *Barthes: Selected Writings*, London, Fontana/Collins.

Stubbs, M. (1983), second edition, *Language, schools and classrooms*, London and New York, Methuen.

Valéry, P. (1957), *Oeuvres*, Tome 1, Paris, Pléiade.

Waley, A. (1949), *Chinese Poems*, trans., London, Allen and Unwin.

Whorf, Benjamin Lee (1956), *Language, Thought and Reality*, ed. J.B. Carroll, Cambridge, Mass., M.I.T. Press.

Chapter Two

Barnes, W. (1841), 'Education in Words and Things', *Gentleman's Magazine*,: 22.

Barnes, W. (1854), *Philological Grammar*, London, John Russell Smith.

Campion, G.E. (1969), *A Tennyson Dialect Glossary with the dialect poems*, Lincoln, The Lincolnshire Association.

Eliot, T.S. (1934), *After Strange Gods*, Faber and Faber, London.

Elliott, R.W.V. (1984), *Thomas Hardy's English*, Oxford, Basil Blackwell.

Ellis, A.J. (1869–74), *On Early English Pronunciation*, London.

Gibson, J. (1976), *The Complete Poems of Thomas Hardy*, London, Macmillan.

Hardy, F.E. (1962), *The Life of Thomas Hardy*, London, Macmillan.

Hardy, T. (1974 edition), *Tess of the d'Urbervilles*, London, Macmillan, first published 1891.

Hardy, T. (1978 edition), *The Mayor of Casterbridge*, Harmondsworth, Penguin, first published 1886.

Hardy, T. (1975 edition), *Desperate Remedies*, London, Macmillan, first published 1871.

Hardy, T. (1908), *Selected Poems of William Barnes*, Oxford, Henry Frowde.

Hardy, T. (1883), *The Dorsetshire Labourer, Longman's Magazine*, in Morrison, (1970).

Hynes, S. (1956), *The Pattern of Hardy's Poetry*, North Carolina, Chapel Hill.

Hynes, S. (1984), *The Complete Poetical Works of Thomas Hardy*, 3 vols., Oxford, Clarendon.

Jones, B. (1962), *The Poems of William Barnes*, 2 vol., Sussex, Centaur Press Ltd.

Kingman, Sir J. (1988), *Report of the Committee of Inquiry into the Teaching of English Language appointed by the Secretary of State under the Chairmanship of Sir J.K. Kingman*, London, H.M.S.O.

Larkin, P. (1968), 'A Man Who Noticed Things', *The Listener*, July 25 1968.

Lawson, J.L. (1971), ed. *Robert Bloomfield, Collected Poems, 1800–1822*, Gainesville, Florida, Scholars Facsimile and Reprint.

Leonard, T. (1973), *Poems*, Dublin, E. & T. O'Brien Ltd.

Leonard, T. (1984), *Intimate Voices: Selected Work 1965–1983*, Newcastle upon Tyne, Galloping Dog Press.

Leonard, T. (1987), 'On Reclaiming the Local and The Theory of the Magic Thing': also interviews with Kasia Body (14 November 1986) and with Barry Wood (31 May 1985), *Edinburgh Review*, 77: 40–48, 59–72.

Matthews, W. (1938), *Cockney Past and Present*, London and Boston, Routledge and Kegan Paul.

Mayhew, H. (1981), *The Morning Chronicle Survey of Labour and the Poor: the Metropolitan Districts*, Horsham, Surrey, Caliban Books, first published 1851.

Morrison, D.J. (1970), *Thomas Hardy: Stories and Poems*, London, Dent.

National Curriculum Council (March 1989), *Consultation Report*, 15–17 New Street, York.

Orel, H. (1967), *Thomas Hardy's Personal Writing*, London, Macmillan.

Page, N. (1980), *Thomas Hardy*, London, Bell and Hyman.

Page, N. (1983), *Tennyson: Interviews and Recollections*, London, Macmillan.

Phelp, W.L. (1930), *The Letters of James Whitcomb Riley*, Indianapolis, Boss-Merrill Co.

Pinion, F.B. (1984), *A Tennyson Companion*, London, Macmillan.

Priestley, F.E.L. (1973), *Language and Structure in Tennyson's Poetry*, London, André Deutsch.

Rawnsley, Canon H.D. (1900), *Memories of the Tennysons*, Glasgow, James MacLehose and Sons.

Ray, J. (1664), *Collections of English Words not generally used*, London.

Ricks, C. (1969), *The Poems of Tennyson*, London, Longman.

Ricks, C. (1972), *Tennyson*, New York and London, Macmillan.

Sampson, D. (1984), 'Worsworth and the "Deficiencies of Language" ', *English Literary History*, 1 : 1 53–68.

Shaw, W.D. (1976), *Tennyson's Style*, London, Cornell University Press.

Sisson, C.G. (1965), *Art and Action*, London, Methuen.

Skeat, W.W. (1911), *English Dialects from the 8th century to the present day*, London, Cambridge University Press.

Taylor, D. (1978), 'Victorian philology and Victorian poetry', *Victorian Newsletter*, 53: 13–16.

Tennyson, Hallam Lord (1897), *Tennyson, A Memoir*, London, Macmillan.

Trench, R. (1851), *On the Study of Words*, London.

Trench, R. (1873), *English Past and Present*, 8th edition, London, Macmillan.

Wakelin, M.F. (1972), *Patterns in the Folk Speech of the British Isles*,

London, Athlone.

Wesling, D. (1979), 'Hardy, Barnes, and the Provincial', *Victorian Newsletter*, 55: 18–19.

Wright, Aldis (1870), 'Provincial Glossary', *Notes and Queries*, March, 12: 271.

Wright, D. (1978), *Thomas Hardy: Selected poems*, Harmondsworth, Penguin.

Wright, Joseph (1898–1905), *English Dialect Dictionary*, London.

Zietlow, P. (1974), *Moments of Vision*, Cambridge, Mass., Harvard.

Chapter Three

Abbott, C.C. (1938), ed., *Further Letters of Gerard Manley Hopkins*, London, Oxford University Press.

Barnes, W. (1820), *Poetical Pieces*, Dorchester, G. Clark.

Barnes, W. (1841a), 'Education in Words and in Things', *Gentleman's Magazine*, January: 22.

Barnes, W. (1841b), 'English Philology', *Gentleman's Magazine*, May: 510–11.

Barnes, W. (1844), *Poems of Rural Life, in the Dorset Dialect*, with a Dissertation and Glossary, London, John Russell Smith.

Barnes, W. (1846), *Poems of Rural Life, in National English*, London, John Russell Smith.

Barnes, W. (1847), *Poems of Rural Life, in the Dorset Dialect*, London, John Russell Smith. Second edition with Dissertation and Glossary enlarged. Third and fourth editions were printed in 1862 and 1866, without Dissertation and Glossary.

Barnes, W. (1849), 'Humilis Domus' articles, *Poole and Dorset Herald*, April 12, 19, 26; May 3, 10, 17, 24.

Barnes, W. (1854), *Philological Grammar*, London, John Russell Smith.

Barnes, W. (1859), *Views of Labour and Gold*, London, John Russell Smith.

Barnes, W. (1859), *Hwomely Rhymes*, London, John Russell Smith.

Barnes, W. (1861), 'Thoughts on Beauty and Art', *MacMillan's Magazine*, 4: 126–37.

Barnes, W. (1862), *Poems of Rural Life in the Dorset Dialect*, London, John Russell Smith.

Barnes, W. (1866), 'A View of Christian Marriage', *Ladies' Treasury*, February-June: 82, 136, 195, 259, 327.

Barnes, W. (1867), 'The Old Bardic Poetry', *MacMillan's Magazine*, August: 306–17.

Barnes, W. (1878), *An Outline of English Speechcraft*, London, Kegan Paul.

Barnes, W. (1879), *Poems of Rural Life in the Dorset Dialect*, collected dialect poems, London, Kegan Paul.

Barrell, J. and Bull, J. (1982), eds. *The Penguin Book of English Pastoral Verse*, Harmondsworth, Penguin.

Barthes, R. (1957), *Mythologies*, Éditions du Seuil, in Sontag (1983).

Baxter, L. (1887), see Scott L.

Cassirer, E. (1946), *Language and Myth*, translated by Susanne K. Langer, New York, Dover Publications, originally published in German as Number VI of the *Studien der Bibliothek Warburg*, ed. Fritz Saxl.

Carlyle, T. (1843), *Past and Present*, London.

Champneys, B. (1900), *Memoirs and Correspondence of Coventry Patmore*, 2 vols., London, George Bell and Sons.

Duck, S. (1736), *Poems on Several Occasions*, London.

Forster, E.M. (1951), *Two Cheers for Democracy*, London, Edward Arnold.

Forsyth, R.A. (1963), 'The Conserving Myth of William Barnes', *Victorian Studies*, 6: 325–34.

Grigson, G. (1950), *Selected Poems of William Barnes*, London, Routledge and Kegan Paul.

Grigson, G. (1953), 'Poet of Dorset', *Observer*, 13 May 1953: 12.

Hardin, R.F. (1979), ed. *Survivals of the Pastoral*, Lawrence, University of Kansas.

Hardy, T. (1886), 'The Rev. W. Barnes, B.D.', *Athenaeum*, October: 501–2.

Hardy, T. (1879), 'Poems of Rural Life in the Dorset Dialect', *New Quarterly Magazine*, October: 469–73.

Hardy, T. (1908), *Select Poems of William Barnes*, Oxford, Henry Frowde. Reprinted in 1922 with alterations including a revised version of 'Woak Hill'.

Hardy, T. (1978), *The Mayor of Casterbridge*, Harmondsworth, Penguin, first published in 1886.

Hardy, T. (1974), *Jude the Obscure*, London, Macmillan, first published 1896.

Hearl, T. (1966), *William Barnes The Schoolmaster*, Dorchester, Longmans.

Hertz, A. (1985), 'The Hallowed Pleäces of William Barnes', *Victorian Poetry*, 23, No. 2: 109–14.

Hinchy, F.S. and V.M. (1966), *The Dorset William Barnes*, Blandford, Dorset.

Jacobs, W.D. (1959), 'A Word-hoard for Folkdom', *Arizona Quarterly*, 15:156.

Jones, B. (1962) ed., *The Poems of William Barnes*, 2 vols., Sussex, Centaur Press Ltd.

Keane, P. (1978), 'Prophet in the Wilderness: Rev. William Barnes as an Adult Educator', *Dorset Natural History and Archaeological Society Proceedings*, 100: 8–21.

Levy, W.T. (1960), *William Barnes, The Man and the Poet*, Dorchester, Longmans.

Lyons, J. (1977), *Semantics*, 2 vols., Cambridge, Cambridge University Press.

Massingham, H.J. (1942), 'William Barnes', *Time and Tide*, 16 May: 408–10.

Paley, W. (1802), *Natural Theology*, London.

Palgrave, F.T. (1887), 'William Barnes and his Poems of Rural Life in the Dorset Dialect', *National Review*, February: 818–39.

Paulin, T. (1975), *Thomas Hardy: The Poetry of Perception*, London,

Macmillan.

Quiller-Couch, A. (1934), *The Poet as Citizen, and other papers*, Cambridge, Cambridge University Press.

Scott, L. (Lucy Baxter) (1887), *The Life of William Barnes, Poet and Philologist*, London, Macmillan.

Sisson, C.H. (1965), *Art and Action*, London, Methuen.

Skeat, W.W. (1911), *English Dialects from the 8th century to the present day*, London, Cambridge University Press.

Smiles, S. (1859), *Self-Help*, London, John Murray.

Snell, K.D.M. (1985), *Annals of the Labouring Poor: Social Change and Agrarian England, 1660–1900*, Cambridge, Cambridge University Press.

Sontag, S. (1983), *Barthes: Selected Writings*, London, Fontana/Collins.

Sutton, M.K. (1979), 'Truth and the Pastor's Vision in George Crabbe, William Barnes, and R.S. Thomas', in Hardin (1979).

Wrigley, C. (1977), 'William Barnes and the Social Problem', *Dorset Natural History and Archaeological Society Proceedings*: 19–27.

Chapter Four

Bauman, R. and Sherzer, J. (1974), *Explorations in the ethnography of speaking*, London, Cambridge University Press.

Blom, J.P. and Gumperz, J. (1972), 'Social meaning in linguistic structures: code switching in Norway', in Gumperz J. and Hymes, D., eds., *Directions in Sociolinguistics*, New York, Holt Rinehart and Winston.

Bodine, A. (1975), 'Androcentrism in Prescriptive Grammar', *Language in Society*, 4, No. 2, 129–56.

Bouwer, D., Gerritsen, M. and Dettaan, D. (1979), 'Speech differences between women and men: on the wrong track?', *Language in Society*, 8, 33–50.

Cameron, D. (1985), *Feminism and Linguistic Theory*, London, Macmillan.

Campbell, C. (1988), *Marie Claire*, October: 52–6.

Céline, L.F. (1966–9), *Oeuvres complètes*, ed Henri Godard, 2 vols, Paris, Gallimard.

Cheshire, J. (1982), *Variation in an English Dialect*, Cambridge, Cambridge University Press.

Coates, J. (1986), *Women, Men and Language*, New York, Longman.

Craig, J. with Ayres, D. (1988), 'Girl-friendly or boy-friendly teaching styles?', *Primary Science Review*, 6, Spring, 25.

Crystal, D. (1979), 'Prosodic Development' 33–48 in Fletcher and Garman (1979).

Daly, M. (1978), *Gyn/Ecology: the Metaethics of Radical Feminism*, Boston, Beacon Press.

Ellis, H. (1894), *Man and Woman*, London, Walter Scott Publishing Co.

Engle, M. (1980), 'Language and play: a comparative analysis of parental initiatives', in Giles, Robinson and Smith (1980).

Fishman, P. (1980), 'Conversational insecurity', in Giles, Robinson and Smith (1980).

Fletcher, P. and Garman, M. (1979) *Language Acquisition*, Cambridge, Cambridge University Press.

Friedan, B. (1963), *The Feminine Mystique*, London, Gollancz,

Furman, N. (1985), 'The politics of language: beyond the gender principle?', in Greene and Kahn 1985.

Furlong, M. (1984), *Feminine in the Church*, London, SPCK.

Giles, H., Robinson, W.P. and Smith P.M. (1980), *Language: social psychological perspectives*, Oxford, Pergamon Press.

Greene, G. and Kahn, C. (1985), *Making a Difference*, London, Methuen.

Greif, E.B. (1980), 'Sex differences in parent-child conversations', 253–8 in Kramarae (1980).

Griffin, S. (1982), 'Split Culture', *Resurgence*, November/December 1983: 101.

Griffiths, P. (1979), 'Speech Acts and Early Sentences' 115–120 in Fletcher and Garman (1979).

Gumperz, J. and Hymes, D. (1972), eds., *Directions in Sociolinguistics*, New York, Holt, Rinehart and Winston.

Hamilton, R. (1985), *The Last Jockey*, Frome, Somerset, Bran's Head Books.

Holmes, J. (1984), 'Hedging your bets and sitting on the fence: some evidence for hedges as support structures', *Te Reo*, 27, 47–62.

Humm, M. (1986), *Feminist Criticism: Women as Contemporary Critics*, Brighton, Harvester Press.

Irigaray, L. (1974), *Speculum de l'autre femme*, Paris, Mouton.

Irigaray, L. (1977), 'Women's Exile', interview with Couze Venn in *Ideology and Consciousness*, 1, 62–76.

Irigaray, L. (1985), *'The Sex which is not one'*, originally published 1977 in French under the title *Ce Sexe qui n'en est pas un*, translated by Catherine Porter with Carolyn Burke, Ithaca, Cornell University Press.

Jespersen, O. (1922), Language, its Nature, Development and Origin, London, Allen and Unwin.

Katriel, T. (1986), *Talking Straight: Dugri speech in Israeli Sabra culture*, Cambridge, Cambridge University Press.

Keenan, E. (1974), 'Norm-makers, norm-breakers: Uses of speech by men and women in a Malagasy community' in Bauman and Sherzer (1974).

Key, M.R. (1975), *Male/Female Language*, Metuchen, Scarecrow Press.

Kirkby, J. (1971), *A New English Grammar*, New York, John Wiley and Sons, first published 1746.

Kramarae, C. (1980), *The Voices and Words of Women and Men*, Oxford, Pergamon Press.

Kramarae, C. (1981), *Women and Men Speaking*, Rowley, Newbury House.

Kristeva, J. (1974), 'Revolution in Poetic Language', extracts from her doctoral thesis *La Revolution du langage poetique*, translated by Margaret Waller (1984), *Revolution in Poetic Language*, Paris, Éditions du Seuil, and reprinted in Moi 1986.

Kristeva, J. (1982), 'Psychoanalysis and the Polis', *Critical Inquiry*, 9, No. 1, translated by Margaret Waller and reprinted in Moi 1986.

Lacan, J. (1982), *Feminine Sexuality: Jacques Lacan and the école freudienne*, edited by J. Mitchell and J. Rose and translated by J. Rose, London, Macmillan.

Lacan, J. (1966), *Écrits*, Paris, Editions du Seuil (a selection translated by Sheridan 1977).

Lakoff, R. (1975), *Language and Women's Place*, New York, Harper and Row.

Leet-Pellegrini, H.M. (1980), 'Conversational dominance as a function of gender and expertise', 97–104 in Giles, Robinson and Smith (1980).

Liebermann, P. (1967), *Intonation, Perception and Language*, Cambridge, Mass., M.I.T. Press.

Lonsdale, R. (1989), *Eighteenth Century Women Poets: an Oxford Anthology*, Oxford, Oxford University Press.

Mallarmé, S. (1945), *Oeuvres complètes*, Paris, Gallimard.

McConnell-Ginet, S., Borker, R. and Furman, N. (1980), *Women and Language in Literature and Society*, New York, Praeger.

Milroy, J. and Milroy, L. (1978), 'Belfast: change and variation in an urban vernacular', in Trudgill (1978).

Milroy, L. (1980), *Language and Social Networks*, Oxford, Basil Blackwell.

Mini Sagas (1985), Gloucester, Alan Sutton Publishers.

Moggach, D. (1988), 'Courting Disaster', *Woman*, 1 November: 38–41.

Moi, T. (1985), *Sexual/Textual Politics: Feminist Literary Theory*, London, Methuen.

Moi, T. (1986), *The Kristeva Reader*, Oxford, Basil Blackwell.

Morley, J. (1984), ' "The Faltering Words of Men": Exclusive Language in the Liturgy', in Furlong (1984).

O'Barr, W. and Atkins, B. (1980), ' "Women's language" or "powerless language"?', 93–110 in McConnell-Ginet, Borker, and Furman (1980).

Palmer, F. (1981), *Semantics*, second edition, Cambridge, Cambridge University Press.

Revised English Bible (1989), London and Cambridge, Cambridge University Press and Oxford University Press.

Ruskin, J. (1907), *Sesame and Lilies*, London, J.M. Dent, first published 1865.

Sheridan, A. (1977), *Jacques Lacan: Écrits. A selection translated from the French*, London, Tavistock Publications.

Shimberg, E. (1971), *APA Monitor*, 2, No. 10, 2, 9.

Smail, B. (1984), *Girl-friendly science avoiding sex bias in the curriculum*, Schools Council Programme 3, London, Longman,

Smith, R.D. (1984), ed. *The Writings of Anna Wickham. Free Woman and Poet*, London, Virago.

Spencer, J. (1986), *The Rise of the Woman Novelist: From Aphra Behn to Jane Austin*, Oxford, Basil Blackwell.

Spender, D. (1980), *Man Made Language*, London, Routledge and Kegan Paul.

Spender, D. (1986), *Mothers of the Novel*, London, Routledge and Kegan Paul.

Swacker, M. (1975), 'The sex of the speaker as a sociolinguistic variable', 76–83 in Thorne and Henley (1975).

Thorne, B. and Henley, N. (1975), *Language and Sex: difference and dominance*, Rowley, Massachusetts, Newbury House.
Trudgill, P. (1974), *The Social Differentiation of English in Norwich*, Cambridge, Cambridge University Press.
Trudgill, P. (1978), *Sociolinguistic Patterns in British English*, London, Edward Arnold.
Welldon, E. (1988), *Mother, Madonna, Whore: The Idealisation and Denigration of Motherhood*, London, Free Association Books.
Wickham, A., in Smith (1984).
Wittig, M. and Zeig, S. (1979), *Lesbian People's Material for a Dictionary*, New York, Avon.
Zimmerman, D., and West, C. (1975), 'Sex roles, interruptions and silences in conversation', 105–29 in Thorne and Henley, (1975).

Chapter Five

Austin, J.L. (1962), *How to do things with words*, London, Oxford University Press.
Barthes, R. (1977), 'Introduction to the Structural analysis of narratives', *Image-Music-Text*, London, Fontana.
Bandler, R., and Grinder, J. (1975), *The Structure of Magic*, Palo Alto, California, Science and Behavior Books Inc.
Bandler, R., and Grinder, J. (1979), *frogs into PRINCES*, Moab, Utah, Real People Press.
Bandler, R., and Grinder, J. (1982), *ReFraming: Neuro-Linguistic Programming and the Transformation of Meaning*, Moab, Utah, Real People Press.
Burton, D. (1980), *Dialogue and Discourse*, Routledge and Kegan Paul, London.
Cole, P., and Morgan, J.L. (1975), *Syntax and semantics, 3. Speech acts*, New York and London, Academic Press.
Dickinson, E. (1975), *The Complete Poems*, edited by Thomas H. Johnson, London, Faber and Faber.
Freedle, R. (1979), *New Directions in Discourse Processing*, Norwood, N.J., Ablex.
Greimas, A. (1966), *Sémantique Structurale*, Paris, Larousse.
Grice, H.P. (1975), 'Logic and Conversation' in Cole and Morgan (1975).
Halliday, M.A.K. (1973), *Explorations in the Functions of Language*, London, Edward Arnold.
Helms, J. (1967), ed., *Essays on the Verbal and Visual Arts*, Seattle, University of Washington Press.
Kress, G. and Hodge, R. (1979), *Language as Ideology*, London, Routledge and Kegan Paul.
Labov, W. (1972), *Language in the Inner City*, Philadelphia, University of Pennsylvania Press.
Labov, W. (1982), 'Speech actions and reactions in personal narrative' in D. Tannen (1982), 12–44.

Labov, W. and Fanshel D. (1977), *Therapeutic Discourse*, Orlando, Academic Press, Inc.

Labov, W. and Waletzky J., (1967), 'Narrative analysis: oral versions of personal experience', in J. Helms (1967).

Lakoff, G. and Johnson, M. (1980), *Metaphors We Live By*, Chicago and London, University of Chicago Press.

Mancuso, J.C. and Adams-Webber, J.R. (1982), *The construing person*, New York, Praeger.

Maranda, E.K. and P. (1970), *Structural models in folklore and transformational essays*, The Hague, Mouton.

Michotte, A.E. (1963), *The perception of causality*, translated by T.R. Miles and E. Miles, New York, Basic Books. (Original work published 1946.)

Mini Sagas (1985), Gloucester, Alan Sutton Publishers.

Mishler, E.G. (1986), 'The Analysis of Interview-Narratives', in Sarbin (1986), 233–56.

Morris, J. (1956), *A Ten-Years' Anthology*, London, Nonesuch Press.

Ong, W.J. (1982), 'Oral remembering and narrative structures' in Tannen, D. (1982).

Opie, I. and P. (1974), *The Classic Fairy Tale*, London, Oxford University Press.

Peterson, C. and McCabe, A. (1983), *Developmental Psycholinguistics: Three Ways of Looking at Child's Narrative*, New York, Plenum Press.

Pinter, H. (1983), *Harold Pinter, Plays: One*, London, Methuen.

Polanyi, L. (1978), *The American story: Cultural constraints on the structure and meaning of stories in conversation*, unpublished doctoral dissertation, University of Michigan.

Polanyi, L. (1981), 'Telling the Same story twice', *Text*, 1, 315–36.

Pratt, M.L. (1977), *Towards a Speech-Act Theory of Literary Discourse*, Bloomington, Indiana University Press.

Quine, W.V. (1963), *Two Dogmas of Empiricism*, New York, Harper and Row.

Quine, W.V. (1969), 'Natural Kinds', in *Ontological relativity and other essays*, New York, Columbia University Press.

Robinson, J.A. and Hawpe, L. (1986), 'Narrative Thinking as Heuristic Process', in Sarbin, (1986), pp. 111–29.

Rothery, J. and Martin, J. (1980), *Writing Project, Papers 1 (Narrative: Vicarious Experience) and 2 (Exposition: Literary Criticism)*, Sydney, Department of Linguistics, University of Sydney,

Sarbin, T.E. (1986), *Narrative Psychology: The Storied Nature of Human Conduct*, New York, Praeger Publishers.

Schafer, R. (1976), *A New Language for Psychoanalysis*, New Haven and London. Yale University Press.

Searle, J.R. (1969), *Speech Acts*, Cambridge, Cambridge University Press.

Tannen, D. (1979), 'What's in a frame?', in Freedle, (1979), 137–81.

Tannen, D. (1982), *Analyzing Discourse: Text and Talk*, Washington D.C., Georgetown University Press.

Wardhough, R. (1985), *How Conversation Works*, Oxford, Blackwell.

Webb, V. (1979), *Personal Narrative as Experiential Organization: A Linguistic study with Philosophical Implications*, unpublished M.A. thesis, Birmingham University.

Index